Psychological Models in
International Politics

Other Titles in This Series

Presidents, Secretaries of State, and Crises in U.S. Foreign Relations: A Model and Predictive Analysis, Lawrence S. Falkowski

U.S. Policy in International Institutions: Defining Reasonable Options in an Unreasonable World, edited by Seymour Maxwell Finger and Joseph R. Harbert

Congress and Arms Control, edited by Alan Platt and Lawrence D. Weiler

Crisis Resolution: Presidential Decision Making in the Mayaguez *and Korean Confrontations*, Richard G. Head, Frisco W. Short, Robert C. McFarlane

U.S.-Japan Relations and the Security of East Asia: The Next Decade, edited by Franklin B. Weinstein

Communist Indochina and U.S. Foreign Policy: Postwar Realities, Joseph J. Zasloff and MacAlister Brown

National Interests and Presidential Leadership: The Setting of Priorities, Donald E. Nuechterlein

Arms Transfers to the Third World: The Military Buildup in Less Industrial Countries, edited by Uri Ra'anan, Robert Pfaltzgraff, Jr., and Geoffrey Kemp

Political Leadership in NATO: A Study in Multinational Diplomacy, Robert S. Jordan

Lend-Lease, Loans, and the Coming of the Cold War: A Study of the Implementation of Foreign Policy, Leon C. Martel

Nuclear Energy and Nuclear Proliferation: Japanese and American Views, edited by Ryukichi Imai and Henry S. Rowen

Presidential Decisionmaking in Foreign Policy: The Effective Use of Information and Advice, Alexander L. George

The Security of Korea: U.S. and Japanese Perspectives in the 1980s, edited by Franklin B. Weinstein and Fuji Kamiya

Westview Special Studies in International Relations

Psychological Models in International Politics
edited by Lawrence S. Falkowski

The authors—among the most eminent researchers and scholars working in this area—evaluate the various psychological models used in international politics and foreign policy. Providing a broad overview of the different approaches and types of analysis current in the field, the contributors compare them in terms of their descriptive, explanatory, and predictive potency. Most if not all of the major approaches to the subject are given ample space, and some extremely novel approaches are included as well. None of the material has been published elsewhere.

Lawrence Falkowski is assistant professor of political science at Louisiana State University. He is author of *Presidents, Secretaries of State, and Crises in U.S. Foreign Relations* (Westview Press, 1978).

Psychological Models in International Politics
edited by Lawrence S. Falkowski

Westview Press / Boulder, Colorado

Westview Special Studies in International Relations

All rights reserved. No part of this publication may be reproduced or transmitted in any form or by any means, electronic or mechanical, including photocopy, recording, or any information storage and retrieval system, without permission in writing from the publisher.

Copyright © 1979 by Westview Press, Inc.

Published in 1979 in the United States of America by
  Westview Press, Inc.
  5500 Central Avenue
  Boulder, Colorado 80301
  Frederick A. Praeger, Publisher

Library of Congress Cataloging in Publication Data
Main entry under title:
Psychological models in international politics.
  (Westview special studies in international relations)
  1. International relations—Research. I. Falkowski, Lawrence S. II. Series.
JX1291.P8   327'.01'9   79-13670
ISBN 0-89158-377-7

Printed and bound in the United States of America
Paperback edition published in September 1980 by Westview Press, Inc.
Paperback ISBN: 0-86531-043-2

To the memory of my mother,
Alice Szersin Falkowski

Contents

Acknowledgments..................................xiii

1. Introduction: Evaluating Psychological Models,
   Lawrence S. Falkowski...............................1

   The Motivation of the Scholars of Motivation............1
   Problems of Psychological Analysis....................3
   Plan for This Volume 11
   References..13

2. Who Becomes a Political Leader? Some Societal and
   Regime Influences on Selection of a Head of State,
   Margaret G. Hermann 15

   Methodology......................................22
   Results 34
   Conclusions......................................44
   Notes..45
   References.......................................46

3. Predicting Flexibility with Memory Profiles,
   Lawrence S. Falkowski..............................49

   Introduction......................................49
   The Importance of Individual Variables in
      Foreign Policy..................................52
   Flexibility in Foreign Policy Behavior: A Framework
      for Analysis....................................55
   The Measurement of Flexibility 60
   Testing the Framework: The Ability to Predict
      Flexibility.....................................64
   References.......................................67

4. Signal Leakage and the Remote Psychological
   Assessment of Foreign Policy Elites,
   Thomas C. Wiegele 71

   The Concept of Signal Leakage 72
   Some Examples of Signal Leakage 73
   The Scientific Foundations of Voice Stress Analysis 78
   Examples of Voice Stress Measurement 81
   Research Applications of the PSE 82
   Conclusions 89
   Notes 90
   References 90

5. The Causal Nexus between Cognitive Beliefs and
   Decision-Making Behavior: The "Operational Code"
   Belief System, *Alexander L. George* 95

   Cognitive Psychology and the Operational Code
     Belief System Approach 96
   The Role of Operational Code Beliefs in Decision-
     Making: Two Theoretical Premises 101
   Procedures for Assessing the Impact of Operational Code
     Beliefs on Decisional Choices 104
   Notes 119
   References 121

6. Operational Codes and Crisis Outcomes,
   Steven W. Hoagland and Stephen G. Walker 125

   Introduction 125
   The Analysis of Operational Codes 127
   The Analysis of Crisis Bargaining 131
   Soviet Crisis Bargaining Propositions 139
   U.S. Crisis Bargaining Propositions 143
   Data Analysis 147
   Operational Codes and Crisis Outcomes 156
   Conclusion 160
   Notes 162
   References 165

7. National Role Conceptions and Systemic Outcomes,
   Stephen G. Walker 169

   Introduction 169

Role Theory and the Analysis of Foreign Policy 173
Analytical Procedures and Findings. 192
Conclusion 199
Notes. 205
References. 207

8. Elite Values and Foreign Policy Analysis:
   Preliminary Findings, *Gerald W. Hopple* 211

   Overview. 211
   Value Analysis. 213
   Findings 224
   Conclusion 240
   Notes. 244
   References. 245

9. Small-Group Dynamics and Foreign Policy Decision-
   Making: An Experimental Approach, *Andrew K.
   Semmel and Dean Minix* 251

   Choice Shifts. 252
   Experimental Research 257
   Methodology. 260
   Findings 261
   Discussion. 270
   Conclusion 274
   Appendix A. 276
   Notes. 279
   References. 281

10. Psychological Models and Systemic Outcomes,
    Lawrence S. Falkowski 289

    The Systemic Impact of Psychological Models 290
    The Nexus between Psychological Models and
        International Behavior. 292
    The State of Psychological Models: What We Know and
        What We Suspect. 294
    Let the Buyer Beware: Correlation, Causation, and
        Spurious Relations 304
    References. 306

Index. 307

Acknowledgments

An edited volume relies for its content on many scholars. The contributors to this volume have done much more than merely submit chapters; they have been part of this work both intellectually and spiritually since its inception. I wish to extend my heartfelt thanks and appreciation to each of them. I would also like to thank my research assistants, Paul Lambert and L. Keith Milam. Josephine Scurria served as the departmental secretary during the preparation of this manuscript and deserves special thanks for her obvious ability and her valiant attempt to keep an absent-minded academic more or less on schedule. My wife, Carol, has been so encouraging and so willing to tolerate the insanity and the telephone bills that come with an edited volume that she deserves many thanks.

A publication requires the faith and encouragement of friends, scholars, and critics. I was fortunate to find one individual who could fulfill all these roles. John Pollock provided the support, insight, and criticism that immeasurably aided in the completion of this manuscript.

Lastly, I wish to thank the people at Westview Press, especially Lynne Rienner, Frederick Praeger, Lynn Lloyd, and Brad Kava, without whose confidence and support this work could not have been printed.

Lawrence S. Falkowski

Psychological Models in
International Politics

1
Introduction: Evaluating Psychological Models

Lawrence S. Falkowski

The use of psychology in international politics is not new. For many years scholars have been employing psychologically based models in the study of international politics and foreign policy. In fact, the student of international politics is presented with a series of models based on different aspects of psychology. The purpose of this volume is to bring together the work of a number of scholars to see if we can draw any overall conclusions from these approaches. This volume contains several psychological models that are being used in international politics; they vary in their level of abstraction as well as in the subject matters examined and the individuals studied. It is now time to examine the general utility of these approaches and models.

The Motivation of the Scholars of Motivation

Implicit in all psychologically based models of international politics is a concern with motivation. We are constantly asking why certain types of behavior occur. What is it that causes leaders or nations or other international actors to behave the way they do? What forces cause a particular nation to wage war on its neighbor? Why was the U.S. government unable to comprehend the intensity of anti-Shah feelings in Iran? In international politics the number of responses to these kinds of questions border on the infinite. Some scholars argue that the environment determines behavior, and their answers to these questions will involve in-depth studies of the nature of international systems. Others argue that the answers are to be found in ideological factors. Still others contend that since the motives behind behavior are individual in nature, one must examine the motivations of the individuals to find the reasons behind a particular series of behaviors.

If we want to study individual motivation, we really need to study individual psychology. Scholars differ as to which psychological variables they consider primary, but all who accept the importance of individual motivation agree that psychological variables are important. All these scholars contend that the functioning of the human brain is a crucial element in the study of international politics. This is a simplistic but telling statement. To accept the importance of the individual in international politics and foreign policy is to accept a microanalytic view of international politics, which in turn implies a certain mode of investigation.

To say that individuals are central to political analysis does not necessarily mean that it is the individual or specific personality characteristics that are important. Although it is ultimately individuals who make decisions, their decisions may be more directly related to external factors such as perceived roles, governmental variables, systemic relationships, and the like (see Rosenau 1971).

In effect, scholars who deal with psychological variables tend to operate within the overall context of the decision-making approach to international politics and foreign policy. Their emphasis is on the process of making decisions and the elites involved in those processes. Thus, what seems to motivate the scholars of motivation are two related questions: First, what psychological mechanisms operate in the decision-making context, and second, what is the importance of these variables as compared to other factors influencing the behavior ultimately exhibited?

The statement, "Foreign policy results from the decision-makers' perceptions of presented or expected problems in the relationships between a nation and its environment (both human and nonhuman)" (Hermann 1972:72), sums up the problem we face, but it does not offer a solution. Indeed, given the current state of the art in using psychology in the international politics context, we may need to address more basic concerns. First: what are the psychological mechanisms involved in foreign policy decision-making, and how do we operationalize them? Only when we have reliable information on these mechanisms can we evaluate their relative weight in the process. Alexander George puts the dilemma in perspective in terms of operational code analysis:

> Operational code beliefs are only one variable cluster within a rich, complex, casual framework for explaining decision-making. Thus, as is well known, in making foreign policy decisions a policy maker may be

influenced by personal considerations, domestic politics, and/or organizational interests as well as his conception of the national interest. This complicates, of course, the task of establishing the casual weight that operational code beliefs have in any particular decision.

The scholars in this volume reflect both the advances in the field and the intellectual tradition of which they are a part. All the contributors see the work of Synder, Bruck, and Sapin (Rosenau 1969) in the area of decision-making as important and address, at least in part, the questions of psychological mechanisms, measurement problems, and comparative value. In Chapter 2 Margaret Hermann discusses the psychology of heads of state; in Chapter 3 I examine U.S. presidents and secretaries of state. Thomas Wiegele (Chapter 4) discusses methodologies that can be employed in "measuring elites while they are engaged in an act of foreign policy behavior," and Alexander George (Chapter 5) examines the place of cognitive variables in foreign policy decision-making. Steven Hoagland and Stephen Walker (Chapter 6) report the findings of operational code analysis of U.S. and Soviet leaders, and in Chapter 7 Walker investigates elite role conceptions. Gerald Hopple (Chapter 8) analyzes the relationship between psychological variables and behavior, and Andrew Semmel and Dean Minix (Chapter 9) associate experimental results with small-group dynamics.

Problems of Psychological Analysis

Applying psychological analysis to international politics necessitates the solving of a number of problems. The first and most basic problem concerns the universe of individuals to be studied. Although most scholars would contend that elites are the primary focus of attention, the definition of elites raises some questions.

The first of these questions deals with the distinction between elites and masses. Stated differently, how can we tell whether a given individual is part of an elite? Some research projects have dealt with only the top decision-makers (Hermann, Falkowski). Does this mean that only heads of state are appropriate for psychological study? Of course not! The question of elites can be dealt with in two ways. One approach is to argue that an elite is composed of only those individuals involved in a particular decision process. This includes a number of individuals who might be excluded if other definitions were employed. For example, if we defined elites as those individuals holding high governmental positions we might exclude the leaders of political opposition parties, corporate executives, and the like. By adopting a decision-making perspective we can include such individuals in studies of election strategy or of the degree of personal involvement in corporate investment decisions.

If we use this definition of elites, we must also construct our models in a manner that is applicable to a wide range of individuals. Margaret Hermann suggests variables that may be important in the selection of political leaders, but it does not require a great deal of imagination to see how her model could be used in other contexts. It would be necessary to change some variable names, but the underlying dimensions would remain unaltered. Thus if Hermann turned her attention to the corporate "heads of state" who seem to have an increasing impact on international events, she might have to change the first two personal characteristics she mentions from training in foreign affairs and nationalism to training in oversees operations and company loyalty, but, in terms of the model, the changes would be more semantic than substantive.

My own work is another example of the broad applicability of psychological models for international politics. If my findings are supported, it is conceivable that one could look at the secretary of defense or a candidate for political office in the same way that I examine presidents and secretaries of state. One can also see how the concept of "process tracing" could easily be applied to non-traditional international actors as well as governments.

But we must ask whether broad applicability can be carried too far. Suppose we were to discover that the models used in international politics could also be used successfully in the study of local government or family relations? Are we then saying that international politics and foreign policy are irrelevant and that the psychology of decision-making is the important thing? If these models have utility outside international politics, does that negate their utility for international politics? I think not. If we discover that certain psychological variables are important in predicting international behaviors in general, we may also discover that behavior in international politics has unique aspects that do not exist in other contexts. For example, we might discover that the perceptions of international decision-makers are affected by certain environmental constraints to a greater or different degree than are those of local mayors. In other words, there may be some basic principles of human interactions, and behaviors we usually associate with international politics are but one manifestation of these basic principles.

This volume contains a great many suggested psychological mechanisms, and it might appear that there is little commonality between them. However, this seeming diversity is more apparent than real. It is possible to be misled by the proliferation of variable and concept names into assuming that the models have very little in common. A careful examination will reveal that, although the models have certain unique aspects, there is a fair degree of overlap between them.

The commonalities are based on the assumed psychological mechanisms that operate within the decision-making process. Consider for a moment the following sequence of events. First we determine the individual or group that is important in a particular decision. Having done so, we examine the personality traits of the individuals or groups involved in order to determine their perceptual or belief pattern. At this stage a number of other variables come into play. They might include information about the type of situation, the nature of the opponent, the type of responses suggested, the positions of various advisors, the consequences of similar decisions in the past, and so forth. Having weighed some or all of these factors, the individual or group then makes a decision. That decision is implemented, and the consequent behavior varies from the letter and spirit of the decision relative to the effectiveness of those designated to implement the decision and possible resistance by groups outside the decision unit. At each stage in the process different variables may be more or less important, depending to some degree on the perceptions and personalities of the decision-makers involved. Not all scholars agree on which personality variables or what perceptual mechanisms are most highly related to what ordering of situational and systemic variables, but all the contributors share the hunch that they are related in some way. Thus, researchers in this field share the search for mechanisms and their effects while diverging on what constitute the most salient mechanisms for study.

Implicit in Hermann's work is the belief that variation in the personal characteristics of leaders is associated with some foreign policy behaviors. This leads to an interesting speculation. Leaders may be chosen with some implicit idea of representing the norms and values of their societies (based on Hermann's notion of congruence), while in reality they may act differentially because of variations in the societies from which they were selected.

I contend that since the most crucial aspect of ultimate behavior is the definition of a situation the decision-maker uses, it is rather important to discover what variables are central in shaping that definition. My model suggests that memory is one of those central variables, and a knowledge of a decision-maker's memory can be used to predict how that decision-maker will behave. The model must be viewed in light of two other studies contained in this volume. Semmel and Minix believe that another crucial element in the decision process is the dynamics of the decision-making group. From experimental data they conclude that some types of individuals are more likely to change their decisions after a process of group dynamics has been experienced. Although these two approaches to psychological mechanisms are not necessarily antithetical—the people who exhibit the largest degree of choice shift might be the type that I would argue are most flexible anyway—the principle of parsimony would have us determine which of these factors are the most important and concentrate on those factors.

Hoagland and Walker deal with the same type of mechanism problems at a slightly more general level. Their studies test more elaborate and concrete models in specific situations. It is the addition of situational variables (which are only dealt with to a degree by myself and by Semmel and Minix) that allows the researchers to address questions of systemic relevance. Another facet of the process of generalization is examined by Hopple. He treats the question of psychological mechanisms and the variables associated with them not as assumptions of his models but rather as subjects for empirical investigation: "A more reasonable question is not *are* psychological variables relevant but *how successfully* do such factors explain behavior *compared to* other clusters?"

Perhaps the best way to sum up is to borrow an insight from Alexander George. If viewed in an information-processing context, the models presented in this volume might fulfill the promise that George suggests:

> The convergence of so many important subfields of psychology into a common information-processing framework promises not only to produce a more fruitful synthesis of psychological theories relevant to the study of decision-making; we are on the threshold—indeed already

beyond it—of a new wave of research in psychology that promises to be even more directly relevant and useful for study of political decision-making than these subfields, individually or collectively, have been in the past.

Viewed in this light, much of the research in this volume can be seen as concentrating on essential segments of the information-processing model.

If we can find some consistency in the theoretical approaches to the use of psychology in international politics and foreign policy, we will have a basis from which to launch an examination of the operationalizations and measurement techniques used in the various studies. All research in international politics suffers from problems of data access. Whether dealing with the individual level of analysis or with decision-making groups, the problems of data access and hence measurement techniques are always complex. To get the information they need, researchers have to rely on indirect measures and cope with all the problems this entails.

It would be wonderful if we could gain the cooperation of decision-makers for all our psychological testing. The information that could be gained is essential, but in reality it is simply unavailable. In order to generate appropriate kinds of data, researchers have developed content analysis techniques, special experimental designs, and unobtrusive measures. The specific operationalizations may differ, but most, if not all, the techniques employed have been devised to measure psychological variables at a distance.

The methods reported in this volume are representative of the types of measurement techniques used in the field. Although only Wiegele's chapter (Chapter 4) is explicitly methodological in its orientation, all the other contributors either develop their own measurement techniques or employ techniques that they feel are appropriate to their particular study. Wiegele assumes the degree of stress or anxiety is important in the context of decision-making (especially in crisis situations) and argues that direct yet unobtrusive measures of the level of stress may go far in helping us understand the nature of the decisions that are made. Although we might question whether stress is the only variable that needs to be examined, the importance of reliable direct measurement of individual variables is a common concern. As Wiegele says:

> I have argued that it is important for the student of foreign policy to work more intensely at the individual level of analysis. At this level,

however, elites are often inaccessible to the analyst. If we want to measure individuals directly, such a situation requires that we develop a repertoire of methods of remote psychological assessment based on the leakage of certain kinds of signals from human beings.

Most of the studies in this volume use a content analysis approach to creating data. Admittedly, the exact operationlizations vary a good deal, ranging from the use of pure event data to a type of thematic content analysis. All the studies seem to indicate that public statements by decision-makers are a useful, if flawed, source of data. The problems of content analysis are manifold, but I will mention only those that seem most directly related to the issue of measuring psychological variables.

The primary question of concern to us is whether content analysis procedures give an accurate picture of decision-makers' perceptions and beliefs. Hopple argues that we have some evidence to indicate that public statements may be less truthful than private ones. However, he also admits that these same statements can impose constraints on future actions. In short, when analyzing statements made for public consumption, the researcher must make every effort to recognize and account for possible or probable bias. Since all of these studies are quite careful in the use of data and have built in as many controls as possible, our task is to see whether or not these controls are sufficient to deal with the data problems.

The obvious way to test this proposition is to get access to the private conversations or statements of these same decision-makers and compare their public and private statements. If a difference exists, we might not be able to tell if they were lying in public or in private, but at least we would have some idea of the degree of difference. To date, this type of test is virtually impossible, so we must rely on less definitive tests of reliability and validity.

An associated difficulty is whether the independent and dependent variables in a content analysis study are really independent of each other. No series of correlations, regardless of strength, are meaningful if the way in which they were associated is inherently tautological. If we are measuring a decision-maker's attitudes or beliefs or memory using information gleaned from observable behavior and we are measuring what they are actually doing by reference to the same series of behaviors, are we not simply running in a circle?

In order to answer this question we must delve more deeply

into the distinction between personality characteristics and observable behavior. No one would argue that it is possible to code an entire series of variables from a single data source, yet in the area of leadership perception the normal approach to data is called into question. A finding that suggests leaders are capable of engaging in a pattern of deception might be as important as finding a robust relationship between attitudes and behavior. Hopple avoids even the appearance of tautology by using one data source for independent variables and another for dependent and intervening variables. While he clearly recognizes the difficulty of creating value-based data, he also recognizes the importance of solid empirical work in this area. As he so aptly states, "Even a pattern of lies can be of some importance in monitoring and attempting to predict elite behavior."

In short, as long as we can see conceptual and theoretical differences between the personality variables we are trying to measure and the behavior we are trying to predict, we can build research designs that avoid tautology. Further, if we find that certain statements of attitudes tend to be highly related to subsequent behavior, are we not increasing our ability to predict even if we are not totally clear on how the two variables are causally related?

Before discussing the way the chapters have been presented in this volume I would like to look at two other examples of measurement techniques. The first is the one offered by Semmel and Minix and the second is the one outlined by Alexander George. Semmel and Minix are able to get hard reliable data by using an experimental approach to the subject of small-group dynamics. They conduct a series of tests and experiments, controlling for as many extraneous factors as possible. The results they produce are quite impressive, but the simplifying assumptions they make may open their work to some criticism. If we accept the notion that one can analogize from a foreign policy decision group to an experimental one, and then repeat the analogy in the opposite direction to make statements about foreign policy decision-making, then Semmel and Minix have made great strides in operationalizing the work of Irving Janis (Janis 1972). If we argue that this type of analogy is inappropriate, then the research reported by these authors is of only passing interest.

It remains to be seen whether the approach used by Semmel and Minix can be correlated to a series of foreign policy decisions. A general implication can be drawn, however. If we examine both the experimental work and the content analysis work, we may be able to construct a multi-method approach to the study of psychological mechanisms that would produce breakthrough results. If the analogy between foreign policy decision groups and experimental groups can be supported, and if we can show a link between psychological variables and foreign policy outcomes, it may then be possible to predict the probable outcomes of an entire series of decisions in the future. We might even reach the stage where it is possible to conceive of a research design which would *integrate* a variety of approaches and *build on* prior work (see Chapter 8).

One way in which an integrated research design might be created is discussed by Alexander George. Not only does this suggestion touch on a number of the studies contained within this volume, but it also indicates how the various techniques might be employed:

> "Process-tracing" seeks to establish the ways in which the actor's beliefs influenced his receptivity to and assessment of incoming information about the situation, his definition of the situation, his identification and evaluation of options as well as, finally, his choice of a course of action.

George argues for specific controlled comparisons, but if we impressionistically take his procedures we can see how a number of these chapters can be compared. In the area of an actor's beliefs and his definition of situation, we can look at the work of Hermann, at my chapter, and, to some degree, that of Wiegele. For evaluating options and instrumental beliefs, we can match up the work of George, Hoagland and Walker, and Walker; and in terms of the choice of actions and behavior we can compare Hopple and Walker.

Another and more interesting cross-examination could be made not in terms of exact controlled experiments but in terms of applying different psychological models to the same real-world situations. It is quite apparent that a number of the scholars in this volume are examining their models in terms of their applicability and predictability in crisis situations. On this basis alone some impressionistic comparisons can be made. In fact, a case can be made for the proposition that if personality factors are going to be important, a crisis situation is likely to occur where these factors will be most important. In addition, a number of these authors deal with the same historical crises. Although it would be rather unfair to make a detailed comparison of the psychological approaches to see which one seems most appropriate, it is not unfair to examine how these crises looked through the various psychological lenses offered by the authors. This is not the type of comparison suggested by George, but it is perhaps the first step on the way to such comparisons.

In conclusion, I suggest that the reader can examine the similarities and differences among the various models by looking for the variations in basic assumptions, operationalizations, measurement techniques, and types of data. This is not a particularly novel idea, but the series of original studies presented in this book provide a unique opportunity to sample a wide variety of models and experimental results in this relatively new field. I have tried to avoid specific result-oriented comparisons in order to let the reader judge the results for himself and also to allow a natural synthesis to develop. Only one task remains for the introduction—to explain the inclusion and the ordering of the contributions.

Plan for This Volume

Given the variety of topics that the contributors to this volume address, any attempt at organization must appear to be just a bit arbitrary. I hope that the organization I have chosen is helpful to the reader and not given over to unthinking categorization. Chapters 2, 3, and 4 deal with psychological models at a very modest level of abstraction. In each of these chapters the emphasis is on the individual himself.

Chapter 2, by Margaret Hermann, deals with personality variations among heads of state and how this variation might be related to the types of societies and governments these individuals are associated with. In Chapter 3, I investigate the relationship between variations in the memory profiles of U.S. presidents and secretaries of state since the end of World War II and the behavior change exhibited by these individuals. The results seem to indicate that individual differences are important and, further, that it is possible to predict how a president is likely to react before he encounters a crisis. Chapter 4, written by Thomas Wiegele, focuses on ways in which we can begin to directly measure stress and possibly the effects of stress on foreign policy elites. This chapter deals with methods of voice stress analysis and signal leakage, and it evaluates the implications of this methodology for foreign policy analysis. Taken as a unit these three chapters provide three insights into the selection and functioning of individual decision-makers.

The next functional section of the volume also includes three chapters. These three chapters are written at a slightly higher level of abstraction and deal not only with the individual decision-maker but also with other variables contained within the decision process. They deal with operational codes and national role conceptions, and examine series of specific rules and beliefs used by decision-makers in the process of arriving at decisions. This type of analysis has the advantage of being more policy relevant than the individual-level studies, but research problems in this approach are only recently being addressed adequately.

Chapter 5, by Alexander George, deals with probable causal links between operational codes and decisions but has implications of a far greater scope. George not only puts forth an extremely insightful treatise on operational codes but also analyzes the value of the cognitive mapping approach in psychology and its potential utility to international politics. Chapter 6, coauthored by Steven Hoagland and Stephen Walker, focuses on the relationship between the operational codes of key American and Soviet decision-makers and the outcomes of the first and second Berlin crises. The actions of Acheson, Stalin, Kennedy, and Khrushchev are compared, and the hypotheses relating the individual elements and overall structures of these "OPCODES" to the tactical outcomes of various stages in the two crises are formulated and tested. The research objectives are to assess the congruence between descriptions of American and Soviet operational codes and their crisis behavior; to test the generalizability of the OPCODE construct from an individual to an aggregate (national) level of analysis; and to relate the dispositional traits of decision-makers to systemic (dyadic) outcomes.

Chapter 7, by Stephen Walker, can be considered either the last chapter of the second section or the first chapter of the third. Walker stresses the relationships between national role conceptions of foreign policy makers and the interaction patterns among their respective nations. The study includes American and Soviet decision-makers as well as the relationships these groups have with nations in Europe, Asia, Africa, the Middle East, and Latin America. The mode of analysis adapts many of the insights from role theory and cognitive balance theory.

The third section is not really a section at all, but is rather a logical extension of all that has gone before. The only difficulty is that the section represents logical extensions in two rather different directions. Gerald Hopple, in Chapter 8, approaches something akin to national role conceptions by examining the belief systems of various elites and then comparing the differences in those belief systems with differences in actual behavior. Other variables that have been assumed to be important in foreign policy—i.e. societal or interstate factors—are added to the equation, and possible relative weights for each factor are discussed.

Chapter 9, by Andrew Semmel and Dean Minix, takes a completely different approach. These researchers try to examine why decision-making groups tend to act differently than individuals might act on their own, and they rely on experimental techniques to investigate this problem. Although their study is not as aggregate in form as the work of Hopple, their approach also tends to build on the extant literature in the field and to push the insights found within that literature as far as possible.

In Chapter 10 I have attempted to integrate the findings contained within the rest of the volume and address the question of where this type of research goes next. The chapter is speculative in nature and personal in tone.

On balance, this volume presents the major approaches to international politics using psychology as a base, and it looks to see if we have progressed over the last several years in insights and methodology. No attempt has been made to be exhaustive in the selection of materials and no claim is made in that regard. The modest purpose of this volume is to present an overview of the types of research that are current in the field.

References

Janis, Irving, *Victims of Groupthink*. Boston: Houghton Mifflin, 1972.
Rosenau, James N., ed. *International Political and Foreign Policy*. 2nd ed. New York: Free Press, 1969.
Rosenau, James N. *The Scientific Study of Foreign Policy*. New York: Free Press, 1971.

2
Who Becomes a Political Leader? Some Societal and Regime Influences on Selection of a Head of State

Margaret G. Hermann

Who becomes a political leader? This question continues to intrigue students of political psychology. Researchers have usually sought to answer the query in one of two ways: by comparing the personal characteristics of political leaders to those of their constitutents or by describing the personal characteristics of specific groups of political leaders. Thus, we have studies by Hennessy (1959), Browning and Jacob (1964), and Hedlund (1973) comparing political leaders' responses to questions about their personal characteristics with the responses of constitutents. These researchers were interested in examining some common-sense notions about political leaders such as "political leaders are extroverts," "political leaders seem to be more power hungry than the ordinary citizen," "political leaders are more dogmatic than most people." We also have descriptions of the personal characteristics of specific groups of political leaders—for example, in Matthews' (1960) discussion of U.S. senators, Frey's (1965) study of the deputies to the Grand Assembly in Turkey, Barber's (1965) research on Connecticut state legislators, and Lasswell and Lerner's (1965) look at revolutionary political leaders.

More recently, a third way of exploring who becomes a political leader has received some attention. At issue is how politicians' personal characteristics, the requirements of the political role, and aspects of the political recruitment process interrelate to influence who emerges as a political leader. Political roles are likely to differ in the personal characteristics they demand for their execution;

An earlier version of this chapter was presented at the annual meeting of the Northeastern Political Science Association, South Egremont, Mass., November 11-13, 1976. The research was supported by grants from the National Science Foundation (GS-40356) and the Mershon Center of Ohio State University.

different recruitment processes probably elicit different personal characteristics from those being recruited.

In his theoretical discussion of elite political recruitment, Seligman (1971) suggests how personal characteristics, political role, and the recruitment process may affect one another in the choice of a political leader. He lists a series of questions one must seek answers to in studying elite recruitment. Given a particular political role we are interested in studying, the first thing we need to know is the opportunity the role affords. Who can hold the position? In other words, what are the formal requirements for the role (e.g., age, training needed, party affiliation, time involved) and what are the informal expectations about the position (e.g., the power inherent in the role, the flexibility of the role, the usefulness of the role as a stepping stone to higher office)? By learning about the opportunities the role offers, we can begin to propose what personal characteristics might be compatible with holding that role. In effect, we can say something about who might be interested in such a position.

A second question that needs to be asked concerns the risks that are involved in trying for the role. What is the probability of winning the position; what are the costs for not getting the position; what must one give up in order to assume the position; what does one gain by taking the role? All of these queries revolve around the uncertainties that are part of deciding whether or not to try for a position. Let us say the answers to these questions indicate high risks in trying for the role. Then a person who was interested in the position *and* who was fairly confident, who enjoyed situations involving high stakes, and who believed he had some control over events might be more likely than his opposite to try for the role. Whereas information about the opportunities that a role offers suggests who can and might be interested in the political role, information about the risks involved indicates who might try for the role.

There is also the issue of the selection process itself. Who does the selecting (e.g., a political party, a political leader, an electorate)? How is selection generally made (e.g., through cooptation, through conscription, through self-selection)? How complex is the selection process—how many stages or steps are there? What happens in the selection process suggests the control that others have over the position. If control is tight, the personal characteristics demanded of the role occupant will be those desirable to the "selectors" or sponsors. They will set the criteria for selection. Under such circumstances personal characteristics like loyalty, conformity, and a match in political beliefs and motivations with the sponsor will probably be important. In examining the opportunities the role affords and the risks involved in trying for the role, we can begin to make judgments about what the candidates for the position will be like and, in turn, what the chosen candidate will be like.

Researchers like DiRenzo (1977), Stewart (1977), Welsh (1977), and Ziller et al. (1977) have begun to systematically explore the ways in which personal characteristics, role requirements, and recruitment processes can interrelate in determining who becomes a political leader. DiRenzo was interested in whether different types of "selectors" (electorates) in the recruitment process choose different types of political leaders. He looked at political leaders and electorates in the United States and Italy. Ziller et al. were also interested in this question with regard to the election process for state legislators in the United States. Stewart examined whether or not a change in the informal requirements of a political role influences who is recruited. He studied American presidents and British prime ministers. Welsh focused on the characteristics of Latin American political leaders who come to power by extra-legal means, namely through *coups d'état*.

The present study follows in this tradition. Of interest is specification of the conditions that may affect the types of individuals who become heads of state. In particular, are different types of heads of state selected in small as opposed to large nations, in modernized as opposed to modernizing nations, in certain areas of the world (Middle East, Africa, Asia, Europe), in nations with high as opposed to low societal stress, in nations with high as opposed to low degrees of political competition, or in nations whose governments came to power illegally or through legal means?

We want to learn if there are differences in the personal characteristics of heads of state who are selected under these varying circumstances. We will examine seven personal characteristics: training in foreign affairs, nationalism, belief in own ability to control events, conceptual complexity, need for power, need for affiliation, and distrust of others (suspiciousness). I propose that these personal characteristics interrelate to form six orientations to foreign affairs. These orientations are the expansionist, active independent, influential, mediator/integrator, opportunist, and participative. The orientations are viewed as predisposing the heads of state to deal with foreign policy problems in certain ways. Students of politics have suggested that these seven personal characteristics and six orientations are relevant to being a political leader. For a review of this literature, see Hermann (1976, 1977, 1978).

Before proceeding further, let us present brief definitions of the personal characteristics and orientations to foreign affairs examined in this study. The personal characteristics can be defined as follows:

1. *Training in foreign affairs:* Training is indicated if an individual has held some previous political or governmental position that would give him or her some knowledge about foreign affairs and foreign policy making.
2. *Nationalism:* A view of the world in which one's own nation holds center stage. There are strong emotional attachments to the nation-state; one's own nation is perceived as the best, while other nations are perceived in less positive terms. Moreover, there is an emphasis on the importance of maintaining national honor and national sovereignty.
3. *Belief in one's own ability to control events:* A view of the world in which one perceives some degree of control over the situations in which one is involved. What happens to an individual is contingent upon his or her own behavior and characteristics.
4. *Need for power:* This refers to an individual's concern for "establishing, maintaining, or restoring one's power—that is, one's impact, control, or influence over another person, group of persons, or the world at large" (Winter 1973:250).
5. *Need for affiliation:* Conceptualized as a concern with "establishing, maintaining, or restoring warm and friendly relationships" (Atkinson 1958:685) with other persons or groups.
6. *Conceptual complexity:* Refers to the degree of differentiation a person shows when observing or contemplating his or her environment (cf. Crockett 1965; Scott 1963). The individual who is high in conceptual complexity can see varying reasons for a particular position, is willing to entertain the possibility that there is ambiguity in the environment, and is flexible in reacting to objects or ideas in the environment. The person who is low in conceptual complexity classifies objects and ideas into good-bad, black-white, either-or dimensions, is unwilling to perceive ambiguity in the environment, and tends to react unvaryingly to objects and ideas in the environment.

7. *Distrust of others:* Distrust or suspiciousness is characterized by a general feeling of doubt, uneasiness, misgiving, and wariness of others—that is, by an inclination to suspect and doubt the motives and actions of others.

Next we will define the orientations to foreign affairs and suggest how the personal characteristics interrelate to form those orientations:[1]

1. *Expansionist:* Indicates a willingness to urge one's own government or like-minded parties to consider enlarging their territorial or resource claims. Persons who have a need to manipulate and control others (high need for power), have little ability to consider a range of alternatives in making a decision (low conceptual complexity), are distrustful of others (high distrust of others), have a strong interest in maintaining their nation's sovereignty and identity (high nationalism), have little need to have friendly relations with others (low need for affiliation), and have a distinct willingness to initiate action (high belief in own control over events) are likely to exhibit an expansionist orientation. Expansionists perceive that aggressiveness is the appropriate means for achieving their ends. For them conflict is the "name of the political game."

2. *Active independent:* This individual has interest in participating in the international community but on his or her terms, without endangering a dependent relationship with any other government, group, or organization. Holsti (1970:262) suggests that political leaders with this orientation "emphasize at once independence, self-determination, possible mediation functions, and active programs to extend diplomatic and commercial relations to diverse areas of the world." Traits such as a strong desire to maintain national sovereignty (high nationalism), ability to consider a wide range of alternatives in making a decision (high conceptual complexity), little distrust of others (low distrust of others), a belief in own ability to control events (high belief in own control), and a need to establish and maintain friendly relations with others (high need for affiliation), with little need to control others (low need for power), comprise the active independent orientation.

3. *Influential:* This orientation centers around an interest in and desire to have an impact on other nations' foreign policy behavior, to play a leadership role in the international arena. Politicians with this orientation want to shape the nature of events in the foreign

policy arena, to have their goals become the goals of certain other nations in the international system. As Holsti (1970:161) notes, the political leader with an influential orientation perceives "special responsibilities . . . for itself [his nation] in relation to states in a particular region with which it [his nation] identifies, or to cross-cutting subsystems such as international communist movements." The interest may also be in leading nations concerned with a specific issue (e.g., oil). Politicians with an influential orientation are characterized by a need for power or control over others (high need for power), a need to establish and maintain friendly relations with others (high need for affiliation), a belief that they can control events (high belief in own control), little ability to consider a range of alternatives in making decisions (low conceptual complexity), little distrust of others (low distrust of others), and no overriding concern with maintaining their own individual identity separate from others (low nationalism). Such individuals have great impetus to lead but are not so ideologically committed that they cannot be responsive to those they are trying to lead.

4. *Mediator/integrator:* Such an individual is concerned with reconciling differences between nations and has an interest in playing a "go-between" role (see Holsti 1970:265). Politicians with this orientation want to gain a reputation for third-party politics as they try to resolve problems in the international system; they perceive themselves and their nations as the peacemakers of the international arena. Traits that probably characterize these individuals are an ability to consider a wide range of alternatives (high conceptual complexity), a belief in one's own ability to control events (high belief in own control over events), a need to establish and maintain friendly relations with others (high need for affiliation), little distrust of others (low distrust of others), no overriding concern with national identity or sovereignty (low nationalism), and little need to control or dominate others (low need for power). They enjoy the "behind the scenes" aspects of foreign policy making, having an impact on the decision without seeming to interfere or to control others.

5. *Opportunist:* Someone with this orientation shows a willingness to be expedient, to take advantage of present circumstances. Ziller et al. (1977) have proposed that this orientation is an important aspect of the political man. Politicians with this orientation are situation-sensitive—they are guided by what they perceive to be the demands and opportunities of the moment and are little tied

to ideological commitments. Individuals with the opportunist orientation have an ability to consider a range of alternatives in making a decision (high conceputal complexity), little distrust of others (low distrust of others), little need to control or dominate others (low need for power), little need to establish or maintain friendly relations with others (low need for affiliation), little belief in their on ability to control events (low belief in own control over events), and no overriding concern with the maintenance of national identity and sovereignty (low nationalism). They continuously monitor the environment, seeking information to confirm or disconfirm the relevance of a particular action or decision.

6. *Participative:* This orientation is evidenced by a desire to facilitate one's nation's involvement in the international arena "to the fullest." Politicians with this orientation have the following personal characteristics: a need to establish and maintain friendly relations with others (high need for affiliation), an ability to consider a wide range of alternatives in making decisions (high conceptual complexity), little distrust of others (low distrust of others), no overriding concern with national sovereignty (low nationalism), little belief in their own ability to control events (low belief in own control of events), and little need to control or dominate others (low need for power). Such individuals are likely to be interested in having their nations interact with other nations, in learning what other nations have of value for their nation and find valuable about their nation, and in seeking a wide range of alternative solutions to problems jointly plaguing their nation and other nations.

Although for the most part this study is viewed as a mapping exercise (an exploration of a new terrain), some propositions guide the research. Thus, heads of state with strong beliefs in their own ability to control events, high needs for power, expansionist orientations, active independent orientations, or influential orientations are more likely in nations that have a low level of modernization and in nations with a low level of political competition. These characteristics and orientations are useful under such conditions—they are congruent with the situation. Characteristics and orientations that are suggestive of responsiveness to the environment (need for affiliation, conceptual complexity, mediator/integrator orientation, opportunist orientation, participative orientation) are probably more likely in heads of state in societies and governments where being in tune with what is going on is an asset (e.g., societal stress is high, political competition is high). By maintaining a sensitivity to their environment, such political leaders can gain and keep a sufficient power base. Training in foreign affairs and the ability to integrate a variety of information (high conceptual complexity, opportunist orientation) are probably more prevalent in heads of states in complex societies and governments (e.g., large nations, modernized or developed nations). The number of issues, problems, and stimuli facing large and modernized nations demand some complexity or experience on the part of the prospective head of state. Characteristics and orientations indicating a self focus (nationalism, distrust of others, expansionist orientation, active independent orientation) are likely in governments seeking their own identity or place in the international system (e.g., in Third World countries and illegal regimes).

We are arguing that there will be a congruence between the characteristics of the head of state and the conditions of the nation and government he or she administers. The heads of state emerging from the recruitment process exhibit characteristics appropriate to the circumstances in which they find themselves. There is some support for this notion of congruence in the research of Browning and Jacob (1964), Edinger (1965), and Stewart (1977). Stewart found that the birth order of American presidents and British prime ministers has been appropriate to the crisis or noncrisis tenor of the times; Browning and Jacob report that local political leaders high in need for power and achievement were found in cities where power and achievement were built into the positions and not in cities where the roles lacked such characteristics; Edinger in his study of a defeated candidate for head of state, Kurt Schumacher of West Germany, suggests that the incongruity between the times and Schumacher's personality was his undoing. The general hypothesis of our study is that the individuals who become heads of state will have personal characteristics relevant to the demands of the nations and governments in which they come to power.

Methodology

Measuring the Personal Characteristics of Political Leaders

Procedure. Content analysis was used to assess the personal characteristics of the heads of state who were the subjects of this research. It has proven useful in measuring personal characteristics of political leaders who are virtually inaccessible for personality testing or clinical interviewing (see Eckhardt and White 1967; Hermann 1974, 1975, 1977; Shneidman 1963; Winter and Stewart 1977). The material which was content analyzed consisted of responses by heads of state to reporters' questions, generally in a press-conference setting. The U.S. Foreign Broadcast Information Service (FBIS) *Daily Report* (a document containing verbatim transcripts of material gleaned from U.S. monitoring of foreign broadcasts) and the *New York Times* were the basic sources used in collecting the interview responses.[2]

Press interviews with heads of state were used because they appear to contain the most spontaneous *public* material available on such political leaders. Spontaneous material is desirable because it minimizes the effects of "ghost writing" and planned communication. Materials such as speeches and letters are often written for the head of state by others and are generally designed to convey a specific image to a certain audience. As a consequence, the researcher who is analyzing these materials for content will learn what the ghost writer is like or what image the political leader would like to reflect. In the press-conference setting, the head of state is usually the author of his or her responses and often has little time in which to plan a response. Several content analysis studies suggest that the link between personal characteristics and spontaneous material is stronger than that between personal characteristics and planned material. Osgood and Anderson (1957) found that the more carefully and deliberately planned a communication was, the more remote the relationship was between the subject's attitudes and the content of the communication. LeVine (1966) has reported that more valid motive scores result from coding spontaneous (i.e., a report of a dream) as opposed to controlled (i.e., an essay) communications.

The FBIS *Daily Report* and the *New York Times* were searched for material on sixty-seven heads of state who held office during the decade 1959-68 in the thirty-six nations comprising the Comparative Research on the Events of Nations (CREON) Project sample. A list of these heads of state was compiled by checking such sources as the *Statesman's Year-Book* (1959-69), *The International Year Book and Statesman's Who's Who* (1959-61), and the *Political Handbook and Atlas of the World* (1959-68). By consulting area specialists, an attempt was made to consider as heads of state only those individuals with apparent final authority on matters of state. In other words, titular heads of state (e.g., the king of Belgium, the president of India) were not included.

At least fifteen interview responses were found during a head of state's period in office for forty-five (67 percent) of the heads of state in the CREON sample. In order to ascertain the stability of the personal characteristics across time and issues, interviews at more than one point in time were considered desirable. Table 1 shows the heads of state whose personal characteristics were examined, the years during which they held office, the number of interview responses which were content analyzed, the number of interviews represented in the responses, and the number of different years in which the interviews were conducted. Fifteen interview responses were not available for heads of state from seven of the CREON nations (i.e., Belgium, Iceland, Italy, Lebanon, Norway, Switzerland, and Uruguay). Thus, they were not included in the sample. Several comments will help the reader's understanding of Table 1. Whereas the FBIS *Daily Report* generally contains a verbatim transcript of press interviews with heads of state, the *New York Times* often summarizes such interviews. For purposes of the present study, only verbatim interview responses were included in the content analysis. Because there were usually in a *New York Times* report of an interview only one or two verbatim responses, some of the heads of state showed only a few responses per interview for analysis. Due to the amount of material available for several of the leaders (e.g., the U.S. presidents), a sampling procedure was employed. Every fifth interview response was included in the content analysis. In most cases only interviews which occurred during a head of state's tenure in office were used in order to assure the assessment of current personal characteristics. For a few heads of state who were in office for a very short time during the 1959-68 decade (e.g., Trudeau of Canada), interviews up to two years preceding their tenure were included.

The following process was used in doing the content analysis. All the interview responses to be content analyzed were put into machine-readable form. The cards for each leader were then run through the Key Word in Context (KWIC) Concordance program, which reports the frequency of occurrence of each word and reproduces each word in alphabetical order with the six to eight words which come before and after it (the word's context). The coding categories for the personal characteristics were designed to be used with the concordance output. In effect, this content analysis was viewed as a preliminary step to the construction of a dictionary for each of the personal characteristics, so future content analyses could be done by computer.

TABLE 1

Nature of Sample and Materials Used
In Content Analysis

NATION and Head of State	Years in Office 1959-1968	Number of Responses Analyzed	Number of Interviews	Years Covered
CANADA:				
Diefenbaker	1959-Apr,63	37	16	5
Pearson	Apr,63-Apr,68	22	17	6
Trudeau	Apr,68-	47	17	3
CHILE:				
Frei	Nov,64-1968	27	8	5
CHINA:				
Chou En-Lai	1959-Aug,66	25	6	4
Lin Piao	Aug,66-1968	19	8	3
COSTA RICA:				
Orlich	May,62-May,66	24	8	4
CUBA:				
Castro	1959-1968	49	8	4
EAST GERMANY:				
Ulbricht	1959-1968	30	5	2
EGYPT:				
Nasser	1959-1968	76	25	9
FRANCE:				
De Gaulle	1959-1968	31	7	5
GHANA:				
Nkrumah	1959-Feb,66	17	3	3
GUINEA:				
Toure	1959-1968	22	10	6
INDIA:				
Nehru	1959-May,64	94	17	7
Gandhi	1966-1968	43	8	3
ISRAEL:				
Ben-Gurion	1959-Jun,63	73	23	4
Eshkol	Jun,63-1968	28	6	3
IVORY COAST:				
Houphouet-Boigny	1960-1968	21	6	4
JAPAN:				
Kishi	1959-Jul,60	21	7	2
Ikeda	Jul,60-Nov,64	21	8	3
Sato	Nov,64-1968	22	5	4
KENYA:				
Kenyatta	Dec,63-1968	21	13	5

TABLE 1
(con't.)

Nature of Sample and Materials Used
In Content Analysis

NATION and Head of State	Years in Office 1959-1968	Number of Responses Analyzed	Number of Interviews	Years Covered
MEXICO:				
Mateos	1959-Nov,64	21	11	5
NEW ZEALAND:				
Holyoake	Dec,60-1968	15	11	5
PHILIPPINES:				
Garcia	1959-Dec,61	28	11	3
Macapagal	Dec,61-Dec,65	26	17	4
Marcos	Dec,65-1968	37	18	3
SOVIET UNION:				
Khrushchev	1959-Oct,64	77	11	3
Kosygin	Oct,64-1968	32	6	3
SPAIN:				
Franco	1959-1968	34	14	7
THAILAND:				
Kittikachorn	Dec,63-1968	15	6	5
TUNISIA:				
Bourguiba	1959-1968	37	10	2
TURKEY:				
Gursel	May,60-Oct,61	23	13	2
Inonu	Nov,61-Feb,65	15	3	2
Demirel	Oct,65-1968	24	8	4
UGANDA:				
Obote	Oct,63-1968	20	7	4
UNITED STATES:				
Eisenhower	1959-Jan,61	96	48	3
Kennedy	Jan,61-Nov,63	127	63	3
Johnson	Nov,63-1968	79	39	5
VENEZUELA:				
Betancourt	Feb,59-Nov,64	39	16	5
WEST GERMANY:				
Adenauer	1959-Oct,63	93	24	5
Erhard	Oct,63-Oct,66	43	11	4
Kiesinger	Nov,66-1968	34	6	1
YUGOSLAVIA:				
Tito	1959-1968	64	13	6
ZAMBIA:				
Kaunda	Oct,64-1968	46	23	5

Coding Categories for the Personal Characteristics. The coding schemes for the personal characteristics are described briefly in what follows. A more complete coding manual for each of the personal characteristics is available from the author. In describing the coding categories for the personal characteristics, two types of reliability are reported—inter-coder reliability and trait reliability. Inter-coder reliability refers to agreement among the coders on the coding of the interview responses for the various personal characteristics. In determining inter-coder reliability, the interview responses for three of the leaders were scored by all four coders involved in the content analysis.[3] Average percent of agreement among the coders is listed for each characteristic. Trait reliability refers to the stability of the personal characteristic across time and issues. This reliability was calculated by dividing the interview responses for each head of state on each personal characteristic into odd and even responses. Scores for these odd and even responses were intercorrelated across heads of state for each characteristic. These correlations, corrected for length by the Spearman-Brown formula, are listed for each characteristic. The higher the correlation between scores for odd and even interview responses, the more stable the characteristic appears to be across time and issues.

Nationalism. In coding for nationalism, a search was made of the concordance printout for references to the speaker's own nation and to other nations. Such references were coded for nationalism if they met any of the following criteria: (a) was a reference to the speaker's nation preceded by a favorable modifier (e.g., "prosperous," "peace-loving," "good"); (b) was a reference to the speaker's nation which contained in its context mention of the need to maintain national honor and sovereignty (e.g., "We, Ghanians, make our own rules."); (c) was a reference to another nation preceded by an unfavorable modifier (e.g., "weak," "unfriendly," "hostile"); (d) was a reference to another nation which contained within its context mention of the meddlesomeness of the referent in the affairs of others (e.g., "The U.S. always tries to interfere in our country's problems."). The score for nationalism was the number of references which met the specified criteria divided by the total number of references to own and other nations made. Average inter-coder reliability for nationalism was .88. The trait reliability was .77.

Belief in One's Own Ability to Control Events. In coding for belief in one's own ability to control events, the coders focused on verbs or action words. An assumption was made that when an individual takes responsibility for planning or initiating an action, he or she perceives some control over the action and outcome. The context for each verb was checked to see if it indicated that the speaker or a group with which he identified accepted responsibility for initiating or planning any action denoted in the verb. Consider an example: "We *proposed* a treaty and *asked* them to join with us." Since the speaker's group is identified as the actor, both verbs are coded as indicating belief in own ability to control events. The score for belief in own ability to control events was the number of verbs indicating the speaker assumed responsibility for the action divided by the total number of verbs found. Average inter-coder reliability for this personal characteristic was .91. Trait reliability was .75.

Need for Power.[4] Verbs were also checked in coding for need for power. Of interest was whether or not a verb and its context suggested an attempt to establish, maintain, or restore power. If a verb and its context indicated *any* of the following activities, it was scored as denoting need for power: (a) verb and context indicate strong, forceful actions which affect others, such as assaults, attacks, verbal insults, threats, reprimands; (b) verb and context suggest giving help, advice, or assistance to another when not solicited by the other; (c) verb and context denote an attempt to control another person or group by regulating their behavior or the conditions of their lives or by seeking information that would affect another's life or actions—such as investigating or checking up on another; (d) verb and context indicate an attempt to influence, persuade, convince, bribe, make a point, or argue with another person or group, as long as the concern is not with reaching agreement or avoiding misunderstanding; (e) verb and context suggest an attempt to impress another person or group or to create a public display in order to gain fame and/or notoriety; (f) verb and context denote concern for one's reputation or position. The need for power score for a head of state was the number of verbs meeting the above criteria divided by the number of verbs used. The average inter-coder reliability for need for power was .86. Trait reliability was .73.

Need for Affiliation.[5] As with need for power, the verb was the focus of attention in scoring need for affiliation. When a verb was encountered in the concordance output, its context was checked to see if *any* of the following conditions were met: (a) the verb and context indicate a positive feeling for another person or group

—in other words, indicate liking, the desire to be liked, the desire to be accepted; (b) verb and context suggest reaction to a disruption of a relationship, such as a wish to restore a relationship, a desire to reach agreement, a desire to negotiate; (c) verb and context denote companionate activities such as making visits, attending summit conferences, engaging in personal diplomacy, requesting joint action; (d) verb and context indicate nurturant acts, such as helping another person or group or being concerned about the well-being of another person or group. The score for need for affiliation was the percentage of verbs meeting the above criteria. Average inter-coder reliability for need for affiliation was .91. Trait reliability was .71.

Conceptual Complexity. In coding for conceptual complexity, the concordance output was examined for the frequency of occurrence of two sets of words—one set indicating low conceptual complexity (e.g., "absolutely," "always," "definitely," "only," "without a doubt") and one set indicating high conceptual complexity (e.g., "approximately," "depends," "may," "possibly," "sometimes," "tend"). If the context of the word indicated a negation of the word or that the speaker was quoting someone else, the word was not counted. The conceptual complexity score for a head of state was the ratio of the number of high conceptual complexity words to the number of low conceptual complexity words present in the interview response. Thus, the higher the score, the higher the head of state's conceptual complexity. Average inter-coder reliability for conceptual complexity was .99. Trait reliability was .90.

Distrust of Others. In coding for distrust of others, all nouns and pronouns referring to groups or persons other than those with whom the speaker identifies were checked to see if their context indicated doubt, misgiving, uneasiness, or wariness about what those others were doing, saying, or planning. An example is the statement, "This is part of the Americans' scheme to enlarge the war." The speaker's concerns could also take the form of statements suggesting that these other persons or groups were doing something harmful or detrimental to the speaker, the speaker's group, an ally of the speaker, or a cause important to the speaker; for instance, "That rebel group is going to force our downfall." The score on distrust of others for a head of state was the percentage of references to other persons or groups (with whom the speaker *did not* identify) that satisfied either of these two conditions. Average inter-coder reliability was .88. Trait reliability was .90.

Training or Experience in Foreign Affairs. To determine the amount of training or experience the heads of state in Table 1 had in foreign affairs, a search was made of sources such as *Statesman's Year-Book* as well as autobiographies and biographies. All past political and governmental positions were noted. From this biographical record on the heads of state, the number of years each held positions involving foreign affairs (e.g., foreign or defense minister, ambassador, in foreign or defense ministry, representative to UNESCO or Common Market) was determined. The score for training or experience in foreign affairs was calculated by finding what percentage of the years a head of state had been in politics involved holding a position concerned with foreign affairs or foreign policy making.

Orientations to Foreign Affairs. Elsewhere the author (Hermann 1976) has suggested that the first six personal characteristics described above interrelate to form six orientations to foreign affairs. By learning the degree to which a political leader is nationalistic, believes in his or her own ability to control events, has a need for power, has a need for affiliation, is conceptually complex, and is distrustful of others, we can begin to propose how he is likely to define a situation and the style of behavior he is likely to emphasize. By examining how the traits combine, we can suggest how a particular type of head of state will be predisposed to act when confronted by a foreign policy making task.

Table 2 indicates the bases on which the personal characteristics were interrelated to form the orientations for the present study. The "Hi" in the table refers to being high on that characteristic; the "Lo" refers to being low on the characteristic. To determine scores for the orientations, the heads of state's scores on each of the six personal characteristics were ranked. The appropriate ranks were then summed. The ranks ranged from 1 for the lowest score to 45 for the highest score, when a high score was indicated by the orientation rationale, and from 1 for the highest score to 45 for the lowest score, when a low score was indicated by the orientation rationale. Scores on the orientations could range from 6 to 270. An example of how the orientation scores were calculated may prove helpful to the reader. In determining a head of state's score on the expansionist orientation, for instance, his or her ranks on nationalism, belief in own control over events, need for power, and distrust of others (in each case 1 was assigned to the lowest score among the heads of state and 45 to the highest score) were

TABLE 2

Bases for Orientation to Foreign Affairs

PERSONAL CHARACTERISTIC	ORIENTATION					
	Expansionist	Active Independent	Influential	Mediator/Integrator	Opportunist	Participative
Nationalism	Hi	Hi	Lo	Lo	Lo	Lo
Belief in Own Control of Events	Hi	Hi	Hi	Hi	Lo	Lo
Need Power	Hi	Lo	Hi	Lo	Lo	Lo
Need Affiliation	Lo	Hi	Hi	Hi	Lo	Hi
Conceptual Complexity	Lo	Hi	Lo	Hi	Hi	Hi
Distrust of Others	Hi	Lo	Lo	Lo	Lo	Lo

summed. The individual's ranks on need for affiliation and conceptual complexity (in each case 45 was assigned to the lowest score and 1 to the highest score) were also summed. These two sums were added together for the orientation score.

Measuring Possible Societal and
Regime Influences on Recruitment

Six possible societal and regime influences on recruitment were examined in the present study. These six were the size of the nation, its level of modernization, the degree of societal stress present, the degree of political competition evident for the government, the genesis of the regime, and the region of the world in which the nation is located. The six variables were operationalized in the following ways.

Size of the Nation. By size of the nation is meant the total resources within a nation—the "raw resources" that are available, the "power potential" of the nation. The measure of size was taken from East (1975). Each of the twenty-nine nations in Table 1 was given a size score based on its factor score as defined by the following seven variables: total population, total area, agricultural area, gross national product, energy consumption, military manpower, and defense expenditures. Data on these seven variables were taken from *World Handbook II* (Taylor and Hudson 1973) for the year 1965.[6]

Level of Modernization. Level of modernization refers to a nation's degree of economic development, its level of urbanization, and its quality of life. The measure of level of modernization, like that for size, was taken from East (1975). As with size, level of modernization was indicated by a factor score on a factor defined by the following eight variables: literacy rate, students in higher education per million population, percent of gross domestic product originating in industry, newspapers per capita, population in cities over 100,000, gross national product per capita, energy consumption per capita, and protein intake per capita per diem. Data on these variables were found in *World Handbook II* (Taylor and Hudson 1973), *Cross-Polity Time-Series Data* (Banks 1971), U.N. *Statistical Yearbook*, and *World Economic Survey*. Data were collected for the year 1965.

Degree of Societal Stress. Societal stress is conceptualized as the "persistent problems in the society which cannot be continually ignored by the government if the society is to continue" (East 1975:10; see also Haas 1968). The societal stress measure used in our study came from East (1975). Degree of societal stress was represented by the sum of a nation's factor scores on two factors which emphasized the following four variables: ethno-linguistic fractionalization, deaths by political violence, political strikes, and inflation rate. Data on these four variables were found in *World Handbook II* (Taylor and Hudson 1973) and the U.N. *Statistical Yearbook*. Data were collected for the year 1965.

Degree of Political Competition. Degree of political competition refers to the level of participation in the political process of a nation's legislature or parliament, of its political parties, and of its citizenry. In effect, degree of political competition is one indicator of the constraints under which a regime and head of state must operate. The greater the degree of political competition, the more attention the head of state must pay to the desires and wishes of others in order to maintain a base of power. Degree of political competition was measured using an additive index composed of four ordinal level variables: effectiveness of the legislature, competitiveness of the nominating process, presence of legislative coalitions, and extent of party legitimacy. This index was taken from the *Cross-Polity Time-Series Data* (Banks 1971). Scores on the index can range from 0 to 11 and were available on the twenty-nine nations in Table 1 for the years 1959-66. An average degree of political competition score was determined for those heads of state in office more than one year during this period.

Genesis of Regime. By genesis of regime is meant how a particular government came to power—by legal or illegal means. A legal government or regime is one that came "into existence as a result of lawful elections, hereditary succession, or other internally sanctioned mechanisms for obtaining political leadership, such as cabinet reshuffles within the confines of the law; illegal regimes are those which gain power in a manner outside the law, such as by revolution, *coup d'état*, or civil war" (Salmore and Salmore 1972:7). Data on genesis of regime were taken from Salmore and Salmore (1972). A code of one was given to a head of state in Table 1 who came to power by legal means; a code of zero was assigned to those who came to power by illegal means.

Region of the World. The twenty-nine nations in Table 1 were categorized into the regions of the world they represent based on the *Dimensionality of Nations* (Rummel 1972) regional classification. The nations represented six regions: Asia, Middle East, Eastern Europe, Atlantic Community, Latin America, and Africa.

Results

Relationships Among Personal Characteristics and Orientations

How do the personal characteristics relate to one another? What are the relationships between the personal characteristics and the orientations? Do the personal characteristics correlate with the orientations in the directions expected in Table 2? Table 3 presents the means, standard deviations, and intercorrelations among the personal characteristics and orientations. It shows that for this sample of heads of state, nationalism, need for power, and distrust of others are significantly correlated. The head of state who was highly nationalistic was also likely to have a high need for power and to be distrustful of others. Conceptual complexity and need for affiliation are significantly inversely correlated—high conceptual complexity was associated with low need for affiliation.

A comparison of the bases for the orientations from Table 2 with the intercorrelations between the personal characteristics and orientations in Table 3 reveals that with only two exceptions the personal characteristics are related in the predicted direction to the orientations. The two exceptions are nationalism in the active independent orientation and need for affiliation in the expansionist orientation. These discrepancies probably occur because of the rather strong positive correlations we have just noted between nationalism and need for power and nationalism and distrust of others as well as the negative relationship between need for affiliation and conceptual complexity.

As their rationales would suggest, the mediator/integrator, opportunist, and participative orientations come out like mirror images of the expansionist orientation. Of the three for this sample of heads of state, the opportunist orientation is the most mirror-like. The intercorrelations among the orientations indicate that the influential orientation is least like the other orientations. At this point we might lend some face validity to the orientations by listing the two leaders with the highest scores on each orientation. They are Lin Piao of China and Nkrumah of Ghana on the expansionist orientation, Sato of Japan and Trudeau of Canada on the active independent orientation, Kenyatta of Kenya and Chou En-lai of China on the influential orientation, Gandhi of India and Eisenhower of the United States on the mediator/integrator orientation, Marcos of the Philippines and Holyoake of New Zealand on the opportunist orientation, and Pearson of Canada

TABLE 3

Data on Personal Characteristics and Orientations

Personal Characteristics	Mean	SD	1	2	3	4	5	6	7	8	9	10	11	12	13
1. Nationalism	.14	.09	--												
2. Believe Control Events	.59	.15	-.06	--											
3. Need Power	.19	.10	.54*	.01	--										
4. Need Affiliation	.07	.06	-.09	-.07	.15	--									
5. Conceptual Complexity	.67	.50	.00	-.20†	-.14	-.34**	--								
6. Distrust Others	.15	.15	.63*	.13	.28*	-.21†	-.13	--							
7. Training	.48	.25	.15	-.35**	-.04	.06	.13	.02	--						
Orientations															
8. Expansionist	138.96	40.58	.58*	.39*	.61*	.17	-.45*	.60*	.03	--					
9. Active Independent	138.18	23.65	-.26*	.27*	-.53*	.14	.27*	-.43**	-.11	-.48**	--				
10. Influential	138.03	35.83	-.39*	.36*	.25*	.57**	-.48*	-.41**	-.19	.10	.12	--			
11. Mediator/Integrator	138.03	39.93	-.69*	.20†	-.60*	.11	.18	-.61**	-.23†	-.74**	.77	.37**	--		
12. Opportunist	138.54	42.87	-.51*	-.32*	-.60*	-.45*	.52*	-.48*	-.07	-.95*	.35**	-.27*	.63*	--	
13. Participative	139.09	36.17	-.54**	-.48*	-.32*	.22†	.32*	-.69**	-.01	-.88*	.44**	.19	.69**	.71**	--

†p < .10; *p < .05; **p < .01

and Kiesinger of West Germany on the participative orientation.

With regard to training in foreign affairs, only the correlation with belief in own control over events was significant. The more highly trained the head of state was, the lower his belief in his own or his nation's ability to control events. Experience may lead to a realization of the range of variables affecting foreign policy over which one can have little control.

Possible Societal and Regime Influences on Head-of-State Selection

Before examining the interrelationships between what the heads of state are like and the types of nations and regimes in which they come to power, let us look at the correlations among the possible societal and regime influences on head-of-state selection. Table 4 shows the means, standard deviations, and intercorrelations for the proposed influences on head-of-state selection that are continuous rather than dichotomous variables—i.e., size of nation, level of modernization, degree of societal stress, and degree of political competition. It indicates that for this sample of twenty-nine nations, size of nation and level of modernization are significantly correlated, as are level of modernization and degree of political competition. The larger nations tend to have higher levels of modernization; the nations with higher levels of modernization tend to have a higher degree of political competition.

Examining the relationships between the dichotomous variables —genesis of regime and region of the world—and the continuous variables by analysis of variance, we also find three significant correlations. Genesis of regime is related (.47 eta-square[7]) to degree of political competition. Less political competition was found in illegal as opposed to legal regimes. Moreover, region of the world is correlated (.20 eta-square) with level of modernization and with degree of political competition (.19 eta-square). In this sample of twenty-nine nations, lower levels of modernization were found in nations in the African and Latin American regions than in countries in the other regions. A higher degree of political competition was evident in Atlantic Community nations than in nations in other regions.

Relationships Among Personal Characteristics and Possible Selection Influences

Do the heads of state in the present study have characteristics relevant to the nations and regimes in which they find themselves?

TABLE 4

Data on Possible Influences on Head of State Selection

Proposed Influence	Mean	Standard Deviation	1	2	3	4
1. Size	.99	2.25	--			
2. Level of Modernization	.65	1.22	.56**	--		
3. Degree of Societal Stress	.93	0.26	-.24†	.07	--	
4. Degree of Political Competition	6.02	4.56	.07	.49**	.14	--

†p <.10; *p <.05; **p <.01

Tables 5, 6, and 7 present some answers to this question. These tables indicate the interrelationships among the personal characteristics (both as individual characteristics and as orientations) and the possible societal and regime influences we are examining. What do the data in these tables suggest?

There appears to be little relationship between size of nation and the characteristics of heads of state. Correlations between size of nation and the personal characteristics are reported in column two of Table 5. Only three of the correlations are significant or approach significance. These suggest that heads of state high in nationalism are found in small rather than large nations and that heads of state with mediator/integrator and opportunist orientations are found in large as opposed to small nations. Nationalism is probably a more useful characteristic to the head of state of a small nation struggling to survive and maintain its identity than in a larger, more resource-rich country whose survival is not a problem. The nationalistic leader in the small nation is less likely to give up the struggle and will continue to urge, cajole, or order the people to work harder for the state. With regard to the mediator/integrator orientation, larger nations provide the resource and power base to allow such leaders the possibility of assuming a third-party role. As a result of their size, large nations probably include a wide range of interest groups with demands and desires that make responsiveness important in the leader. The sensitivity to environmental cues of individuals with opportunist orientations may make them relevant choices under such circumstances.

Seven of the thirteen correlations between the personal characteristics and level of modernization are moderately large and sig-

TABLE 5

Relationships Between Personal Characteristics, Orientations, and Possible Selection Influences

		Possible Selection Influences		
Personal Characteristics	Size	Modernization	Societal Stress	Political Competition
Training	-.15	-.09	.05	-.27*
Nationalism	-.29*	-.40**	.10	-.41**
Belief in Own Control of Events	.00	-.21†	-.19	-.02
Need Power	-.18	-.31*	.12	-.28*
Need Affiliation	-.11	-.10	.21†	-.13
Conceptual Complexity	-.14	.07	-.10	.11
Distrust of Others	-.18	-.35**	-.09	-.41**
Orientations				
Expansionist	-.19	-.50**	.04	-.52**
Active Independent	-.01	.21†	-.06	.37**
Influential	.15	.01	.07	.07
Mediator/Integrator	.22†	.38**	-.15	.48**
Opportunist	.20†	.49**	-.09	.53**
Participative	.12	.45**	.06	.44**

†p <.10; *p <.05; **p <.01

nificant (see column three of Table 5). Heads of state high in nationalism, high in need for power, high in distrust of others, and with an expansionist orientation were found in nations with lower levels of modernization—nations in the process of modernizing. On the other hand, heads of state with mediator/integrator, opportunist, or participative orientations were found in nations with higher levels of modernization.

One consequence of a low level of modernization is a small bureaucracy. It, in turn, offers a greater chance for the head of state to exercise control over policy. In many cases policy is made by a small group including the head of state and some close associates. A need for power and distrust of others become functional characteristics in such a setting. By providing a rationale for his activities, nationalism helps the head of state in the modernizing nation to maintain control. Since nationalism, need for power, and distrust of others are important features of the expansionist orientation, it is not surprising to find a relationship between an expansionist orientation and level of moderization. One way to sustain and nurture national identity and to increase one's perceived power in a modernizing nation is through advancing an expansionist world view—"Our nation deserves more and we are going to get more."

Higher levels of modernization provide the necessary support systems for leaders with mediator/integrator and participative orientations. The resources and technologies are available to allow the leaders to participate actively in the international system and to play a mediator role. As with size, a higher level of modernization may introduce a degree of complexity that makes sensitivity to the environment important in a leader. Thus, an opportunist orientation becomes more relevant the higher the level of modernization.

An examination of column four in Table 5 shows that, overall, the correlations between degree of societal stress and personal characteristics are quite low. None of the correlations is significant; the relationship for need for affiliation approaches significance. Heads of state with high needs for affiliation are more likely to be found in nations with high as opposed to low societal stress. High affiliation motivation is suggestive of much energy directed toward maintaining good relations with others—e.g., members of one's government, ethnic constituents, party regulars, dissidents—and, thus, attempting to ameliorate the causes of the stress.

Nine of the thirteen correlations between the personal characteristics and degree of political competition are fairly high and significant (see column five of Table 5). In a similar pattern to that for modernization, heads of state high in nationalism, high in need for power, high in distrust of others, and with an expansionist orientation appear more likely in nations where political competition is low; heads of state with mediator/integrator, opportunist, and participative orientations are more likely in nations with a high degree of political competition. In addition, heads of state with more training in foreign affairs are found in nations where political competition is low; leaders with active independent orientations are more likely in nations with a high degree of political competition.

The higher the political competition in a government, the more constrained the leaders of that government are in what they can do (see Salmore and Salmore 1972). When political competition is low, on the other hand, the leaders have more freedom to make and control policy. Thus, need for power, nationalism, and distrust of others are probably more useful characteristics for heads of state where competition is low; these characteristics probably become dysfunctional when competition is high. In a similar manner, an expansionist orientation, emphasizing aggressive control of foreign policy, is more functional when competition is low. Orientations focusing on cooperative coping with the environment (i.e., active independent, mediator/integrator, opportunist, participative) are more useful when competition is high.

The training relationship suggests that where domestic political competition is "hot and heavy," expertise in foreign affairs may be a little prized virtue in coming to power. On the other hand, where competition is less keen, training in foreign affairs may be viewed as a relevant part of any head of state's grooming or apprenticeship program.

Table 6 reports means for personal characteristics of the heads of state in the present sample who came to power illegally and legally. An analysis of variance was used with the dichotomous genesis of regime variable to determine relationships with the personal characteristics. The pattern of results for genesis of regime is similar to that for degree of political competition. This was not entirely unexpected, given the strong relationship between political competition and genesis. The strongest relationships were found with nationalism (eta-square = .11; remember eta-square is equivalent to r^2 or R^2—see note 7), need for power (eta-square = .11), expansionist orientation (eta-square = .12), active indepen-

TABLE 6

Means for Personal Characteristics and Orientations
by Genesis of Regime

Personal Characteristics	Genesis of Regime[a]		F
	Illegal (N=9)	Legal (N=28)	
Training	.61	.43	3.51†
Nationalism	.17	.12	4.25*
Belief in Own Control of Events	.58	.58	0.00
Need Power	.25	.17	4.42*
Need Affiliation	.06	.07	0.09
Conceptual Complexity	.78	.64	0.46
Distrust of Others	.20	.12	3.06†
Orientation			
Expansionist	139.44	106.45	4.97*
Active Independent	121.78	141.54	5.80*
Influential	132.89	138.27	0.16
Mediator/Integrator	108.11	145.80	8.55**
Opportunist	117.00	147.59	3.49†
Participative	95.89	120.66	3.85*

†$p < .10$; *$p < .05$; **$p < .01$

[a] The Salmore and Salmore (1972) genesis data did not contain information on eight heads of state in the present sample

dent orientation (eta-square = .14), mediator/integrator orientation (eta-square = .20), and participative orientation (eta-square = .10). Heads of state coming to power illegally were more nationalistic than those coming to office by legal means; they had a greater need for power, were more expansionistic, and were less likely to have an active independent, mediator/integrator, or participative orientation.

For the present sample of nations and heads of state, it appears to take a highly nationalistic or power-oriented individual—a person who is willing to be expansionistic—to try to assume leadership by other than legal means. The predominant illegal means of coming to power for the sample of heads of state examined here was by revolution. Heads of state with orientations that emphasized a more cooperative coping with the environment (i.e., active independent, mediator/integrator, participative) were more likely to come to office through legal means.

Table 7 shows means for each of the personal characteristics by regions of the world represented by the heads of state in the twenty-nine nations of this sample. It indicates that there are regional differences on nationalism, distrust of others, expansionist orientation, mediator/integrator orientation, opportunist orientation, and participative orientation. Analyses of variance reveal significant or near significant differences for these six variables. Heads of state in the Middle East and Africa were more nationalistic than heads of state in other regions. The least amount of nationalism was found among leaders in the Atlantic Community nations. Like nationalism, distrust of others was greatest among heads of state in the Middle East and Africa and least among heads of state in Atlantic Community nations. An expansionist orientation was more prevalent among heads of state in the Middle Eastern, African, and Eastern European nations and least prevalent among heads of state in the Atlantic Community nations. The mediator/integrator orientation was found more often among heads of state from Atlantic Community, Asian, and Latin American countries and least often among heads of state in Middle Eastern countries. An opportunist orientation was more likely in leaders in Asian, Atlantic Community, and Latin American countries and least likely in African nations. A participative orientation was more prevalent among heads of state in Atlantic Community nations and least prevalent among heads of state in Middle Eastern nations. These results suggest that there are differences in the

TABLE 7

Means for Personal Characteristics and Orientations by Region

Personal Characteristics	Asia (N=12)	Middle East (N=6)	Eastern Europe (N=4)	Atlantic Community (N=11)	Latin America (N=5)	Africa (N=7)	F
Training	.36	.48	.53	.55	.35	.65	1.74
Nationalism	.12	.20	.11	.09	.13	.21	3.25*
Belief in Own Control of Events	.65	.60	.54	.53	.64	.58	0.87
Need Power	.20	.27	.19	.13	.18	.21	1.72
Need Affiliation	.06	.06	.08	.06	.04	.11	0.83
Conceptual Complexity	.89	.56	.47	.72	.67	.43	0.99
Distrust of Others	.10	.25	.15	.07	.16	.25	2.39†
Orientations							
Expansionist	109.25	146.58	124.25	82.14	118.40	141.43	3.76**
Active Independent	146.04	124.17	119.38	145.64	142.70	132.50	1.64
Influential	143.17	131.00	141.13	132.73	140.90	139.79	0.14
Mediator/Integrator	149.46	106.33	125.88	159.41	139.50	117.93	2.32†
Opportunist	147.58	110.50	126.38	169.36	141.30	103.64	3.55**
Participative	119.17	86.33	109.50	143.23	103.90	99.71	3.07*

†$p < .10$; *$p < .05$; **$p < .01$

personal characteristics and orientations of heads of state who come to power in the various regions of the world.

Conclusions

In general, the results indicate that there is a relationship between political leaders' personal characteristics, role requirements, and recruitment processes. Different types of heads of state were found in modernizing as opposed to modernized societies, in governments where political competition was high as opposed to low, in different regions of the international system. Moreover, different types of heads of state came to power illegally as opposed to legally. Most of the differences in the present study centered around three individual characteristics—nationalism, need for power, and distrust of others—and four orientations to foreign affairs—expansionist and its mirror images, the mediator/integrator, opportunist, and participative orientations. In most instances, there appeared to be a congruence between these characteristics and the setting. Heads of state had those characteristics most likely to be functional and rewarding in the setting in which they came to power.

This study has been exploratory and to a certain extent raises more questions than it answers. For example, where the personal characteristics of heads of state are incongruent with the setting, are they less likely to remain in office long? Are the personal characteristics of the citizenry of these different types of nations reflected in their leaders' characteristics? As a society or government changes, are there congruent changes in the characteristics of the leaders? In our study we assessed the personal characteristics of heads of state from their responses to press interviews held during their tenure in office. Are our findings merely the result of their assuming the rhetoric of their particular roles, or would we find similar characteristics prominent in their responses to the press prior to coming to office? Clearly, there is much more research yet to be done relating personal characteristics to role requirements and recruitment conditions and processes.

Once we learn what linkages there are between societal and regime conditions and the selection of heads of state, a further intriguing issue comes to mind. In another study (Hermann 1976) we found that the personal characteristics and orientations considered here are related to particular national foreign policy behaviors. If certain types of leaders come to office in certain types of nations, can we develop models to suggest the effects on foreign policy behavior? Studies like this one can help bring us one step closer to the development of such models.

Notes

1. Only six of the personal characteristics are used in defining the orientations. Training in foreign affairs is not included, since it is viewed as acting in a more general fashion on the behavior of heads of state. A high degree of training in foreign affairs is viewed as increasing the repertoire of possible responses and comparable events that a head of state may rely on in dealing with a foreign policy situation and, thus, as decreasing the impact of the head of state's personality on political behavior. Heads of state with little training in foreign affairs are influenced more by their predispositions. For more on this point, see Hermann (1978).

2. These two sources were supplemented by material from "Meet the Press" and "Face the Nation" television interviews when such were available. Material on the U.S. presidents was taken from the *Public Papers of the Presidents*. The *Public Papers of the Presidents* includes verbatim transcripts of all press conferences held during a president's tenure in office.

3. The author would like to express her appreciation to Petra Donofrio, Danny Donofrio, Joanne Farley, and Beverly Gatliff for their aid with the content analysis.

4. The coding scheme for this variable was developed by Winter (1973: 247-345) who, with his associates, has used it to analyze inaugural addresses of twentieth-century American presidents (see Donley and Winter 1970; Winter and Stewart 1977).

5. This coding scheme has been used extensively in personality research. The complete coding scheme is found in Atkinson (1958:685-776). Winter and Stewart (1977) have applied the scheme to the inaugural addresses of twentieth-century American presidents.

6. The East measures used in our study were developed as part of the Comparative Research on the Events of Nations (CREON) Project, which focuses on an examination of the foreign policy behavior of thirty-six nations during the decade 1959-1968. (The personal characteristic measures described in this chapter were also developed as part of the CREON Project.) Because aggregate data were most complete for these thirty-six nations in the year 1965, the measures focus on this year. A comparison with data on several of the variables for 1960 indicated little change in the variables across time (see East 1975).

7. Eta-square is an analysis of variance equivalent to r^2 or R^2. It indicates the proportion of variance in the dependent variable accounted for by the independent variable(s) (see Cohen and Cohen 1975). The other type of correlation used in this chapter is the product moment correlation. Whenever a

correlation is listed but is not preceded by the notation "eta-square," it is a product moment correlation.

References

Atkinson, J. W. *Motives in Fantasy, Action, and Society.* Princeton: Van Nostrand, 1958.

Banks, A. *Cross-Polity Time-Series Data.* Cambridge, Mass.: M.I.T. Press, 1971.

Barber, J. D. *The Lawmakers.* New Haven, Conn.: Yale University Press, 1965.

Browning, R. P. and Jacob, H. "Power Motivation and the Political Personality." *Public Opinion Quarterly* 23 (1964):75-90.

Cohen, J. and Cohen, P. *Applied Multiple Regression/Correlation Analysis for the Behavioral Sciences.* Hillsdale, N.J.: Lawrence Erlbaum Associates, 1975.

Crockett, W. H. "Cognitive Complexity and Impression Formation." *Progress in Experimental Personality Research* 2 (1965):47-90.

DiRenzo, G. J. "Politicians and Personality: A Cross-Cultural Perspective." In *A Psychological Examination of Political Leaders,* edited by M. G. Hermann, pp. 149-173. New York: Free Press, 1977.

Donley, R. E., and Winter, D. G. "Measuring the Motives of Public Officials at a Distance: An Exploratory Study of American Presidents." *Behavioral Science* 15 (1970):227-236.

East, M. A. "Explaining Foreign Policy Using National Attributes." Paper presented at the annual meeting of the American Political Science Association, San Francisco, Sept. 2-5, 1975.

Eckhardt, W., and White, R. K. "A Test of the Mirror-Image Hypothesis: Kennedy and Khrushchev." *Journal of Conflict Resolution* (1967):325-332.

Edinger, L. J. *Kurt Schumacher: A Study in Personality and Political Behavior.* Stanford University Press, 1965.

Frey, F. W. *The Turkish Political Elite.* Cambridge, Mass.: M.I.T. Press, 1965.

Haas, M. "Social Change and National Aggressiveness, 1900-1960." In *Quantitative International Politics,* edited by J. D. Singer. New York: Free Press, 1968.

Hedlund, R. D. Psychological Predispositions: Political Representatives and the Public. *American Journal of Political Science* 17 (1973):489-505.

Hennessy, B. "Politicals and Apoliticals: Some Measurements of Personality Traits." *Midwest Journal of Political Science* 3 (1959):336-355.

Hermann, M. G. "Leader Personality and Foreign Policy Behavior." In *Comparing Foreign Policies: Theories, Findings, and Methods,* edited by J. N. Rosenau, pp. 201-234. New York: Sage-Halsted, 1974.

——. "Explaining Foreign Policy Behavior Using Personal Characteristics of Political Leaders." Paper presented at the annual meeting of the American Political Science Association, San Francisco, Sept. 2-5, 1975.

———. "The Effects of Political Leaders' Orientations to Foreign Affairs on Foreign Policy Behavior." Paper presented at the annual meeting of the Peace Science Society (International), Midwest Section, Chicago, April 29–May 1, 1976.

———. *A Psychological Examination of Political Leaders*. New York: Free Press, 1977.

———. Effects of Personal Characteristics of Political Leaders on Foreign Policy. In *Why Nations Act: Theoretical Perspectives for Comparative Foreign Policy Studies*, edited by M. A. East, S. A. Salmore, and C. F. Hermann, pp. 49-68. Beverly Hills, Calif.: Sage Publications, 1978.

Holsti, K. J. "National Role Conceptions in the Study of Foreign Policy." *International Studies Quarterly* 14 (1970):233-309.

Lasswell, H. D., and Lerner, D. *World Revolutionary Elites: Studies in Coercive Ideological Movements*. Cambridge, Mass.: M.I.T. Press, 1965.

LeVine, R. A. *Dreams and Deeds: Achievement Motivation in Nigeria*. University of Chicago Press, 1966.

Matthews, D. R. *U.S. Senators and Their World*. Chapel Hill, N.C.: University of North Carolina Press, 1960.

Osgood, C. E., and Anderson, L. "Certain Relations Among Experienced Contingencies, Associative Structure, and Contingencies in Encoded Messages." *American Journal of Psychology* 70 (1957):411-420.

Rummel, R. J. *The Dimensions of Nations*. Beverly Hills, Calif.: Sage Publications, 1972.

Salmore, B. G., and Salmore, S. A. "Structure and Change in Regimes—Their Effect on Foreign Policy." Paper presented at the annual meeting of the American Political Science Association, Washington, D.C., Sept. 5-9, 1972.

Scott, W. A. "Cognitive Complexity and Cognitive Behavior." *Sociometry* 26 (1963):66-74.

Seligman, L. G. *Recruiting Political Elites*. New York: General Learning Press, 1971.

Shneidman, E. S. "The Logic of Politics." In *Television and Human Behavior*, edited by L. Arons and M. A. May, pp. 177-199. New York: Appleton-Century-Crofts, 1963.

Stewart, L. H. "Birth Order and Political Leadership." In *A Psychological Examination of Political Leaders*, edited by M. G. Hermann, pp. 206-236. New York: Free Press, 1977.

Taylor, C. L. and Hudson, M. *World Handbook of Political and Social Indicators*, vol. 2. New Haven: Yale University Press, 1973.

Welsh, W. A. "Effect of Career and Party Affiliation on Revolutionary Behavior Among Latin American Political Elites." In *A Psychological Examination of Political Leaders*, edited by M. G. Hermann, pp. 276-310. New York: Free Press, 1977.

Winter, D. G. *The Power Motive*. New York: Free Press, 1973.

Winter, D. G. and Stewart, A. J. "Content Analysis as a Technique for Assessing Political Leaders." In *A Psychological Examination of Political Leaders,* edited by M. G. Hermann, pp. 28-61. New York: Free Press, 1977.

Ziller, R. G., Stone, W. F., Jackson, R. M., and Terbovic, N. J. "Self-Other Orientations and Political Behavior." In *A Psychological Examination of Political Leaders,* edited by M. G. Hermann, pp. 176-204. New York: Free Press, 1977.

3
Predicting Flexibility with Memory Profiles

Lawrence S. Falkowski

Introduction

This chapter presents a framework for studying flexibility and offers the results of employing this framework on presidents and secretaries of state since the end of World War II. Several issues related to the nature and prediction of flexibility are addressed, including the importance of the individual in foreign policy and the degree to which the flexibility of decision-makers in crisis can vary.

Flexibility may be viewed as the ability of a decision-maker to change the direction and intensity of his behavior when faced with new information. In one sense, it describes the degree to which a decision-maker is more or less "closed minded" when compared to other decision-makers. The degree to which a leader changes his policies, goals, and even the examples that he utilizes are indicative of that leader's flexibility.

The study of individual decision-makers is not novel. Most scholars would agree with the statement by Patrick Morgan that "for purposes of research the nation is at any given time its [own] decision-maker" (Morgan 1972: 113-14). Most disagreement arises, not in the fact that decision-makers are important, but rather in considering whether or not the individual differences among decision-makers are crucial to an understanding of foreign policy formulation and change.

The framework offered here owes much to the insights and assumptions of decision-making analysis. This approach assumes that the decision-maker is important to an understanding of foreign policy and that individual decision-makers vary in their response to new information. The variation among decision-makers is attributable, at least in part, to variations in perception. This contention is summed up dramatically by Charles Hermann: "Foreign

Policy results from the decision-makers' perceptions of present or expected problems in the relationship between a nation and its international environment (both human and nonhuman)" (Hermann 1972:72).

It is the perception rather than the "reality" of the environment, then, that is crucial to an understanding of how decisions are made (Sprout and Sprout 1962:48-49; Lovell 1970:9-10; Deutsch 1966:101; Holsti, North, and Brody 1968:128). As individual perceptions differ, so should the behavior of decision-makers. Thus, a decision-maker who views an event as beneficial will probably behave in a very different way from a decision-maker who perceives the event as threatening.

Although within the decision-making tradition, the framework we shall use attempts to avoid several of the problems contained within the decision-making approach. One problem is that decision-making structures are often examined at the expense of individual motivation. In fact, much of the literature assumes that decision-makers will (or ought to) act in a rational way. Perhaps the difficulty with assuming rationality is that the scholars who use the concept rarely define what rationality means, to whom, and for whom.

Conventionally, rationality means that a decision-maker will choose the best of all possible alternatives. If one does not have "perfect" information, however, one cannot determine what is the best alternative. In most situations perfect information is impossible to obtain; even the cost of obtaining more information is so prohibitive that it tends to bring into question the validity of the rational assumption (Verba 1955).

A second difficulty with the rational assumption is the question of rational to whom. Much of the decision-making literature claims that rationality is something determined by the analyst. However, perceptions differ, and, therefore, perceptions of what is rational should also differ. Thus, awareness of perceptual variables seems important to a determination of "rationality" (North and Chourci 1968; Holsti 1965; Wallace 1971; East 1971).

The aspect of rationality labelled "for whom" is concerned with the motivation of an individual decision-maker vis-à-vis the decision. If a decision-maker is more concerned with his career than with the "successful" or rational conclusion of a situation in terms of the "national interest," he may seek an outcome that others would judge as only partially successful. His bureaucratic superiors, though, might judge the same action as both rational and successful in terms of the agency or bureau in which they operate. A "rational" bureaucrat may be the one who secures an increase in his agency's budget, thereby winning approval and increasing his probability of promotion.

Still another general problem with the decision-making approach is that in some versions it tries to explain everything and succeeds in explaining very little. One of the earliest models of decision-making was offered by Richard Snyder, H. W. Bruck, and Burton Sapin in 1969. They identified five clusters of factors which are considered important: *A.* Internal Setting of Decision-Making; *B.* Social Structures and Behavior; *C.* Decision-Making Process—Decision-Makers; *D.* Action; *E.* External Setting of Decision-Making. Snyder and his colleagues contended that the key to understanding why a state behaves "lies in the way its decision-makers as actors define their situation," and that this is achieved through the interplay of three elements: "perception, choice, and expectations" (Snyder, Bruck and Sapin 1969:201). Their model, however, is merely descriptive and lacks "if-then" hypotheses (Rosenau 1971:270-71). Perhaps an additional difficulty lies in the fact that the Snyder model sought to explain decision-making in general; instead what may be needed is a series of models based on differences in setting and situation.

The Snyder model led to further research by other scholars. They tended to emphasize one or another element of the original model and claimed that whatever element they were researching was the most important. One group focused on the perceptual aspects of the Snyder model (Holsti, North, and Brody 1968; Lovell 1968; Morgan 1972). A second argued that situation or context was of great importance (Hermann 1972; Paige 1968, 1972; Robinson and Snyder 1965; George, Hall, and Simons 1971). Yet other researchers offered several "models" of decision-making and examined the explanatory power of each in given situations (Allison 1971; McCormick 1975).

Implicit in much of the recent decision-making literature and especially in the work of Allison is that decision-making must be viewed in light of its ability to adequately explain a variety of decisions. In short, no one model can explain all situations. No one variable can totally explain the multitude of decisions that are reached.

To date the decision-making literature has not really offered a predictive framework that considers both perceptual and situational variables. The framework that we employ examines perceptions of U.S. decision-makers and one type of situation—crisis. The aspects of crisis and its impact on decision-makers is key to this framework. These variables have a hypothesized relationship to the degree of flexibility that a decision-maker is likely to exhibit. Included are variables such as the perceptual net of a decision-maker, the relationship between the net and flexibility, and the effects of crisis and failure on the perceptual net.

The Importance of Individual Variables in Foreign Policy

Even if individuals are ultimately the actors who make decisions, the study of idiosyncratic variables is not necessarily the most practical or profitable method for understanding how foreign policy is made. Yet the claim that the flexibility of decision-makers is important assumes that individual variables are also important.

Rosenau suggests that such variables are important to an understanding of foreign policy and includes individual variables as one of his five clusters of variables (Rosenau 1971:113). He argues that in large developed open countries, such as the United States, the individual cluster is the least "potent" of the five clusters in terms of explanation. Although he does not claim that individual variables have no importance, he indicates rather strongly that only in "underdeveloped countries" are the individual variables likely to be the most potent. Perhaps in different contexts different variables are likely to be more important. It may be that in certain contexts individuals will be extremely important even though Rosenau's caveat would be that such circumstances are unlikely to exist in the United States.

Ernest May contends that crisis causes decision-makers to employ axioms instead of calculations to reach their decisions. These axioms are of individual creation. May declares:

> [An axiom's] sources are nearly always historical. Some have roots that go very deep.... The axiomatic policy that governs the Korean decision... is derived from the experience of the 1930s.... Moreover, while historical experience is the substance of an axiom, it is not the molder. People read into history more or less what they want to read, and they exercise some discretion about the precepts they apply to particular cases (May 1962).

Implicit in May's analysis is that the individual decision-makers in the Korean case were important. It was their axioms that were employed to reach a decision. The Korean decision exemplifies what is meant by a crisis encompassing those situations which:

> (1) threaten high-priority goals of a decision-making unit; (2) restrict the amount of time available for response before the decision is transformed; and (3) surprise the members of the decision-making unit by its occurrence. Threat, time, and surprise all have been cited as traits of crisis. . . . Underlying the proposed definition is the hypothesis that if all three traits are present, then the decision process will be substantially different than if only one or two of the characteristics appear. (Hermann 1972:9).

Crises are therefore situations in which many of the normal restraints on decision-makers do not apply. Fred Greenstein suggests that under certain conditions individual personality variations are likely to be very important. These conditions involve the nature of leadership and the nature of situation. When Greenstein's propositions are compared to the definition of crisis, they suggest that in crisis, leaders will be active participants and will tend to act with reference to their own personalities.

Leadership, for Greenstein, is a position that has loose role expectations. As such, individual differences are likely to be important. Since leaders tend to become involved in crises, the individual differences are likely to have an impact on the decisions reached (Greenstein 1969:56; Levinson 1959).

The element of high threat or "high value consequences" (Robinson and Snyder 1965:442) may also be related to high levels of personal involvement (Greenstein 1969:54). Short time and surprise usually mean that a great deal of information must be handled quickly, leading in large measure to conditions of ambiguity.

> Ambiguous situations leave room for personal variability to manifest itself. . . . Three types of ambiguous situations [are] (a) the "completely new situation in which there are no familiar cues" . . . (b) "a complex situation in which there are a great number of cues to be taken into account" . . . (c) "a contradictory situation in which different elements suggest different structures." (Greenstein 1969:50-51).

This hypothesis is supported by other psychological research (Sherif 1963:211). During a crisis, the need for information increases dramatically. In order to supplement and organize incoming information, decision-makers tend to employ analogies.

This easily accessible information about the past aids the decision-maker by reducing the apparent novelty and complexity of the current situation (Paige 1968:47). The analogies used by a decision-maker are very similar to what we shall call referents. Such referents are highly related to the degree of flexibility that a decision-maker is likely to exhibit.

Flexibility is linked to behavior and crisis decision-making in terms of the leader's ability to handle and respond to feedback information. An individual's behavior can be reinforced by incoming information or can be altered by it. This alteration can affect both his policies and his goals. Only humans are capable of changing goals. A change in goals represents what Deutsch calls "second-order" feedback (Deutsch 1966:92). Second-order feedback requires a more sophisticated information net than first-order feedback. In order for a system to have second-order capabilities, it must have information about the external realm, information about itself, and a lasting memory of past events. Without these capabilities the unit in question could not be autonomous and would have no second-order potential (Deutsch 1966:128-29). The differences among individuals are partly a function of memory. The degree of difference in individual memory is likely to predict differences in the intensity and direction of flexible behavior.

Individual decision-makers can differ in many important ways. Some may stubbornly refuse to change their goals or their policies. Others may be willing to change their policies as long as goals remain intact. Still others may be willing to change both their goals and their policies in the light of a current situation. Two decision-makers who are subjected to the same incoming information may nevertheless differ because of differences in memory. For example, during the first few days of the Cuban missile crisis, Robert Kennedy and Dean Acheson both had access to the same information and yet chose to advocate different policies in part because of different prior experience (Kennedy 1971:16). Although both men were interested in a "successful" solution to the problems at hand, Acheson chose examples and axioms based on his feeling that the United States *must* guarantee security, whereas Robert Kennedy did not want to see the president become another Tojo. The process of selection and abstraction that both men experienced is connected with memory. The lessons that an individual learns from history may serve at a later date as a filter for new information, and he may allow only that information that conforms to a past analogy to enter his decision process. In effect, he may block out other relevant information, thereby precluding any possibility of change at the time.

Many analysts from a wide diversity of backgrounds have viewed memory as playing a role similar to what we have described in the decision process (Morgenthau 1966; Allison 1971; Paige 1968; de Rivera 1968; Greenstein 1969). The problem is: although many scholars believe that individual memory is important, there has been little empirical investigation on the subject.

There are several possible explanations for this anomalous situation. Memory may simply be too difficult and too time-consuming to operationalize and research in this context. It would be impossible to do a psychobiography of all major leaders. Even if memory is analytically useful, it may be difficult to operationalize in a meaningful fashion. Finally, memory as a single concept may be too broad to be useful and may have to be reduced and segmented before it can be productively investigated.

Flexibility in Foreign Policy Behavior:
A Framework for Analysis

By systematically analyzing the statements of decision-makers before and after a crisis, we can assess the degree of flexibility that they exhibit and then compare the intensity and direction of change for several decision-makers. The response of a decision-maker to feedback is indicative of his flexibility. By controlling for situation and for type of feedback, we can ensure that negative feedback is being directed at the decision-maker. Crisis failure can be viewed as a set of conditions in which the decision-maker receives large amounts of feedback with a negative impact. Such a situation is one in which we would expect the highest degrees of flexbility to be exhibited. To the degree that a decision-maker does not change his behavior, it may be contended that his perceptual filters are such that only information which reinforces his position is being allowed to enter, thereby eliminating or deemphasizing the negative feedback being directed at him.

The perceptions and perceptual screens of a decision-maker can be viewed as being closely related to memory. These filters serve several functions, the most important of which is the selecting out of unneeded information or "static." If these filters do not operate, as in the case of an LSD "trip," one's ability to function is severely limited.

Although it is possible to speak of memory in general, we can also view memory as being composed of several distinct elements. Ole Holsti suggests that memory can be considered as "the belief system composed of a number of 'images' of past, present, and future, includ(ing) 'all accumulated, organized knowledge that the organism has about itself and the world'." (Holsti 1962:251) At the most general level, memory consists of two major elements: referents and themes.

Referents refer to those cognitive objects used by a leader; of these, events form a significant part. Referents themselves consist of several significant dimensions. The first of these is temporal. Referents can be classified as past, present, or future. Past referents are those objects or events that existed before the period under examination; present referents are those that exist during the time period being considered; and furture referents are those events which are perceived as likely to occur after the period.

Decision-makers who tend to use the most past referents are least likely to behave flexibly. The referents that they select are temporally incongruent with the crisis. Therefore, their filters are less sensitive to accurate and precise selection and abstraction. The crudeness of selection and abstraction may lead to a "loss" of the negative feedback being directed at the decision-maker. In contrast, a leader using present referents is more likely to exhibit flexible behavior because the temporal dimension of referent is likely to be more congruent with the subject at hand. The decision-maker who chooses future referents may or may not exhibit flexible behavior depending on the other dimensions of the referent at hand. One leader may be concerned with the possibility of reelection and may therefore ignore signals concerning the crisis except as they refer to his campaign, whereas a second leader may be viewing the long-term situation in the area of the crisis and will therefore be very sensitive to all incoming information from that area.

Location constitutes a second dimension of referent. Thus, referents may be either foreign or domestic in origin. Domestic referents are those objects or events which are internal to the decision-maker's society; foreign referents are objects or events which originate outside that society or involve actors originating outside the society. Decision-makers who make use of domestic referents are less likely to exhibit consistent patterns of flexible response. The international crisis and the subject of their referent have different origins. This type of decision-maker is more autistic; he may be ill-informed about foreign affairs and therefore rely on information from a domestic context to inform his judgment. On the other hand, he may have knowledge of foreign affairs but be primarily concerned with domestic problems and therefore view foreign situations only in relation to their impact on domestic matters. In either case, the decision-maker's pattern of behavior may be motivated by a different set of stimuli than the substance of the crisis, leading to erratic behavior patterns in terms of flexibility.

Leaders who employ foreign referents have a higher probability of exhibiting consistent patterns of flexibility or rigidity than leaders who use domestic referents. A leader who uses foreign referents may be more sensitive to current foreign situations or he may be firmly rooted in foreign events that occurred many years before.

The final dimension of referent is that of affect. A referent may be either positive or negative. A positive referent is one that is looked upon favorably by the decision-maker; a negative referent, in contrast, is one that is deplored and would be eschewed by him. Generally speaking, neither positive nor negative affect by itself predicts flexibility. However, in terms of a specific decision-maker, the knowledge of his affect toward a referent can be quite instructive. If two decision-makers use the same historical event as a referent, we would expect that they would exhibit the same degree of flexible behavior. However, if the first viewed the referent as positive and the second negative, the direction of the resultant behavior is likely to be different.

The hypotheses concerning the dimensions of referent should not be viewed as exclusive—rather, one dimension can serve to reinforce or modify another. This is especially true in terms of the temporal and spatial dimensions. For example, we might hypothesize that decision-makers who use foreign referents are likely to be consistent in their behavioral responses. We also indicated that individuals who use present referents are likely to be flexible. Therefore, leaders who use present foreign referents are most likely to exhibit consistent patterns of flexible behavior in terms of both goals and policies.

A second major element of memory is that of theme. Theme may be more a product of memory than an element of memory itself. However, that distinction, if it exists, is not germane to the problem we are considering. Theme consists of the lessons or attitudes that a decision-maker associates with or attributes to a referent. Theme itself can be subdivided into goal and policy theme. Goal theme refers to the desired future state that the decision-maker seeks, the "what" of foreign policy. Policy theme refers to the means to be employed in pursuance of the "what"; policy theme thus becomes the "how."

It is the relationship among and the appearance of different referents and themes that first determines the state of a decision-maker's perceptual network and later allows us to determine whether there has been any change in that network. In terms of goals, for example, if a decision-maker has only one goal of broad character, it is unlikely that we would see a great change in goals over time. If one's goal in foreign policy is to "stop communism," one might change policies from time to time, but it is unlikely that that goal is likely to change. This is due, in part, to the highly abstract nature of the single goal.

The intellectual baggage that a decision-maker brings to a crisis can be considered as constituting the independent variables in this framework. These variables include the dominant referents and themes that a decision-maker exhibits during a period before a crisis.

The intervening variables in the framework are crisis and failure. The use of crisis ensures that the decision-maker will be important and will be receiving high levels of feedback, and the use of failure increases the probability that the feedback will be negative in nature. The intervening variables have been chosen in order to enable us to tap the question of flexibility without ignoring the equally important question of situation. In addition, the combination of the two intervening variables allows the concept of flexibility to be measured adequately because it ensures both high salience and negative affect.

Finally, the dependent variables are the intellectual baggage that a decision-maker carries with him from a crisis. These include the revised themes and referents used by the decision-maker after a crisis.

Flexibility is determined by the degree of change which occurs in referents, goal themes, and policy themes before and after the crisis. Not all changes are equally significant; therefore we must determine a way of measuring relative importance. The following rules are utilized in this regard. Decision-makers who exhibit change in *both* goal themes and policy themes are considered to have undergone the most significant change regardless of referent.

Change in both indicates first- and second-order feedback.

The second most significant change encompasses a change in goal theme while referent and policy theme remain relatively stable. This would be a case of what Deutsch calls "second-order purposes" of a feedback net.

> By a second-order purpose would be meant that internal and external state of the net that would seem to offer the net the largest probability (or predictive value derived from past experience) for the nets' continued ability to seek first-order purposes. This would imply self-preservation as a second-order purpose of the net, overriding the first-order purposes. It would require a far more complex net (Deutsch 1966:93).

The third most significant change is that of referent while goal and policy theme remain stable. This would indicate the utilization of primary feedback.

Finally, the least significant change is that of referent while goal and policy theme remain stable. In such a case, it is probable that the subject is engaging in rhetorical justification much as a debater would shift arguments or restate points to persuade a particular audience.

The relationship between the elements in the framework may also aid in predicting flexible behavior. One important relationship in this regard is that between referent and the subject matter of the crisis itself. This relationship is similar to the one posited for type of referent, but is more detailed and stresses the concept of congruence. Thus, the greater the congruence between the issue at hand and the example used by the decision-maker, the greater is the likelihood that information will be filtered more precisely and harmoniously. If, for example, a decision-maker were speaking on the subject of an economic boycott of an Asian nation and were using referents of past military invasions of Europe, it could be assumed that that leader would exhibit little flexibility. It might even be hypothesized that the greater the congruence between referent and crisis, the greater the flexibility of behavior that will be exhibited.

As was the case with degrees of change, we must be able to determine degrees of congruence. Congruence is viewed in six dimensions: geographic, foreign-domestic, temporal, societal involvement, policy type, and issue. Geographic congruence refers to determination of whether the crisis event and the referent occurred in the same geographic region. Foreign-domestic congruence pertains to whether the crisis and the referent refer to the same space as viewed from the United States (internal or external). Temporal congruence is obtained when the referent is a present one rather than a past or future one. Societal involvement asks the question is the United States a direct or indirect participant in both referent and crisis? Policy type can be defined by whether the means employed in the analogized event (economic, military, diplomatic, etc.) is congruent with the means employed in the crisis. Lastly, issue refers to the degree of agreement between referent and crisis in terms of the subject matter of the event. Do they both refer to the spread of communism or European security, and so forth?

In summary, consider the following scenario. When a decision-maker receives initial information about crisis and failure, he is likely to choose an object or event (referent) to sort out information. After passing through this screen, the abstracted and selected information is allowed to combine with those aspects of the memory called goal theme and policy theme. The amount of negative feedback that is allowed through the screens will determine the degree to which a decision-maker is likely to exhibit flexible behavior. These changes in behavior are directed outward, and additional feedback is then sent back to the initial perceptual screens. The decision-maker who has chosen his examples to block out all information that disagrees with his own position is likely to be akin to John Foster Dulles. According to Ole Holsti, John Foster Dulles virtually ignored all tension-reducing overtures by the Soviet Union. In response to Soviet troop reduction, Dulles replied, "Well, it's a fair conclusion that I would rather have them standing around doing guard duty than making atomic bombs" (Holsti 1962:244-52). This statement is indicative of the type of behavior that led Holsti to conclude:

> These findings have somewhat sobering implications. . . . They suggest the fallacy of thinking that peaceful settlements of outstanding international issues are simply a problem of devising good plans. Clearly as long as decision-makers on either side of the Cold War adhere to rigid images of the other party, there is little likelihood that even genuine bids to decrease tensions will have the desired effect. . . . To the extent that each side undeviatingly interprets new information, even friendly bids, in a manner calculated to preserve the original image (memory screen) the two-nation system is a closed one (Holsti 1962:251).

The Measurement of Flexibility

For the framework to have more than "heuristic" value, it must be made operational, and the hypotheses generated by it must be testable. The additional problem of data source exists when we are discussing perceptual variables.

The source of data that seems most appropriate for this framework is public documents. For the independent and dependent variables these include speeches, transcripts of news conferences, testimony before congressional committees, and the like. Public documents can be considered "valid" sources of data for perceptual variables and have been used before for perceptual variables with success (Holsti 1962; Gutierrez 1973).

One criticism of the use of public documents in this manner involves the possibility of obtaining a skewed sample. It is usually assumed that public statements by decision-makers would tend to skew the sample toward consistency, since it is difficult to back away from a statement which was made publicly. However, this very skewing, if it does exist, tends to aid rather than hinder our efforts. We are looking for change; if change is found in a sample skewed toward consistency, even more confidence can be placed in the change that is revealed.

Of the intervening variables, crisis is operationalized in a manner adapted from Thomas Brewer (Brewer 1973:89-114). Brewer's data source is the *New York Times Index*; we can adopt the same sources and many of the same procedures that he employed. His statement concerning the validity of the *New York Times* and, by implication, the *Index* as a data source for the determination of crisis is most enlightening in this context.

> The validity of any given data set is the degree to which it does indeed measure what it is purported to measure. Three types are commonly distinguished: predictive (or criterion), content (or face), and construct. . . .
> One can argue and adduce evidence that the data also have content validity. The argument is based largely on the observation that the American policy process . . . tends to be rather open and public and that, therefore, the *New York Times* constitutes a defensible data source. . . . The data have also been found to have construct validity inasmuch as the variables within each of the clusters . . . positively intercorrelate (Brewer 1973:98-99).

The data source for failure is newspaper editorials sampled during the crisis. Newspaper editorials are chosen for their quick response time to situations and their role as opinion molders. The subscription sample used was chosen because it reflects the newspapers that the president and his secretary of state are most likely to read. Failure occurs when the sampled editorials do not approve of the actions of the president, his secretary of state, or their official representatives.

The independent variables—referent, goal theme, policy theme— are measured by coding the various speeches, news conferences, and so forth for each post-war president and secretary of state. The sample period for the independent variables is six months, ending the day before a crisis.

The first of the independent variables to be coded is referent. A determination is made for each referent used as to its temporal, spatial, and effect dimensions. In a general sense, all the nouns contained within a particular document can be considered as referents. After each document for a given period has been coded, several procedures for aggregation are employed. Raw scores for each type of referent are calculated as are scores of percentages of total referents. Both raw scores and percentages are calculated for the period as a whole and for each speech. This technique allows for the determination of overall behavior patterns for the period as well as incremental change within each period.

The desired future state or goal theme is expressed in the verb or verb phrase in much the same way as referents are expressed as nouns. Usually the goal is contained within a conditional clause— for example, "In order to stop communism and make the world safe for democracy, I have . . . ." Goal theme is determined by thematic analysis: each paragraph of a speech is coded by making a judgment as to the goal theme(s) contained within it.

Policy themes can be measured on a scale from conciliation to belligerence. Coding schemes which have been devised to handle "event data" can be adapted for use in coding policy themes. We employ the twenty-two categories and general method used in the World Events Interaction Survey (WEIS) (McClelland 1969:711-24).

Policy themes are weighted on the assumption that actions are more important than words and words are more important than mere participation. Deeds are assigned a value of 3, verbal behavior a value of 2, and participation a value of 1. Any action that can be considered as cooperative is assigned a "+" sign and any action deemed conflictive a "−" sign. Participation is assigned a plus based on the assumption that participation, though low in terms of commitment, is still minimally supportive.

The first major intervening variable is that of crisis. Although we employ the definition offered by Hermann (Hermann 1972:9), we add the stipulation that the crisis must be initiated by an actor external to the United States. Crisis itself is operationalized by adapting a method devised by Thomas Brewer (1973:92-93). Brewer examines and suggests measurements for the three elements of crisis. We are adopting his procedures for a determination of short time and surprise, but have developed a different measure for high threat. High threat may be viewed as situations of high value consequences and, as such, issues of high salience. High salience and therefore high threat are determined by coding the *New York Times Index* for the period of the crisis. An event is considered high threat if the *Index* contains a minimum of three entries for each day of the crisis. An additional minimum requirement of ten total entries, regardless of days, is also required to avoid the possibility of an event being intensely discussed for only a short time. The method of assessing high threat differs markedly from the scheme employed by Brewer, who requires that judgments be made based on the likelihood that a change in the value inventory will occur, the distance into the future that such a change will occur, and the magnitude of change that is foreseen.

Short time depends on the complexity of the problem and clock time. Clock time is defined as the amount of time in the conventional sense—days, weeks, etc.—that will elapse before the situation will significantly make the circumstance of any decision less advantageous. Clock time is considered short if the situation would change after no more than one month. Complexity of the problem is measured by the number of people involved and the number of tasks to be performed, and it is determined on the basis of whether or not the situation involved more than one agency or major program of the U.S. government.

Finally, surprise is operationalized in terms of the amount of precedent for the situation: in short, whether there was any advance notice that this particular situation might develop. Specifically, precedent is determined by examining the *New York Times Index* for a period of one month prior to the onset of the event in question. If any precedent exists within that month, except for the last week—where the decision-makers state the event in question might occur—then the event itself is not considered a surprise.

Failure is measured by coding newspaper editorials for negative affect only. We are interested in the newspapers' disagreement with presidential actions. We are not interested in the newspapers' advice. These newspaper editorials are coded for the period of time beginning with the onset of a crisis and lasting two weeks after the crisis has been concluded. This additional two-week period ensures the inclusion of the "post-mortem" type of editorial which usually follows the conclusion of a major event. Only those editorials that relate directly to the crisis are coded. Failure exists when the editorials are characterized by a predominance of negative words in a manner similar to the scheme used for coding policy theme. A crisis is deemed a failure when 75 percent or more of the editorials indicate that the actions of the president, his secretary of state, or their representatives were mistaken.

Turning to the dependent variables in the study: Level of flexibility is determined by the difference in the direction and intensity of referents, goal themes, and policy themes after a crisis has occurred. The differences are measured as the change in overall behavior in terms of referent and theme from the base period. The same data sources and coding techniques are used for the dependent variables as were used for the independent variables. The only change between the two samples is the sample dates. The dependent variables are determined for a period of six months beginning the day after the end of the crisis.

Testing the Framework:
The Ability to Predict Flexibility

Before reporting the results of our research, it is necessary to describe the data set which has been collected. For each administration, crisis and failure verification was undertaken according to the rules and procedures described above. It was determined that the following incidents could be verified as crises and failures: Truman—Czechoslovakia; Eisenhower—Lebanon; Kennedy—Berlin; Johnson—Tet; Nixon—1973 Middle East War. The individuals who served as secretary of state during the crises mentioned were also included in the study.

Having established the events to be examined, we then collected the data for the independent and dependent variables. The coding of public speeches for each individual for each period yielded a total of 308 coded units (most of which were complete speeches). The major source for the coding was the *New York Times.* Only when a speech or news conference was *not* transcribed in full was the original tesimony or transcript referred to.

The first interesting and somewhat unexpected finding is demonstrated by an analysis of the number of speeches given by each of the individuals in the study. With the exception of President Kennedy, who gave the same number of speeches before and after the Berlin crisis, and Secretary of State Kissinger, who gave more speeches after the Middle East War, all the individuals in the study gave significantly fewer speeches after the crisis than before it. In the case of Kissinger, he was not appointed secretary of state until after the beginning of the pre-crisis sample period and, therfore, the fact that he gave more speeches is quite understandable. We might suggest that this result shows that most of the individuals in our study became more conservative in their statements after experiences of failure. They seemed to be much more cautious after they had stumbled, possibly because they did not want to stumble again so soon.

There is another possible explanation for this finding. It may be that in psychological terms these leaders were demonstrating "avoidance." Avoidance in this sense means the intentional or unintentional denial of the importance or reality of a certain class of situations. After failure it is possible for a decision-maker to avoid the source of failure (foreign policy) and seek more successful areas of activity. This finding is supported by other research on crisis. Charles McClelland discovered that during the period of "crisis abatement," the average of all types of behavior decreases when compared to the pre-crisis period. (McClelland 1972:97-100).

In order to test our hypotheses concerning the predictive power of our independent variables, it is necessary to measure the amount of change, if any, which occurred for each individual in terms of his goals, policies, and referents. After determining the degree of change in each of the variables mentioned, an overall indicator of change was developed by weighting goal change by a factor of five, policy change by a factor of three and referents by a factor of one. This has the effect of transforming the data from nominal to ordinal.

We argue that the more a decision-maker is able to test reality, the more flexible he is likely to be. This leads to two complementary hypotheses. The first is that the greater the number of present foreign referents used by a decision-maker, the more flexible he will be. The second, the more past referents that a decision-maker uses, the less flexible he will be. In order to test this hypothesis, rank order correlation was performed between present foreign referents and overall change and a second rank ordering was done for past referents and overall change. The rank order correlation between present referents and overall behavior change was a dramatically high +.74. The correlation between past referents and overall behavior change was +.16.

The correlation between present referents and behavior change was in the expected direction and tends to support the hypothesis. When compared to the very low correlation between past referents and change, one has even more confidence in the predictive ability of referents.

A second series of hypotheses suggested by the research framework refers to a variable we have called congruence. Congruence is a measure of fit along six dimensions of referents and goals during the pre-crisis period. The congruence score is determined by dividing the number of matches on the six variables by the total number of variables. After the congruence scores for each individual were determined, a correlation between the congruence measures and the overall behavior change was calculated. The rank order correlation was +.798.

This finding is very suggestive. It seems that congruence may be as good and in some cases even slightly better at predicting overall flexibility than present referents. Other research has indicated that present referents are better indicators of any single dimension of change. (Falkowski 1976:199-203). A great deal of additional research is necessary to fully explain how these two variables interrelate. On balance, however, since we set out to predict flexibility, we must consider that we have been at least partially successful.

The results allow us to say that the data have supported the general notion that the aspects of memory which we initially identified are crucial to an understanding of flexibility. More specifically, we have identified two predictive variables. By examining the types of referents that a decision-maker employs, we can predict whether or not he is likely to change his goals, policies, and referents after experiencing a crisis failure. If this scheme does have the value that the data seem to indicate, then it should be possible to predict the post-crisis behavior of other presidents and secretaries of state. In fact, such an analysis was undertaken for Carter and Vance. It was discovered that Carter and Vance demonstrated profiles that should place them in the "very flexible" category. It seems that Carter is likely to react in a very similar fashion to President Kennedy. Thus, if Carter is faced with a crisis failure, his reaction should be similar in direction and intensity to that of Kennedy after the Berlin crisis.

If this prediction is supported, it would increase the support for the framework as a whole and should lead to a series of rather interesting insights. First, it seems that we have supported the notion that relative sensitivity to negative feedback is related to the state of an individual's perceptual filters at any given moment. Second, it may be that the more current the perceptual filters, the more congruent they will be and, in turn, the more the decision-maker will be testing reality. The more he tests reality, the greater the likelihood that he can respond quickly to change in his environment. This suggestion does imply causation and a certain psychological prejudice which we have avoided up to this point.

We should conclude by indicating that the findings offered should not be an end in themselves; rather they serve as a preliminary test. If one were to take this framework to its logical conclusion, it should be possible to investigate in much more precise fashion the motivation of decision-makers on a variety of issues, both foreign and domestic. Having done that, one could then create referent and congruence profiles for decision-makers for a series of issues. This could lead to the type of prediction that would state different levels of flexibility over an entire spectrum of issues.

Once a researcher has developed a detailed issue-flexibility profile for an individual, one could then analyze the position that that individual occupies and, by comparing the two, not only indicate the decision-maker's preference but also begin to predict the decisions and behaviors which might result.

One further expansion of this framework should also be suggested. We now know that we can compare and contrast American foreign policy decision-makers. Based on that work, we could replicate this research for presidents and secretaries of state that held office before World War II. In addition, it is not unreasonable to suggest the inclusion of decision-makers in non-American contexts for the purpose of comparison. Finally, what we have tried to provide is not so much a series of findings on certain individuals, but rather a method by which individuals, especially individuals in leadership roles, can be examined.

References

Allison, G. T. *Essence of Decision.* Boston: Little, Brown, 1971.
Brewer, T. L. "Issue and Context Variation in Foreign Policy." *Journal of*

Conflict Resolution 17 (1973):89-114.
de Rivera, J. H. *The Psychological Dimension of Foreign Policy.* Columbus, Ohio: Merrill, 1968.
Deutsch, K. W. *Nerves of Government.* New York: Free Press, 1966.
East, M. A. "Status Discrepancy and Balance in the International System an Empirical Analysis." In *The Analysis of International Politics*, edited by J. N. Rosenau, V. Davis, and M. A. East. New York: Free Press, 1972.
Falkowski, L. S. "Foreign Policy Flexibility: A Comparative Analysis." Ph.D. Dissertation, Rutgers University, 1976.
George, A. M., D. K. Hall, and W. E. Simons. *The Limits of Coercive Diplomacy, Laos, Cuba, Vietnam.* Boston: Little, Brown, 1971.
Greenstein, F. I. *Personality and Politics.* Chicago: Markham Publications, 1969.
Gutierrez, G. G. "Dean Rusk and Southeast Asia: An Operational Code Analysis." American Political Science Association Paper, 1973.
Hermann, C. F., ed. *International Crises: Insights from Behavioral Research.* New York: Free Press, 1972.
——. "Policy Classification: A Key to the Comparative Study of Foreign Policy." In *The Analysis of International Politics*, edited by J. N. Rosenau, V. Davis, and M. A. East. New York: Free Press, 1972.
Holsti, O. "The 1914 Case." *American Political Science Review* 59 (1965): 365-378.
——. "The Belief System and National Images: A Case Study." *Journal of Conflict Resolution*, vol. 6 (1962).
Holsti, O., R. C. North, and R. Brody. "Perception and Action in the 1914 Case." In *Quantitative International Politics*, edited by J. D. Singer. New York: Free Press, 1972.
Kennedy, R. F. *Thirteen Days.* New York: W. W. Norton, 1971.
Levinson, D. "Role of Personality and Social Structure in Organizational Setting." *Journal of Abnormal and Social Psychology* 58 (1959):170-180.
Lovell, J. P. *Foreign Policy in Perspective.* New York: Holt, Rinehart, and Winston, 1970.
May, E. "The Nature of Foreign Policy: The Calculated versus the Axiomatic." *Daedalus*, Fall 1962, pp. 653-667.
McClelland, C. A. "Conflict Patterns in the Interactions Among Nations." In *International Politics and Foreign Policy*, edited by J. N. Rosenau. New York: Free Press, 1969.
McCormick, J. M. "Evaluating Models of Crisis Behavior: Some Evidence from the Middle East." *International Studies Quarterly*, March 1975, pp. 17-45.
Morgan, P. M. *Theories and Approaches to International Politics.* San Ramon, Calif.: Consensus Publications, 1972.
Morgenthau, H. *Politics Among Nations.* New York: Alfred A. Knopf, 1966.
North, R. C., and N. Chourci. "Background Conditions to the Outbreak of World War I." *Peace Research Society Papers* 9 (1968):125-317.

Paige, G. D. "Comparative Case Analysis of Crisis Decision: Korea and Cuba." In *International Crises: Insights from Behavioral Research*, edited by C. F. Hermann, pp. 41-55. New York: Free Press, 1972.

———. *The Korean Decision*. New York: Free Press, 1968.

Robinson, J. A., and R. C. Snyder. "Decision-Making in International Politics." In *International Political Behavior*, edited by H. C. Kelman. New York: Holt, Rinehart, and Winston, 1965.

Rosenau, J. N. *The Scientific Study of Foreign Policy*. New York: Free Press, 1971.

Sherif, M. "The Concept of Reference Groups in Human Relations." In *Group Relations at the Crossroads*, edited by M. Sherif and M. O. Wilson. New York: Harper and Row, 1963.

Snyder, R. C., H. W. Bruck; and B. Sapin. "The Decision-Making Approach to the Study of International Politics." In *International Politics and Foreign Policy*, edited by J. N. Rosenau. New York: Free Press, 1969.

Sprout, H. and M. *Foundations of International Politics*. Princeton, N.J.: D. Van Nostrand, 1962.

Verba, S. "Assumptions or Rationality and Non-Rationality in Models of International Systems." *The International System: Theoretical Essays*, edited by K. Knorr and S. Verba. Princeton University Press, 1955.

Wallace, M. D. "Power Status and International War." *Journal of Peace Research* 8 (1971):23-36.

4
Signal Leakage and the Remote Psychological Assessment of Foreign Policy Elites

Thomas C. Wiegele

Most social science research on the behavior of elites has dealt with such aspects as operational codes, roles, events, situations, socioeconomic factors, recruitment, perceptions, birth order, style, and so forth. Because they deal with behavioral outputs and with social factors outside of the individual himself, these kinds of researches can be considered as peripheral measures or indices of individual behavior.[1] Granted, many of these aspects are often correlated with individual behavior; nevertheless, they do not constitute *in a primary way* the direct measurement of the individual himself. It is in this sense that they might be considered peripheral to the human being.

This is understandable because there are numerous impediments for the researcher who desires to work at the individual level of analysis. First among these difficulties is the obvious problem of measuring elites while they are engaged in the act of foreign policy behavior. Elites normally will not submit to the intervention of measurement routines in the midst of highly stressful or sensitive decision-making processes. Brody (1969:116) has posed the problem quite directly: "[H]ow can we give a Taylor Manifest-Anxiety Scale to Khrushchev during the Hungarian revolt, a Semantic Differential to Chiang Kai-shek while Quemoy is being shelled, or simply interview Kennedy during the Cuban missile crisis?" Even if elites were to consent to such intervention, the researcher would be forced to use intrusive methods of measurement—these involve the well-known difficulties of subject reaction to the measurement process. This is particularly true of psychophysiological measurement methods.

Confronted by such problems, researchers have typically turned to experimental or simulation techniques (see C. Hermann 1969). In terms of international relations research, the experimental paradigm suffers because the researcher is normally not working with real foreign policy elites.

A second significant limiting factor in attempting to generate individual-level data is time. Longitudinal studies with elites are particularly difficult to achieve because they involve an extended commitment to a researcher—a commitment unlikely to be made. Another vexing problem confronts the foreign policy researcher. If he is working at the individual level, the subjects of his investigations, by the very nature of their role responsibilities, are at the highest echelons of decisional authority and therefore particularly inaccessible.

Therefore, if one is interested in studying the psychological states of elites as they engage in foreign policy making, traditional approaches do not appear to provide satisfactory research strategies. Further, the limiting factors of time and instrument intrusiveness must be dealt with if one desires to engage in some form of direct measurement. An entirely different research focus is needed to shift the analyst away from peripheral measures to more direct but less intrusive measures of the individual elite person under examination. If elites could be measured directly *and* remotely, we could open the door to a range of behavioral indicators that might contribute significantly to an understanding of the political acts of foreign policy elites as well as their psychological states while performing those acts.

The Concept of Signal Leakage

The umbrella conceptualization needed to organize such a retinue of measures has been provided by Ekman and Friesen (1969). They posit the concept of nonverbal leakage that was developed within a context of clues to deception. "Leakage," they stated in 1975, "can be defined as the (un)intended betrayal of a feeling the person is trying to conceal." To Ekman and Friesen (1969:88), in person-to-person deception interactions, the "neuro-anatomy and cultural influences combine to produce spcific types of body movements and facial expressions which escape efforts to deceive and emerge as leakage or deception clues." Certain parts of the body have specific sending capacities which are indexed by the length of time needed to transmit the information, by the "number of discriminable stimulus patterns which can be emitted," and by visibility or the degree to which the analyst is able to observe the leakage content (Ekman and Friesen 1969:93-94).

In order for the leakage concept to become most useful for us, however, we must adjust it somewhat. First, we have a broader interest in the affect states of elites than simply those that might be associated with deception. For this reason, we are interested in that leakage which might provide information on psychological states directly related to foreign policy behavior, such as fear, surprise, etc. Furthermore, as we shall show below, unintended leakage is not necessarily only nonverbal. Thus, we can modify Ekman and Friesen's concept of nonverbal leakage as it applies to deception to a much more comprehensive conceptualization: signal leakage.

Signal leakage can be defined as the unintended verbal or nonverbal emission of a measurable clue to a psychological state by an individual human being. Of course, elites can intentionally leak signals regarding their psychological states or national actions. This kind of predetermined communication is a normal aspect of the study of international relations and need not be discussed here. Our focus is on the unintended leakage of signals that can be remotely obtained and that will provide insights into the affect states of the individual under examination. Such signal leakage constitutes the direct measurement of the person.

Some Examples of Signal Leakage

Without providing an exhaustive list, several types of signal leakage that can be assessed remotely are of interest to international relations researchers.

Language

Unintended signal leakage occurs through language, not in the manifest meanings of words, but through certain underlying structures. Frank (1973:26-27) argues that "verbal behavior can have an inner logic, an 'inner life' and a specific set of psychological functions in which language acts as both tool and symptom that accompany states of psychological affect." With this thought in mind, Frank (1973:27) has constructed a theory of verbal kinesics which holds that "certain semantic forms, including spatial symbols and referential distantiation, universally appear in verbal discourse." Moreover, "these semantic forms represent psycholinguistic tools by which body-environment and body-behavioral responses can be actualized. As such, these forms are symptomatic of underlying psychological states and are isomorphic with parallel behavioral disposition." To use a more concrete formulation, Frank points out that "under periods of stress, the frequency of flight or horizontal symbols used by the speaker will increase as the predisposition to actual physical flight increases."

Decision making under conditions of stress is frequently present in the foreign policy realm. Frank (1973:27) indicates that in a stressed environment an individual "can employ two psycholinguistically distantiating strategies: (1) move the stressor away from self through the use of nonimmediate language, and (2) move the self away from the stressor through the use of horizontal movement symbols." Signal leakage occurs in the theory of verbal kinesics because the use of symbols is not topic-bound, and a message beyond the manifest meanings of words is leaked to the skilled analyst.

To test the theory of verbal kinesics in this context, Frank (1973) analyzed the content of thirty-eight State of the Union messages of U.S. presidents during the 1934-69 period. Even though Frank points out that this work does not constitute a definitive validation of a theory of verbal kinesics, he observes that "spatial symbol patterns do shift, with statistical significance, internal to speeches according to the degree of perceived topic-stress on the part of the speech giver" (1973:35). Frank's theory of verbal kinesics has operational applications in the study of foreign policy crisis statements.

The Eye

The signal leakage provided by the human eye contains a wealth of psychological information which is only beginning to be fully recognized. Although disturbances in the eye have been carefully catalogued by Haessler (1960), it is the psychological dimensions of pupillary response that appear to emit a significant amount of signal leakage. In pupillometry, the change in horizontal or vertical diameter of the pupil from a previously established baseline measure is the measure of signal leakage. As Janisse (1977:14) indicates, however, other measures of the pupil have also been used—e.g., average size, peak size, minimum size, or variance. The technology of measurement includes filming the eye with a movie or television camera, or utilizing an electronic scanning device. Pupillometry has been used to study sexual arousal, attitudes, anxiety, mental effort, nonverbal communication, drug abuse, personality, and abnormal and choice behavior.

As with most forms of psychophysiological measurement, pupillometry evokes a good deal of controversy. What is the meanin of pupil dilation? Janisse (1977:32) observes that "the data from all studies taken together [form] ... a pattern described as an 'intensity-dilation' rather than a 'valence-dilation' hypothesis; that is, the pupil [appears] ... to dilate to all stimuli (except light) as a positive function of the physical or psychological intensity of the stimulus, and not as a function of whether its emotional valence [is] ... positively or negatively toned."

One of the difficulties with pupillometric research has been in developing a satisfactory technology and method for working in applied as opposed to experimental settings. Most of the scholarship in this area has been experimental; but it appears that breakthroughs are likely, such that remote assessment might be done with ease. To students of international crisis, one of the most noteworthy developments is the use of the pupil as an index of fatigue and stress (Janisse 1977:169). It may be possible to assess the leakage of signs of fatigue through remote pupil examination; and this could prove useful for the crisis management process.

The Human Face

The face is also the site of a good deal of signal leakage that can be noted without observer intrusion. The work in this area has been nicely reviewed by Ekman, Friesen, and Ellsworth (1972). Rigorous cross-cultural studies have provided solid research on the facial indicators of surprise, fear, disgust, anger, happiness, sadness, and deceit. (Ekman and Friesen 1975). (This work should not be confused with the uncontrolled and mundane efforts that have so often appeared in the popular press.)

Ekman and Friesen (1975:10-11) view the human as a multisignal, multimessage system. They indicate that the face emits three kinds of signals:

> static (such as skin color), slow (such as permanent wrinkles), and rapid (such as raising the eyebrows). The static signals include many more-or-less permanent aspects of the face—skin pigmentation, the shape of the face, bone structure, cartilage, fatty deposits, and the size, shape, and location of the facial features (brows, eyes, nose, mouth). The slow signals include changes in the facial appearance which occur gradually with time.... The rapid signals are produced by the movements of the facial muscles, resulting in temporary changes in facial appearance.

As a multimessage system, the face provides the careful observer with a range of messages or signals dealing with several psychological orientations including emotion and mood.

Elaborate coding schemes which divide the face into segments have been developed; and with the aid of slow-motion photography, reliable judgments can be made by scorers. Such photography is also an aid in coding brief micro-affect displays which are seldom noted in unaided observation.

In contrast to most other types of signal leakage, facial leakage can be consciously manipulated by a subject under examination. However, this does not imply that facial expressions are always controlled, for, indeed, most often they are not. On the other hand, it should be pointed out that not all signals emitted from the face are controllable; static and slow signals are not.

Speech Disturbances

Disturbance in extemporaneous speech can be conceptualized as the leakage of signals that might provide information on the psychological states of foreign policy elites. Dibner (1956) identified eleven types of disturbances: unfinished sentence, breaking in with a new thought, interrupted sentence, repeating words or phrases, stuttering, "I don't know" (used as exclamation), laughing, voice change, questioning the interviewer, and blocking (word searching with unusual hesitation). His study and the development of his typology were the consequence of his interest in developing some measures for situational anxiety developed in a therapy session for psychologically ill persons.

Mahl (1956) developed a similar list, but identified only eight categories of speech disturbances: the use of "ah," sentence correction, sentence incompletion, repetition, stuttering, intruding, incoherent sound, tongue slips, and omissions. Mahl was also interested in measuring situational anxiety. He reasoned that techniques which attempted only to measure overall patient anxiety (in therapeutic sessions) were likely to obscure much of the rapid variation in anxiety produced during these sessions. This, in turn, might deprive a therapist of much information concerning the possible anxiety-arousing areas in a patient which these techniques purport to measure.

Maclay and Osgood (1959) developed a set of categories which very much resembled Mahl's speech disturbance categories but which included in their set a general category described as "hesitation types": repeats, false starts, filled pauses, and unfilled pauses. Goldman-Eisler (1961) focused on filled and unfilled pauses in an effort to determine their significance for anxiety assessment.

Kasl and Mahl (1965), building on Mahl's earlier research, reexamined Mahl's eight speech disturbance categories and attempted, in an experimental setting, to make a detailed study of the relationship between speech disruption and anxiety. In testing this relationship, Kasl and Mahl (1965:427) used Mahl's earlier type categories but clustered them into "non-ah" speech disturbances and the "ah" speech disturbance. They were: sentence corrections, sentence incompletions, repetitions, stuttering, intruding incoherent sounds, tongue slips, and omissions. The "ah" speech disturbance did not change with experimentally produced anxiety but was sensitive to a change in the audience setting.

In a carefully designed research effort, M. G. Hermann (1977) utilized speech disturbance measures in an attempt to probe the behavior of negotiators during low and high stress situations. She concluded (1977:382) that "although these indices are not problem-free, their problems do not seem insurmountable." Further, she suggests that speech disturbance measures should prove to be "valuable additions to the 'toolbox' of the investigator interested in examining the behavior of political leaders under stress." It is important to underscore that for the foreign policy researcher, speech disturbance measures are probably useful only for the examination of spontaneous speech, such as press conferences and interviews. In prepared speeches, disturbances of the type just discussed are relatively rare.

Eyeblinks, Gross Bodily Movements, and Nods

In a multi-indicator research effort, Frank (1977) combined speech disturbance measures with three nonverbal indicators of leakage: eyeblinks, gross bodily movements, and nods. Based on previous experimental work (Russell and Snyder 1963; Dittman 1962), Frank (1977:69) relates that blink behavior is related to negative affect; that "gross bodily movements represent passive responses to stressful situations"; and that "vertical head nodding is seen as a strong but negative response to stress." All of these measures were coded from videotape recordings.

Frank found that certain indicators were more salient for a particular subject and that certain substantive issues produced higher frequency counts than others. He concluded that "these techniques can help to unearth new and fresh dimensions of actor behavior and orientation which would otherwise be unavailable were the researcher to concentrate solely on an analysis of the image that the subject is consciously trying to portray in his particular sociopolitical role" (1977:79).

A final example of signal leakage involves the use of voice stress analysis. Because I have utilized this technique in foreign policy analysis, a more extended discussion seems appropriate.

The Scientific Foundations of Voice Stress Analysis

Cameron (1958) reported that speech contains nonverbal information that can be detected by acoustic analysis. Building on the work of Cameron, Rubenstein (1966) set out to determine whether vocal responses to psychological stress were detectable by physiological or, as he termed it, electro-acoustical measurement techniques. Verbal responses of subjects were tape-recorded, and a spectral curve for each response was plotted with a Bruel and Kjaer Audio Spectrometer. It is clear from Rubenstein's work that vocal changes result from the stimulus of psychological stress, and that these physiological alterations can be detected by electronic instrumentation. Thus, the intellectual groundwork has been laid for the electronic detection of the physiological manifestations of stress in the human voice. The Psychological Stress Evaluator (PSE) is a recently developed instrument that has been designed specifically for voice stress analysis.

The PSE, because it processes voice modulations, is particularly well-suited to study high ranking elites who are likely to report to their national constitutencies via radio and television broadcasts during critical foreign policy situations. Further, the PSE is an excellent tool for remote examination of signal leakage in the human voice because it utilizes a tape recording that can be made unobtrusively. The following summary of the operation of the PSE draws on Bell, Ford, and McQuiston (1976).

Two types of vocal changes can result when an individual finds himself under strong psychological stress. Bell et al. (1976) refer to the first of these as a gross vocal change—it can be detected audibly by noting variations in rate, volume, voice tremor, change in spacing between syllables, and change in the fundamental pitch or frequency of the voice. It should be pointed out that some subjects are capable of exercising a deliberate and conscious control over the variations just mentioned.

The second type of vocal change is quite different from the first. This change is not detectable by the human ear, but the change nevertheless results when an individual finds himself under a condition of psychological stress. Moreover, this type of vocal change differs from the first in that it is unconscious and uncontrollable by a subject. This unconscious and inaudible manifestation of stress results from a slight tensing of the vocal cords that can take place even under conditions of minor stress and results in a dampening of selected frequency variations. As Bell et al. (1976: 6) state, "when graphically portrayed, the difference is readily discernible between unstressed or normal vocalization and vocalization under mild stress.... These patterns have held true over a wide range of human voices of both sexes, various ages, and under various situational conditions."

The physiology of these vocal changes is best described in the following excerpt from Bell et al. (1976:6):

> There are two types of sound produced by the human vocal anatomy. The first type of sound is a product of the vibration of the vocal cords, which, in turn, is a product of partially closing the glottis by contraction of the lung cavity and the lungs. The frequencies of these vibrations can vary generally between 100 and 300 Hertz, depending upon the sex and age of the speaker and upon the intonations the speaker applies. This sound has a rapid decay time.
>
> The second type of sound involves the formant frequencies. This constitutes sound which results from the resonance of the cavities in the head, including the throat, the mouth, the nose, and the sinus cavities. This sound is created by excitation of the resonant cavities by a sound source of lower frequencies in the case of the vocalized sound produced by the vocal cords, or by the partial restriction of the passage of air from the lungs, as in the case of unvoiced fricatives. Whichever the excitation source, the frequency of the formant is determined by the resonant frequency of the cavity involved. The formant frequencies appear generally about 800 Hertz and appear in distinct frequency bands which correspond to the resonant frequency of the individual cavities. The first, or lowest, formant is that created by the mouth and throat cavities and is notable for its frequency shift as the mouth changes its dimensions and volume in the formation of various sounds, particularly vowel sounds. The highest formant frequencies are more constant because of the more constant volume of the cavities. The formant wave forms are ringing signals, as opposed to the rapid decay signals of the vocal cords. When voice sounds are uttered, the voice wave forms are imposed upon the formant wave forms as amplitude modulations. . . .

A third signal category exists in the human voice and . . . this third signal category is related to the second type of voice change discussed above. This is an infrasonic, or subsonic, frequency modulation which is present, in some degree, in both vocal cord sounds and in the formant sounds. This signal is typically between 8 and 12 Hertz. Accordingly, it is not audible to the human ear. Because of the fact that this characteristic constitutes the frequency modulation, as distinguished from amplitude modulation, it is not directly discernible on time-base/amplitude chart recordings. Because of the fact that this infrasonic signal is one of the more significant voice indicators of psychological stress, it will be dealt with in greater detail. . . .

Both the vocal cords and the walls of the major formant-producing cavities constitute, in reality, flexible tissue which is immediately responsive to the complex array of muscles which provide control of the tissue. Those muscles which control the vocal cords through the mechanical linkage of bone and cartilage allow both the purposeful and automatic production of voice sound and variation of voice pitch by an individual. Similarly, those muscles which control the tongue, lips, and throat allow both the purposeful and the automatic control of the first formant frequencies. Other formants can be affected similarly to a more limited degree.

It is worthy of note that, during normal speech, these muscles are performing at a small percentage of their work capability. For this reason, in spite of their being employed to change the position of the vocal cords and the position of the lips, tongue, and inner throat walls, the muscles remain in a relatively relaxed state. . . . During this relatively relaxed state, a natural muscular undulation occurs typically at the 8-12 Hertz frequency previously mentioned. This undulation causes a slight variation in the tension of the vocal cords and causes shifts in the basic pitch frequency of the voice. Also, the undulation varies slightly the volume of the resonant cavity (particularly that associated with the first formant) and the elasticity of the cavity walls to cause shifts in the formant frequencies. These shifts about a central frequency constitute a frequency modulation of the central or carrier frequency.

It is important to note that neither of the shifts in the basic pitch frequency of the voice or in the formant frequencies is detectable directly by a listener, partly because the shifts are very small and partly because they exist primarily in the inaudible frequency range previously mentioned. . . .

As mentioned above, . . . the array of muscles associated with the vocal cords and cavity walls is subject to mild muscular tension when slight to moderate psychological stress is created in the individual. . . . This tension, indiscernible to the subject and similarly indiscernible by normal unaided observation techniques to the examiner, is sufficient to decrease or virtually eliminate the muscular undulations present in the unstressed subject, thereby removing the basis for the carrier frequency variations which produce the infrasonic frequency modulations.

The recovery of the FM indicator by the PSE allows evaluation of closely spaced stimuli—the sort that occurs in narrative speech. Thus, stress induced by fear, anxiety, or conflict conditions that are prevalent in political decision-making can be detected by the PSE in using the voice as the physiological medium for stress evaluation.

A normal tape recording preserves the speech pattern containing the words that carry the involuntary speech components indicating stress. Using electronic filtering and frequency discrimination techniques, the PSE processes the voice frequencies and displays the inaudible stress-related FM patterns on a moving strip chart. Utilizing interpretation criteria developed by the manufacturers of the PSE, these FM patterns indicate levels of psychological stress.

Examples of Voice Stress Measurement

How is stress represented on a PSE chart? The normal wave form of spoken words under nonstress conditions would appear as in Figure 1.[2] Each individual wave form represents a single word. Note the irregularity of the cycles and that the general configuration resembles a wave. That is, if a line is drawn connecting the top points of each cycle a wave-like pattern will be evident.

Figure 2 illustrates three examples of the charted responses of a person under psychological stress. As stress in an individual becomes stronger, the undulating wave patterns shown in Figure 1 break down into increasingly "squarish" configurations. The patterns in Figure 2 show a degree of rectilinearity proportionate to the degree of stress present. Increasing levels of stress are evident from left to right, with the square blocking configuration of high stress displayed on the far right. It should be pointed out that amplitude (height) is arbitrarily adjusted to fit the tape width by the operator of the instrument.

A researcher employing the PSE prepares a chart for each word in a narrative document. It is a long, tedious, and laborious process. Nevertheless, when it is completed, the analyst has a clear stress profile of a speaker for a particular oral document. It should be mentioned that PSE-generated stress data are easily and perfectly reproduced by individual operators.[3]

FIGURE 1
Three Charts of Unstressed Words

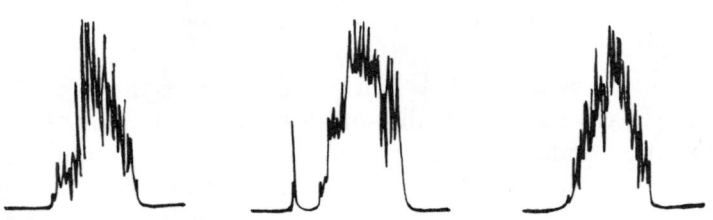

Research Applications of the PSE

The PSE has been used in a variety of research environments, both nonpolitical and political. Because of the great usefulness of this instrument in politically oriented research, let us review the PSE literature in some detail.

Nonpolitical Research

Smith (1973) designed an experiment that measured the responses of fifteen hospital outpatients suffering from general anxiety states to seven phrases referring to common life stressors and three phrases referring to personal life stressors. Each subject was asked to read the ten items in each list twice for test-retest reliability. The responses were recorded and subsequently analyzed by the PSE. It was assumed that the patient's self-report would not always agree with the PSE analysis, and this was found to be true. In general, however, the voice analysis corresponded significantly with the patients' responses to the questionnaire. Smith concluded that the voice analysis method of identifying particular areas of anxiety would significantly enhance psychological evaluation and treatment.

In an attempt to assess levels of stress in various communication responses, Wiggins, McCranie, and Bailey (1975) made recordings of psychiatric interviews with two children. Using the PSE, the experimenters analyzed these verbalizations and organized them into three major response categories. These were: content of communication, responses to therapist-posed questions, and miscellaneous responses. Content responses were further broken down into people, ideas, objects, and actions. An analysis of the children's responses to different people in their environment was also made. Finally, the amount of stress elicited either when responses were given to the therapists' questions or when they

FIGURE 2

Three Charts of Stressed Words

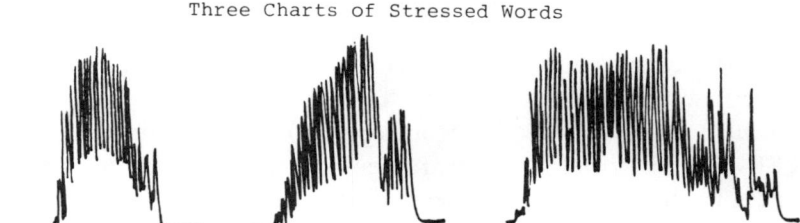

were volunteered was also analyzed. This study concluded that stress in the voice can be detected and assessed and that PSE analysis could lead to new ways of exploring the relationship between psychological stress and content of communication in psychiatric patients.

McGlone (1975) designed three experiments to evaluate the effectiveness of the PSE. Although the results of the first two experiments appear to be inconclusive, a third experiment utilized an ingenious design. Twenty male subjects read "An Apology for Idlers" by Stevenson while experiencing successively increased levels of shock with randomly determined time-intervals between trials. Baseline data words recorded before the administration of shock were compared with words recorded during the administration of the most severe shock trials. It was found that stress could be detected 77 percent of the time through the use of the PSE.

Smith (1973) conducted two related experiments. In the initial experiment, a six-question format was used containing two control questions in the first and fourth positions of the schedule. Subjects were asked to give either a "yes" or a "no" answer to each question. These items (concerning the days of the week) were assumed to produce particular levels of stress, with the first question producing significantly more stress than the second due to an initial "test anxiety." The second type of question was assumed to be relevant or "stressing," since it was concerned with whether the subject had ever pilfered any office supplies. It was hypothesized that these questions would significantly vary in stress when compared to the second control question, but would not be significantly different when compared to the first.

Twenty subjects were analyzed. It was found that the mean stress on the first control question was significantly higher than on the second with $t = 1.83$, $p = 0.05$ (1-tail). The combined mean stress of the relevant questions was also significantly higher than on the second control question ($t = 1.75$, $p = 0.05$, 1-tail). However, the one "stressing" question was significantly more stressed than the control question ($t = 2.11$, $p = 0.025$, 1-tail). The second experiment produced similar results.

Further work by Smith (forthcoming) demonstrated that the PSE could be used as an instrument to detect significant differences in anxiety states. One experiment dealt with a broadcasting situation in which it was assumed that "professional broadcasters would be under a lesser degree of stress because of their experience ... than members of the public, who would be subject to the anxiety of a new experience." Analyzing the PSE traces by both visual schemes and objective rating schemes, ten responses for each of twenty-two professionals and thirteen members of the public were investigated. It was found that the public's responses were significantly more stressed than the broadcasters' (Mann-Whitney U-test, $p = 0.001$) when the visual ratings procedure was utilized. Using objective scoring, a t-test revealed that significant differences could also be found ($p = 0.001$).

In another experiment, Smith divided eighteen neurotic outpatients into two groups. It was assumed that the phobic group would respond to the experimental situation with a higher anxiety level than the nonphobics (obsessionals, hypochondriacs, and mild depressives). Fifteen student nurses and professionals were used in a control group for comparison. Each subject was asked to count aloud from 1 to 10 and was told that the experimenter would be concerned with anxiety levels in his voice. For the visually rated data, using a Mann-Whitney U-test it was found that the phobics were significantly more anxious than nonphobics ($p = 0.01$). However, this test did not reveal any significant differences between the nonphobics and the normals.

In an attempt to explore the possibility of using the PSE as a tool for measuring both anxiety and the effectiveness of anti-anxiety drugs, other researchers (Borgen and Goodman) designed an experiment evaluating eight paid volunteer male prisoners' responses to a Stroop Test. The Stroop Test produces a conflict situation which is assumed to be stress-inducing. The subjects' blood flow, skin potential, and EKG readings were taken during the test, along with a recording of their verbal responses. The subjects also received either 10 milligrams of Diazipan, a tranquilizer, or a placebo two hours prior to the examination, depending on the treatment group to which they were assigned.

The Stroop Test proved to be an effective means of eliciting an arousal state, which was noted by significant increases in blood flow, skin potential, and systolic and diastolic pressures. Subjects also showed appropriate stressed responses to the conflict situation presented in the Stroop Test. Because of the small number of subjects in each group, significant differences in stress responses, as measured by traditional physiological measures and/or the PSE, were not detected. All results, however, showed movement in the appropriate directions (Diazipan reduced the degree of stress as indicated by both types of measurements).

Using the PSE to measure stress reactions during a poem recitation, Brenner (1974) attempted to examine the effects of group size on the intensity of "stage fright." Twenty-five introductory speech students from the University of Michigan were asked to recite a short poem before an empty auditorium. They were then divided into groups and recited a very difficult piece before twenty-two, eight, two, and no spectators from an introductory psychology class. The correlation between the PSE scores and self-reports of arousal was $r = .32$. Stress increased as an almost perfect power function of group size.

The dental profession has long been concerned with the effects of stress during the treatment process. Johnson (1978) conducted an experiment in which eighty-one professionals were divided into four groups based on amount of clinical experience and education in pedodontics. Fifteen slides of both stressing and nonstressing pedodontic situations were shown to each subject. Differing content in the stressor slides included traumatic injuries and congenital malformations. The nonstressing slides were simply textures of various colors which contained no cognitive content. When a slide was projected on a screen, the subject was asked "Do you see the slide?" A tape recording of the subject's "yes" responses was made and then analyzed with the PSE.

Johnson hypothesized that the least-experienced groups would be the most stressed by the stressor slides, and that practicing pedodontists would be the least stressed. Precisely the opposite findings prevailed. In explaining his results, Johnson suggests that the only plausible explanation for the most experienced dental professionals showing the most stress is that it is only they who understand the broad procedural implications of the stressor slides. Thus, their voices conveyed the highest levels of psychological stress. Johnson's work is consistent with previous research involving the physiological monitoring of anxiety states among experienced and inexperienced parachute jumpers (see Tanner 1976: 26-27).

Shearer and Wiegele (1977) hypothesized that successfully conditioned stress words, as determined by the Galvanic Skin Response (GSR), would correlate positively and significantly with stress words as detected in the PSE analysis. Thirty subjects (fifteen male, fifteen female) were asked to read a list consisting of eight one-syllable numbers. For each subject, several words were chosen randomly and were stress-conditioned through the presentation of a high-frequency noise burst for 500 milliseconds in free field 100 dB SPL. A tape recording of the verbal responses for each subject was made, and the second experimenter, who had not witnessed the stress-conditioned GSR, chose the stress-conditioned words on the basis of a PSE analysis. These words were correctly chosen in ten of the thirty subjects, and the chi square value was found significant at the .01 probability level. These results lead to the suggestion that the PSE is capable of detecting stressed words in speakers' voices.

Not all nonpolitical work with the PSE has had positive results, however. McGlone and Hollien (1976) raised questions about the detectability of low frequency tremors in the body. Other researchers have had difficulty in determining stress in experimental situations.

Political Research

In politically oriented PSE research, two types of studies have been done, both on an exploratory basis. The first attempted to examine some emotional aspects of a political leader not involved in foreign policy making, and the second dealt solely with the behavior of foreign policy elites under conditions of high stress.

In the first type of study (Wiegele 1978), I looked at the phenomenon of stress in a political context by selecting for PSE analysis two extemporaneous speeches of Richard M. Nixon during periods assumed to have created intense psychological discomfort or negative affect (stress) in him. These two speeches were his 1962 California gubernatorial concession speech and the 1974 farewell to his staff after his resignation from the presidency. Both speeches were delivered at critical turning points in Nixon's political life: The capture of the California governership was supposed to have provided a base for Nixon to reinject himself into national politics after John F. Kennedy defeated him in the 1960 presidential campaign; and it is an understatement to describe the first forced resignation from the American presidency as a major event in an individual's life.

The findings of the voice stress analysis of these two speeches indicated that the two themes on which Nixon exhibited the greatest amount of signal leakage through the voice dealt with the press and himself as a person. While most of the speech dealt with the reasons for his loss, the nature of the campaign, political issues, and the economy, the two most stressing themes for Nixon (as revealed by voice analysis) dealt with intensely personal issues. "Nixon's words regarding the press made it clear that he was expressing a deep-felt personal anger at what he considered unfair treatment toward himself. His comment that he fought the good fight even though he went down to defeat likewise reflected a concern with himself as an individual" (Wiegele 1978:35).

Nixon's "farewell to his staff" speech was delivered on August 9, 1974, and was a thoroughly extemporaneous effort, in contrast to his prepared resignation speech of the previous evening. Nixon thanked his staff for its faithful service and asked them to support the incoming president. In the very emotional environment of that day, Nixon went on in a rambling fashion offering psychological portraits of his father and mother, reflections on President Theodore Roosevelt's autobiographical account of the death of his wife at a very young age, and insights into his own career.

In the PSE analysis of this oral document, the "sense of the personal" again emerged with clarity. "The loss of the presidency was viewed by Nixon not as a political but as a personal tragedy. Nixon's historical reflections were not about a political leader (Theodore Roosevelt) who experienced a political crisis, but rather about a political leader who experienced a personal crisis: the death of his wife.... The mark of a great man, said Mr. Nixon, is that he can view disappointment as a beginning" (Wiegele 1978: 35-36).

Voice stress analysis of these two speeches revealed that in periods of great emotional tension, Nixon viewed political affairs in highly personal terms rather than in political perspective, as one might expect of a professional politician. The implications of these observations for foreign policy analysis are intriguing: analysis might be able to uncover the normally well-protected psychological exteriors of individual, high-ranking elites through the leakage of physiological signals in the voice. Psychophysiological profiles of individuals might be constructed which would provide an expanded range of data upon which to assess foreign policy—

especially crisis—behavior. Moreover, decisional choices designed to restore personal worth or prestige might be fundamentally different from those directed at the precise resolution of a political problem (Wiegele 1978:36).

Another study (Wiegele, forthcoming) attempted to utilize voice stress analysis to assess the foreign policy behavior of U.S. presidents. This work examined the speeches of Presidents Truman, Kennedy, and Johnson during five crises: Korea (1950), Berlin (1961), Cuba (1962), Tonkin (1964), and Pueblo (1968). All of the speeches were nationally televised presentations to the American people regarding a specific international challenge and the projected U.S. response to it.

In each speech it was possible to identify individual themes that caused the highest amount of stress in the speaker's voice. Truman exhibited the greatest stress when he criticized North Korea for not permitting U.N. observers on its territory. Kennedy, during the Berlin crisis, displayed very high stress when he called for an increase in appropriations for nonnuclear weaponry. As might be anticipated, during the Cuban missile crisis the president revealed the highest stress when he indicated that the launching of a Soviet missile in the Western hemisphere would require full U.S. retaliation. Lyndon Johnson's remarks regarding the Gulf of Tonkin—that U.S. air strikes on North Vietnam were then under way—and during the Pueblo affair—that certain precautionary measures were being taken in the Korean area—resulted in extreme stress levels for him. These brief comments are illustrative of the kind of information that can be generated by the PSE. By themselves they are simply raw data which must be examined along with other PSE data and situational variables.

Some comparisons were also made across the five crisis documents. There is a certain rhetoric in international crisis speeches that appears to demand that the act which precipitated the crisis be spelled out in some detail and with a good deal of strength in order to marshal national support. Our analysis found that the precipitating act themes, in spite of the strong language used, came through as low stress themes. Only one, that of the Gulf of Tonkin speech, could be classified as high stress. The assessment of this was that presidents viewed the precipitating acts as "givens" or clear facts in the crises studied, with the exception of Tonkin—where the realization of what happened apparently had not been established beyond doubt.

Another cross-crisis comparison was done on the "determination themes." Typically, words in such themes (of national determination) were found in crisis speeches, and they indicated that the United States was determined to reach a successful outcome of the crisis. In the Korean, Berlin, and Cuban crises, the determination themes were highly stressful to the speakers, while in the Tonkin and Pueblo crises the determination themes were of very low stress. Our interpretation of this was that in Korea, Berlin, and Cuba, U.S. determination could have led to a "shooting" war—as it in fact did in Korea. On the other hand, in the case of Tonkin, a direct state-to-state confrontation at that time (1964) was not realistic and a war was not imminent. This was also true with regard to the Pueblo affair. With U.S. involvement in Vietnam in 1968 at a near peak, it would have been unreasonable for the United States to open a second war in Korea. Results of this study implied that determination themes are likely to produce high stress in a speaker's voice if he perceives that there is a strong possibility that a situation could lead to war.

To this point, politically oriented work with the PSE can only be described as exploratory. But the promise of this methodology appears great, especially in foreign policy analysis, where remote measurement methods must be employed in the direct measurement of elite decision-makers. More rigorously designed studies currently under way aim at examining an individual speaker over a period of months rather than at a single point in time, as was done in previous work. Such an effort will furnish the analyst with a profile of signal leakage which could, for example, provide clues to the changing levels of stress in a leader or indicate information regarding his state of mental health.

Further, as discussed earlier, other remote indicators of signal leakage such as language, eye, face, speech, etc., could usefully be correlated with voice stress analysis both in experimental and applied research settings. In order to make remote psychological assessment accurate, we need to know the best mix of indices of leakage. It does appear, however, that voice stress analysis is a critical index of leakage for the foreign policy researcher.

Conclusions

I have argued that it is important for the student of foreign policy to work more intensely at the individual level of analysis. At that level, however, elites are often inaccessible to the analyst. If we want to measure individuals directly, such a situation requires that we develop a repertoire of methods of remote psychological assessment which is based on the leakage of certain kinds of signals from human beings.

In creating such a repertoire or toolbox, it is likely that our research will become more basic and perhaps more experimental in character. We will have to acquire some knowledge of psychophysiology and perhaps certain aspects of medicine. In this process, moreover, we will have to design studies that will be truly interdisciplinary in character.

For scholars of international relations, such an orientation might be described as a revolution in the research process. But if we are to proceed to develop direct and accurate measurements of individuals in authoritative foreign policy making roles, employing the concept of signal leakage with appropriate methods appears to open the door to acquiring more precise psychological knowledge for foreign policy analysis.

Notes

1. Foreign policy analysts who have either worked at or encouraged work at the individual level include George and George (1964), Paige (1968), Allison (1971), Holsti (1972), C. Hermann and Brady (1972), Bloomfield (1973), Holsti and George (1976), M. Hermann (1978), and Falkowski (1978).

2. A much abbreviated form of this material appears in Wiegele (forthcoming from Westview Press).

3. The method of scoring PSE data can be found in Wiegele (forthcoming from Westview Press).

References

Allison, G. *Essence of Decision: Explaining the Cuban Missile Crisis.* Boston: Little, Brown, 1971.

Bell, A. D., Jr., W. H. Ford, and C. R. McQuiston. "Physiological Response Analysis Method and Apparatus." U.S. Patent No. 3,971,034, issues July 20, 1976; n.p.

Bloomfield, L. "Theories of State: Analyzing the Policy Process." Washington, D.C.: Departmentof State (November 1973).

Brenner, M. "Stagefright and Steven's Law." Paper presented at the Eastern Psychological Association.

Brody, R. A. "The Study of International Politics Qua Science." In *Contending Approaches to International Politics*, edited by K. Knorr and J. N.

Rosenau. Princeton University Press, 1969.
Cameron, D. E. "Ultraconceptual Communication." In *Psychology of Commumication*. New York: Grune and Stratton, 1958.
Cotter, C. P., ed. *Political Science Annual*, no. 6. Indianapolis: Bobbs-Merrill, 1976.
Dibner, A. "Cue-counting: A Measure of Anxiety." *Journal of Consulting Psychology*, vol. 26 (1956):475-478.
Dittmann, A. T. "The Relationship between Body Movements and Moods in Interviews." *Journal of Consulting Psychology*, vol. 26 (1962).
Ekman, P. and W. V. Friesen. *Unmasking the Face: A Guide to Recognizing Emotions from Facial Clues.* Englewood Cliffs, N.J.: Prentice Hall, 1975.
———. "Non-Verbal Leakage and Clues to Deception." *Psychiatry* 32, no. 1 (February 1969):88-105.
Ekman, P., W. V. Friesen, and P. Ellsworth. *Emotion in the Human Face.* New York: Pergamon Press, 1972.
Falkowski, L. S. *Presidents, Secretaries of State, and Crises in U.S. Foreign Relations: A Model and Predictive Analysis.* Boulder, Co.: Westview Press, 1978.
Frank, R. S. "Nonverbal and Paralinguistic Analysis of Political Behavior: The First McGovern-Humphrey California Primary Debate." In *Political Leaders*, edited by M. G. Hermann and T. W. Milburn. New York: Free Press, 1977.
———. *Linguistic Analysis of Political Elites: A Theory of Verbal Kinesics.* Beverly Hills: Sage Monograph, 1973.
George, A., and J. George. *Woodrow Wilson and Colonel House.* New York: Dover, 1964.
Goldman-Eisler, F. "A Comparative Study of Two Hesitation Phenomena." *Language and Speech* 4 (1961):18-26.
Haessler, F. H. *Eye Signs in General Disease.* Springfield, Ill.: Charles C. Thomas, 1960.
Hermann, C. F., ed. *International Crisis: Insights from Behavioral Research.* New York: Free Press, 1972.
———. *Crises in Foreign Policy.* Indianapolis: Bobbs-Merrill, 1969.
Hermann, C. F., and L. Brady. "Alternative Models of International Crisis Behavior." In *International Crisis: Insights from Behavioral Research*, edited by C. F. Hermann. New York: Free Press, 1972.
Hermann, M. G. "Effect of Personal Characteristics of Political Leaders on Foreign Policy." In M. A. East, S. A. Salamore, and C. F. Hermann, *Why Nations Act: Theoretical Perspectives for Comparative Foreign Policy Studies.* Beverly Hills, Calif.: Sage, 1978.
———. "Verbal Behavior of Negotiators in Periods of High and Low Stress: The 1965-66 New York City Transit Negotiations." In *A Psychological Examination of Political Leaders*, edited by M. G. Hermann and T. W. Milburn. New York: Free Press, 1977.
Hermann, M. G. and T. W. Milburn, eds. *A Psychological Examination of*

Political Leaders. New York: Free Press, 1977.

Holsti, O. *Crisis Escalation War.* Montreal: McGill-Queens University Press, 1972.

Holsti, O. and A. George. "The Effects of Stress on Foreign Policy-Makers." In *Political Science Annual,* no. 6, edited by C. P. Cotter. Indianapolis: Bobbs-Merrill, 1976.

Janisse, M. P. *Pupillometry: The Psychology of Pupillary Response.* Washington, D.C.: Hemisphere Publishing Corp., 1977.

Johnson, J. B. "Stress Reactions of Various Judging Groups to the Child Dental Patient." Thesis submitted in partial fulfillment of the requirements for the degree of M.A. in Pedodontics, University of Iowa, Iowa City, 1978.

Kasl, Stanislav V., and George F. Mahl, "The Relationship of Disturbances and Hesitations in Spontaneous Speech to Anxiety." *Journal of Personality and Social Psychology* 1 (1965):423-433.

Lewis, B., and J. Worth. "Transfer of Stress Through Verbal and Written Communication." Manuscript, Washington and Lee University, 1974.

Maclay, Howard, and Charles E. Osgood. "Hesitation Phenomena in Spontaneous English Speech." *Word* 15 (1959):18-44.

McGlone, R. "Test of the Psychological Stress Evaluator (PSE) as a Lie and Stress Detector." Paper presented at the Carnahan Conference on Crime Countermeasures, Lexington, Ky.

McGlone, R. E., and H. Hollien. "Partial Analysis of Acoustic Signal of Stressed and Unstressed Speech," manuscript (1976).

Mahl, George F. "Disturbances and Silences in the Patient's Speech." *Psychotherapy* 53 (1956):1-15.

Paige, G. *The Korean Decision.* New York: The Free Press, 1968.

Rubenstein, L. "Electro-Acoustical Measurement in Vocal Responses to Limited Stress." *Behaviour Research and Therapy* 4 (May 1966):135-139.

Rubin, B., ed. *Communications Yearbook II.* New Brunswick, N.J.: Transaction Books, 1978.

Russell, P. O., and W. V. Snyder. "Counsellor Anxiety in Relation to Amount of Clinical Experience and Quality of Affect Demonstrated by Clients," *Journal of Consulting Psychology,* vol. 27 (1963).

Shearer, W., and T. Wiegele. "A Comparison of Vocal Stress Analysis and Skin Responses." Paper presented at the annual convention of the American Speech and Hearing Association, Chicago.

Smith, G. "Analysis of the Voice," manuscript (1973).

———. "Lie Detection by Voice Analysis: The Problem of Reliability," manuscript.

———. "Voice Analysis for the Measurement of Anxiety." *British Journal of Medical Psychology,* forthcoming.

Tanner, O. *Stress.* New York: Time-Life Books, 1976.

Wiegele, T. C. "Physiologically-Based Content Analysis: An Application in Political Communication." In *Communications Yearbook II,* edited by

B. Rubin. New Brunswick, N.J.: Transaction Books, 1978.
——. "The Psychophysiology of Elite Stress in Five International Crises: A Preliminary Test of a Voice Measurement Technique." *International Studies Quarterly*, forthcoming.

Wiggins, S., M. McCranie, and P. Bailey. "Assessment of Voice Stress in Children." *The Journal of Nervous and Mental Disease* 160 (1975):402-408.

5
The Causal Nexus between Cognitive Beliefs and Decision-Making Behavior: The "Operational Code" Belief System

Alexander L. George

Specialists on international relations working with decision-making approaches have long emphasized the importance of cognitive variables in the making of foreign policy. It is noteworthy that even some revisionist historians critical of U.S. cold war policy have recently begun to examine and emphasize the importance of cognitive belief systems (Yergin 1977; see also the 1971 effort by Gamson and Modigliani to explain U.S.-Soviet interactions within the framework of cognitive variables). However, progress in incorporating cognitive variables of various kinds into empirical research on decision-making has been relatively slow and uneven. "Existing studies," Ole Holsti notes in a recent review, "are characterized by diversity in conceptualization, sources of theory, research site, subject, and 'data-making' operations (categories, coding rules, data analysis procedures). They range from rather traditional single-case analyses of specific leaders to efforts aimed at developing computer simulations of cognitive processes" (Holsti 1976:36).

Here we shall examine the "operational code" belief-system construct for conceptualizing cognitive variables in decision-making, which differs in important respects from other cognitive approaches. A large number of studies have explored the feasibility and utility of the operational code approach (George and Holsti 1974; Holsti 1977). Most have limited themselves to deriving the beliefs of a particular political leader with respect to the set of

---

Preparation of this chapter was supported by a research grant (No. SOC 75-14079) from the National Science Foundation. I would like to express my appreciation also to the Center for Advanced Study in the Behavioral Sciences, Stanford University. Copyright © 1979 by Alexander L. George.

"philosophical" and "instrumental" issues encompassed by the operational code construct. These studies encounter the familiar problem of inter-coder reliability and validity, which have been attended to in specific studies (Walker 1977; Heradtsveit 1977; Hoagland and Walker 1979) and have been addressed during efforts to develop a standardized codebook (Holsti 1977).

Here, attention is directed, not to these methodological issues, but rather to those associated with efforts to assess the impact of an individual's operational code beliefs on his policy preferences and choices of action. In order to do so, we must first locate the operational code approach within the framework of cognitive psychology and articulate the theoretical premises that guide us in efforts to assess the influence such beliefs have in decision-making.

Cognitive Psychology and the Operational Code Belief System Approach

Cognitive theory includes within its scope attention to (a) cognitive organization or structure; (b) cognitive processes; and (c) cognitive dynamics (Zajonc 1968). Cognitive organization, which is of immediate relevance to the operational code construct, refers in the most general terms to any form of interdependence among cognitive elements, whatever their referent. Various cognitive elements have been employed as units of analysis by social psychologists to characterize the components of cognitive organization—namely, attributes, attitudes, psychological dimensions, categories or concepts, and finally, of particular importance for the present discussion, *schemata*.

Psychologists recognize that cognitive structures can be more or less differentiated, unified, hierarchically organized, or stable. Some psychologists focus attention on the *content* of cognitive concepts, to which we shall return shortly; others have investigated primarily their *structural aspects*—e.g., the properties of "concreteness-abstractness," "category width," "levelling," "assimilation and contrast," "cognitive simplicity or complexity," "open- and closed-mindness"—which are less relevant here.

Whether dealing with substantive content or structural aspects, psychologists have not found it an easy task "to find aspects of cognitive functioning that remain stable from situation to situation, and yet reliably discriminate among individuals" (Zajonc 1968:335).

Of the various characteristics of cognitive structure that have been employed as basic units of analysis, I regard schemata as particularly appropriate and important in studying the role of cognitive variables in the decision-making behavior of political leaders.[1] As the term is employed in cognitive psychology, schemata refers to an individual's generalized principles about social life. These principles exist on a subjective and relatively private level and enable the individual to order his relationship to the social environment.

The construct of the operational code belief system deals with schemata, so defined; but it limits itself to the set of generalized principles about *political* life that an individual acquires and applies in information processing for the purpose of exercising judgment and choice in decision-making.

Schemata differ from attitudes. Although the concept of attitudes has been employed with reference to a broad range of cognitive phenomena, attitudes generally have more specific referents than schemata and operational code beliefs. The latter two refer to generalized principles about social and political life and not, as attitudes presumably do, to predispositions to respond to rather specific or delineated objects.[2]

Incidentally, it is partly for this reason that the concept of attitude has become vulnerable to some of the same criticisms that earlier undermined the traditional "trait approach" to personality. The trait approach was based on the premise that personality traits are underlying dispositions which exert generalized effects on behavior and that, as a result of possessing such traits, an individual behaves consistently in a variety of situations. But with the accumulation of experience indicating that attitudes are poor predictors of behavior, many social psychologists now concede that the failure of attitudes to correlate well with behavior reflects a fundamental gap in attitude theory—namely, a neglect of situational and contextual variables.

Although the cross-situational consistency of behavior tends to be quite low, however, it can not be concluded from this (1) that individuals lack stability and consistency in important components of their cognitive structures over time, or (2) that there is a general lack of consistency between all cognitive beliefs and behavior (but only that the consistency between cognitive variables and behavior is not likely to be located in traits and attitudes); or (3) that cognitive variables do not play a role in influencing behavior.[3]

These are challenging issues in contemporary cognitive psychology, and a brief digression is apporpriate in order to note how they are linked with a reexamination of a number of fundamental premises associated with the "models of man" controversy, the proper conceptualization of personality, the theory and practice of behavior modification, and fundamental epistemological issues. (See, for example, Bandura 1974; Abelson 1976; Bowers 1973; Mischel 1973, 1977; Ross 1977; Bem and Allen 1974.) Of particular interest to political scientists engaged in research on decision-making is the fact that these developments in psychology are producing a major paradigm shift, referred to by some as "a cognitive revolution" in psychology. Recent developments in cognitive balance and dissonance theories, attribution theory, attitude theory, social learning theory, and personality theory are moving or have already moved each of the elements into an information-processing framework.[4]

The convergence of so many important subfields of psychology into a common information-processing framework promises to produce a more fruitful synthesis of psychological theories relevant to the study of decision-making. We are also on the threshold of a new wave of research in psychology that promises to be even more directly relevant and useful for study of political decision-making than these subfields, individually or collectively, have been in the past.

Two important aspects of this paradigm shift should be noted. First is the shift in the fundamental "model of man" assumption—away from the conception of man as a passive agent who responds to environmental stimuli and back to a conception of man as actively and selectively responding to and shaping his environment. (For a reflection of the controversy over this issue, see Bowers 1973.) Second, within the conceptualization of man as an active agent, an additional shift has occurred—away from the fundamental premise of earlier cognitive balance theories, which viewed man as a "consistency-seeker," and toward the quite different premise of recent attribution theory (and other psychological theories as well), which view man as a "problem-solver."

Thus, as attribution theorists stress, man's status has been elevated from that of a mere "consistency-seeker" to that of a "naive scientist"—that is, one who seeks as best he can (applying naive epistemology rather than scientific epistemology!) to infer the causes of social events in everyday life, to discern the attributes of other actors and social phenomena, to predict historical trends and the behavior of other persons—all in order to be able to exercise some control over the outcome of social situations. Hence, there is an emphasis in attribution theory on man as a would-be scientist, on who is engaged in acquiring knowledge and theories by means of which to explain, predict, and control. But at the same time attribution theory reminds us that man often performs as a "naive scientist" because of various flaws, biases, and errors in the epistemology he employs to this end.

It takes very little stretch of the imagination for a political scientist who is exposed to these descriptions of the "naive scientist" (see Ross 1977) to grasp the fact that these are apt descriptions also of the typical policy maker! One can go further and fruitfully define the task of policy science (the task of designing and managing policy-making systems) as that of avoiding, correcting, and/or compensating for flaws, errors, and biases of the kind that the policy maker's naive epistemology introduces into the information processing associated with decision-making.

Let us return now to the apparent dilemma created by the finding that cross-situational consistency of behavior tends to be quite low and that attitudes do not correlate very well with behavior. As was suggested above, it would be unjustified to conclude from this that there is a general lack of consistency between all types of cognitive beliefs and behavior or that cognitive variables do not play a role in influencing behavior. The question may be reformulated: if the influential role of cognitive beliefs and their consistency with behavior is not to be located in "traits" and "attitudes," then where?

At what level of cognitive structure should we look for cognitive beliefs that influence decision-making behavior across situations? One answer to this question is that "central" beliefs are more likely to have these qualities and consequences than beliefs that occupy a secondary or peripheral role in the hierarchy of cognitive belief structure (Bem 1970).

Operational code beliefs have centrality. Unlike attitudes, they are concerned with fundamental, unchanging issues of politics and political action. These central issues were inducted empirically from an earlier study (Leites 1953) of the Bolshevik elite's well-developed, comprehensive approach to politics in an effort to codify and generalize the operational code construct (George 1969).[5] Those who have since employed the operational code construct in studying a variety of other leaders have found the initial identification of central issues adequate and in need of only minor adaptations and additions (George and Holsti 1974).

A distinction is made in the operational code construct between "philosophical" and "instrumental" issues. Philosophical beliefs refer to the assumptions and premises made by an actor regarding:

1. the fundamental nature of politics and political conflict, and the image of the opponent;
2. the general prospects for achieving one's fundamental political values;
3. the extent to which political outcomes are predictable;
4. the extent to which political leaders can influence historical developments and control outcomes; and
5. the role of chance.

Instrumental beliefs, on the other hand, have to do with questions of correct strategy and tactics—such issues as:

1. the best approach for selecting goals for political action;
2. how such goals and objectives can be pursued most effectively;
3. the best approach to calculation, control, and acceptance of the risks of political action;
4. the matter of "timing" of action; and
5. the utility and role of different means for advancing one's interests.

Considerable effort has been given to the refinement and elaboration of beliefs centered on these ten basic issues and to the development of detailed coding categories for each of them in order to facilitate achievement of inter-coder reliability (Holsti 1977).

We have also assumed (and much supporting evidence, mostly of an impressionistic kind, has accumulated in the various studies to support the assumption) that an individual actor's operational code beliefs are not a fortuitous, unconnected collection of beliefs. Rather, they comprise a "belief system" in the sense described by Converse (1964): "a configuration of ideas and attitudes in which the elements are bound together by some form of constraint or functional interdependence. The individual beliefs in an operational code have this kind of internal consistency or interconnectedness for the actor, though not necessarily a logical consistency."

As in Converse's further characterization of "belief systems," the operational code evidences internal interconnectedness in the sense that a change in its central or dominant idea-elements—in particular, the first philosophical belief concerning the nature of political conflict and, related to it, the image of the opponent—seems to require (psychologically from the standpoint of the actor) some compensating change in the status of other beliefs within the configuration. (The operational code's system-like character has been exploited in an effort to derive typologies of operational codes; see in particular Holsti 1977; Heradtsveit 1977). That the first philosophical belief is probably a dominant or "master" belief was noted in the initial formulation of the construct (George 1969) and has received support in some subsequent studies.

The Role of Operational Code Beliefs in Decision-Making: Two Theoretical Premises

Our views regarding the role that operational code beliefs may be expected to play in decision-making follow from the special nature of these beliefs. Of a general rather than a specific character, these beliefs concern fundamental issues of politics, history, and political action; they provide the basic framework within which the actor approaches the task of attempting to process available information and to engage in rational calculation in pursuit of his values and interests.

Our first theoretical premise is that beliefs of this kind influence decision-making indirectly by influencing the information-processing tasks that precede and accompany the decision-maker's choice of action. (Our second theoretical premise, which we shall discuss later, is that such beliefs do not unilaterally determine his choice of action; other variables are also at work in determining what he will do.)

There are several useful ways of identifying information-processing tasks in policy making. One standard terminology characterizes these tasks in functional terms: search, evaluation, and choice. Another depicts these tasks in substantive terms: first, the task of formulating a "definition of the situation"; then the task of "option-development"—that is the formulation and evaluation of options. Both ways of describing information-processing tasks are useful.

Various hypotheses can be advanced as to the effects that different types of operational code beliefs can have on one or another of these functional and substantive tasks of information processing. Let us consider the way in which an actor's "definition of the situation" may be influenced by certain of his operational code beliefs. The particular definition of a new situation formulated by a decision-maker can be of great importance in shaping his response to that situation, so much so that his definition of the situation is likely to eliminate from serious consideration certain policy options and to favor others. We assume (and available empirical evidence of an impressionistic kind supports the assumption) that an actor's image of the opponent (an aspect of the first philosophical belief) is particularly important in shaping his definition of the situation, particularly as regards his assessment of the threat posed by the adversary's behavior.

A general image of one's opponent as being fundamentally hostile encourages the actor to define situations of interaction with that opponent as posing dangers to his side. Ambiguous situations are perceived as threatening or as posing latent crises. Ambiguous information about an opponent's behavior or intentions is likely to be interpreted as evidence of hostility. Discrepant information that challenges the existing image of him as fundamentally hostile is discounted or ignored (Holsti 1967). Thus, an actor's operational code beliefs introduce diagnostic propensities into his information processing.

An actor's operational code beliefs also influence the focus and extent of the search and evaluation aspects of his information processing. Thus, if the actor views the opponent as a "unitary actor" (another aspect of the first philosophical belief), he is likely to engage in less extensive search for information about the adversary's motivations than he would if the opponent were viewed as a pluralistic group of leaders. The latter view raises the likelihood that policy views and preferences on the opposing side are not homogenous in all respects, a possibility that sensitizes and deepens the search for clues as to the opponent's motivations and calculations.

Search can also be affected by the fourth philosophical belief: How much control or mastery can one have over historical development? Thus, an actor who believes that he can exert a significant degree of control over events is more likely to undertake extensive search. His informational requirements are greater than those of an actor who feels he can do little to control and shape the course of events.

Finally, an actor who believes that chance and unforeseeable circumstances govern human affairs and historical development (the fifth philosphical belief) is less likely to engage in extensive search behavior.

In addition to these various diagnostic propensities, an actor's operational code beliefs can also introduce choice propensities into his information processing. For example, choice can be affected by the second philosophical belief: If an actor is essentially optimistic about his ability to achieve his fundamental political values, he is likely to avoid knowingly choosing high-risk options.

Evaluation of options can also be influenced by the third philosophical belief: If one believes that the political future is predictable, one is more likely to engage in extensive analysis of the possible consequences of various policy options.

Choice is also likely to be influenced by the actor's instrumental beliefs regarding correct strategy and tactics. If he is an "optimizer" rather than a "satisficer" in his approach to goal selection (the first instrumental belief), he is more likely to seek to develop and choose options that offer the prospect of greater payoffs.

A final illustrative example of the choice propensities introduced by operational code beliefs is: If the actor believes (as did the old Bolsheviks) that risks of action can generally be calculated and often controlled (the third instrumental belief), he is more likely to pursue amibitious objectives by means of controlled risk options rather than to settle for conservative strategies that trade off the possibility of major payoff in preference for options that entail low risks.

These theoretical premises can be summarized in the observation that by performing certain functional and substantive tasks in information processing, the actor's operational code beliefs introduce two types of propensities, not determinants, into his decision-making: (a) diagonistic propensities, which extend or restrict the scope of search and evaluation and influence his diagnosis of the situation in certain directions; and (b) choice propensities which lead him to favor certain types of action alternatives over others. Thus, our conception of the role of operational code beliefs in decision-making is that they serve as a set of general guidelines—heuristical aids to decision, not a set of mathematical algorithms that are applied by the actor in a mechanical way in his decision-making.[6] Viewed from a slightly different standpoint, a person's operational code beliefs structure and channel the way in which he copes and deals with the cognitive limits on rationality; they serve to define his particular type of "bounded rationality."

Our second theoretical premise is that operational code beliefs, despite the fact that they deal with fundamental issues of politics, history, strategy, and tactics, and despite the fact that they occupy a position of "centrality" in a person's entire set of beliefs and attitudes, do not unilaterally determine the individual's choices of action. Rather, the decisions he makes are sensitive to a variety of other variables as well. Operational code beliefs are only one variable-cluster within a rich, complex causal framework for explaining decision-making. Thus, as is well known, in making foreign policy decisions a policy maker may be influenced by personal considerations, domestic politics, and/or organizational interests as well as by his conception of the national interest. This complicates, of course, the task of establishing the causal weight that operational code beliefs have in any particular decision.

In addition, it leads us to expect that the influence of an actor's beliefs is likely to be more weighty in determining his policy preferences—the option he prefers—than in determining the option he finally chooses. This is the case insofar as the actor's final decision will often be influenced by other variables—domestic politics, organizational considerations, the necessity for compromise, etc.—which run in a direction contrary to his preferred option. It is more useful wherever possible, therefore, to regard the decision-maker's policy preference rather than his final choice of an option as the dependent variable.

Procedures for Assessing the Impact of Operational Code Beliefs on Decisional Choices

In turning to this difficult methodological problem, it is useful to remind ourselves of Philip Converse's remark that "belief systems have never surrendered easily to empirical study or quantification" (1964:206). It is not surprising that most efforts to assess the role of an actor's operational code beliefs in his decision-making have been of an impressionistic and tentative character; recently, however, several investigators have employed more systematic and rigorous assessment methods (Walker 1977, Heradtsveit 1977).

Given the limited opportunities in research of this kind for employing research designs of an experimental or statistical character (Campbell and Stanley 1963), the "softer" methodologies of single case studies and comparative study of a few cases have to be employed. Ways of improving the rigor of causal assessments in case studies are required. We need to introduce into the methodology of single-case explanations the functional equivalent of experimental design. This can be done by requiring causal interpretations in single-case analysis to pass a series of hurdles (questions inspired by the logic of controlled experiments) before granting them plausibility.

Before proceeding, it should be noted that the methodology of explanation in single-case analysis—a problem of long-standing interest to historians—is beginning to receive more attention from other social scientists as well. The reason for this is that in the last decade or so, scholars identified with a variety of disciplines and different research areas have independently come to adopt a more positive view of the contribution that single case studies and "controlled comparisons" of a few cases can make to theory development (see, for example, Verba 1967; Russett 1970; Diesing 1971; Lijphart 1971, 1975; George, Hall, and Simons 1971; George and Smoke 1974; Brown 1974; Campbell 1974, 1975; Eckstein 1975; Cronbach 1975; Lazarus, n.d.).

Two techniques can be employed to assess the impact of a policy maker's operational code beliefs on his decisional choices. The first is the procedure of establishing "congruence" (or consistency) between the content of given beliefs and the content of the decision(s). The second is the procedure of tracing in some detail the steps in the process by means of which given operational code beliefs influence the assessment of incoming information, help to shape the individual's definition of the situation, and influence his identification and evaluation of options. The congruence procedure, insofar as it goes beyond noncausal correlation, relies on a nomothetic-deductive mode of explanation. The process-tracing procedure, on the other hand, follows the pattern model of explanation (Kaplan 1964; Diesing 1971); this, too, makes use of generalizations of one type or another (sometimes of an implicit character and quite restricted in scope) to support each step in the intervening causal sequence.[7]

The Congruence Procedure

The data requirements for these two procedures differ substantially. The congruence technique requires much less information on actual policy making than the process-tracing procedure. Having first established the subject's beliefs on the basis of relevant behavioral data from his prior life-history, the investigator considers whether the subject's policy preferences and decisions are consistent with those beliefs. The effort to do so requires that the investigator decide at what level of concreteness-abstraction to describe the decision in order to establish whether it is consistent with the implications of the operational code beliefs. This determination is obviously of critical importance, and we shall return to it later.

The determination of consistency is made deductively. From the actor's operational code beliefs, the investigator deduces what implications they have for decision. If the characteristics of the decision are consistent with the actor's beliefs, there is at least a presumption that the beliefs may have played a causal role in this particular instance of decision-making.

Two methodological questions, however, must be addressed before the presumption of a causal relationship is granted plausibility. The first question is the familiar one (encountered also in statistical analysis of a large n) of whether the consistency is of genuine causal relevance or is merely fortuitous and spurious. The second question is whether the consistency is explainable largely with reference to antecedent variables other than the operational code beliefs in question. Let us take up each of these methodological problems in turn.

1. *Is consistency genuine or spurious?* Causal interpretation of consistency gains a measure of support if it can be brought within the framework of a nomothetic explanation—that is, if a general law or statistical generalization can be found to support the consistency between the specific beliefs and the specified decisional characteristics. The more specific such a generalization, the more powerfully it supports the causal interpretation. In the absence of a more specific generalization, some support is nonetheless provided by psychological theories of cognitive balance, which call attention to the fact that individuals generally (at least under certain conditions)[8] strive to achieve consistency between their beliefs and their actions.

It should be noted that efforts to apply the congruency procedure to assess the causal role of beliefs will be complicated by the fact that an operational code belief system may contain some ambiguous or inconsistent elements. As noted above, numerous impressionistic studies support the view that operational codes share the characteristics of "belief systems," but this does not exclude the possibility that some of the beliefs within a particular operational code are ambiguous or seemingly inconsistent with one another. A certain element of ambiguity is present, for example, in the Bolshevik operational code that contained instrumental maxims such as the following: "attempt to optimize gains," "push to the limit," "resist from the start." General injunctions of this type lack operational content in that they do not indicate how the maxim is to be applied in specific situations. In addition to this element of ambiguity, some of these beliefs regarding correct strategy and tactics were qualified, if not contradicted, by other maxims in that belief system: "attempt to optimize gains, but don't engage in adventures"; "push to the limit, but know when to stop"; "resist from the start, but don't yield to enemy provocations"; and "be sure to retreat before superior force." As a result, there was what might be called a "tension of opposites" in the cognitive structuring of the problem of action (Leites 1953; George 1969).

The presence of ambiguities, qualifiers, and "tension of opposites" in an actor's belief system complicates the investigator's task of using knowledge of that belief system to explain and to predict his behavior. Ambiguity of certain beliefs offers more of a problem in this respect than qualifiers and tension-of-opposites statements. In any case, even this sort of operational code belief system is of value, especially when combined with situational analysis, for explaining and predicting behavior tendencies. When dealing with a belief system of this kind, the investigator must make appropriate adjustments in his use of the congruency procedure for establishing its causal impact on decision-making.

Confidence that consistency between beliefs and actions is of causal significance is enhanced if it is encountered repeatedly in a sequence of interrelated decisions taken by an actor over a period of time. This was the case in Stephen Walker's ingenious and impressive study (1977) of the role of Henry Kissinger's operational code beliefs in the bargaining with North Vietnam.[9] In this study and in his joint contribution with Steven Hoagland to this volume, Walker has pioneered in developing highly systematic and explicit methods for employing the congruence procedure.

2. *Are beliefs a "necessary condition"?—How much explanatory power do they have?* Turning to the second methodological question, we have to ask and attempt to establish whether the operational code beliefs are a "necessary condition" for, or merely "favor" the decisional output in question.[10] We also have to ask the related question: how much of the explanation is provided by these beliefs as against other antecedent variables?—that is, how much explanatory power can be assigned the operational code beliefs?

The temptation to regard operational code beliefs (or, for that matter other independent or intervening variables, such as role) as a necessary condition when congruence has been demonstrated is often irresistible; therefore, explicit safeguards against a premature, possibly unwarranted interpretation of this kind are necessary. The critical question, of course, is whether the decision could have occurred in the absence of these particular beliefs. Arrangements for assessing this possibility can be built into an experimental design. When the possibility of constructing such a design is not available, the investigator must supplement inspection of the single case in which consistency was found by looking for other cases in which the same value of the dependent variable (the decisional output) occurred in the absence of that particular value of the independent or intervening variable (the beliefs). Since it may be difficult to locate other cases for this purpose, the disciplined single-case analyst may have to rely on analytical imagination to provide a safeguard against a premature, unwarranted inference (which consistency implies) that these beliefs were a necessary condition for the behavior in question. Can he conceive that the same type of decision might have occurred as the result of some other causal pattern, one in which these particular beliefs need not have been present? If so, then the beliefs cannot be regarded as a "necessary condition" (though their presence may still favor the occurrence of that decision).

Thus, in the absence of an experimental or quasi-experimental design, the single-case investigator disciplines the interpretative procedure he is forced to employ by considering a broader range of relevant empirical materials and/or by engaging in what writers on historical explanation sometimes refer to as "mental experiments." This term refers to simulated experiments that the investigator conducts in his own mind, i.e., mental rehearsals in which he varies critical variables in order to estimate variance in outcomes.[11] Well-designed computer simulations may serve the same purpose.

Even if the causal interpretation of consistency survives this type of challenge—i.e., the investigator cannot find or imagine any instances in which the same type of decision occurs in the absence of such beliefs—he cannot claim more than that the beliefs in question *may* be a necessary condition. The causal hypothesis is then more (rather than less) plausible than it would otherwise be. If the grounds for regarding the beliefs as a necessary condition are shaky, it might be advisable to conclude that the beliefs in question *favor* the emergence of certain decisional characteristics, but are not a necessary condition for them.

An important question remains: how much explanatory power can be attributed to the operational code beliefs? Presumptive evidence that certain beliefs are a necessary condition for the decisional outcome can easily encourage an exaggerated notion of their causal weight. To safeguard against this type of error, the total context of the decision must be examined. The investigator must attempt to assess the contribution that other antecedent variables and conditions might have made to the decision in question; one cannot estimate the causal weight of the operational code beliefs without taking into account situational, organizational, and role variables, as well as psychological variables other than operational code beliefs. All of these may be part of a fuller explanation for the emergence of the characteristics of the decision in question. In fact, in certain settings, situational variables may dwarf other variables in determining the decision. In other circumstances, an actor's operational code beliefs may be a function of the role he occupies and hence lack independent causal weight.

But in other types of decisional settings, the actor's cognitive beliefs are neither accounted for nor dwarfed by situational or role variables, and hence their impact on his decisions may be a substantial one. Walker (1977) advances a plausible argument to this effect in his study of the role of Henry Kissinger's operational code beliefs in his conduct of the Vietnam peace negotiations. He holds that Kissinger's beliefs were idiosyncratic in important respects and not easily accounted for by situational or role variables. That is to say, the set of Kissinger's beliefs and the policy actions that were consistent with those beliefs were probably not those that anyone else in his position would have displayed. Walker reminds us that the administration's policy on Vietnam was controversial and that, as a result, there were policy preferences that competed with Kissinger's. Moreover, the role of national security adviser that Kissinger filled at the time was not tightly defined. It permitted considerable latitude to the incumbent. For these and other reasons, Walker concludes that Kissinger's role in the long bargaining process with the leaders of North Vietnam exemplifies both "action indispensability" and "actor indispensability," as defined by Fred Greenstein (1969).

In a recent review of available empirical research bearing on these questions, Ole Holsti (1976) suggests that a decision-maker's beliefs may play an important role in shaping his policy choices and behavior in circumstances of the following kind:

1. Situations that contain highly ambiguous components and are thus open to a variety of interpretations.
2. Non-routine situations that require more than the application of standard operating procedures and decision rules—for example, decisions to initiate or terminate major international undertakings, including wars, interventions, alliances, etc.
3. Situations that require decisions at the pinnacle of the government hierarchy by leaders who are relatively free from organizational and other constraints or who may at least define their roles in ways that enhance their latitude for choice.
4. Events that are unanticipated or contain an element of surprise, in responding to which the decision-maker's initial reactions are likely to reflect his cognitive "sets."
5. Long-range policy planning, a task that inherently involves considerable uncertainty and in which policy makers are likely to differ in their perception of the uncertainties and in their preferred resolution of them.

Thus far in considering the explanatory power of certain operational code beliefs we have called attention to the possibility that antecedent variables other than these beliefs may carry the burden of explaining a particular decision, even when these beliefs are consistent with the decision. Another possibility must also be considered by the investigator when he works with the congruency procedure: namely, that the actor's beliefs would be consistent also with other decisions than the one he took. That there are reasons for assuming that the causal role of given beliefs is not dwarfed by situational, organizational, or role variables does not exhaust the means available to the single-case analyst for assessing the explanatory power of these beliefs. The question remains whether other decisions by the actor in the same situation would also have been consistent with those same beliefs. Since only one value of the dependent variable (the historical outcome) is available to the single-case analyst, it is easy for him to overlook the possibility that other values of the dependent variable could also be consistent with a given independent/intervening variable to which explanatory weight is being attributed. When this is the case, the independent/intervening variable may be part of the explanation, but its ability to discriminate among alternative outcomes and its predictive power are weakened. Thus, the explanatory and predictive power of an independent (or intervening) variable differs considerably, depending on whether it is consistent with one and only one value of the dependent variable or whether it is consistent with several different values of the dependent variable.

A somewhat different question must also be asked: is it possible to conceive of any credible policy options in the same situation that would not have been consistent with those same beliefs? If all the possible actions that the decision-maker might have taken would be consistent with his operational code beliefs, then the explanatory power of those beliefs is negligible. Conversely, if other policy options were available which were not consistent with the decision-maker's own beliefs, then the investigator has additional presumptive evidence of the explanatory power of his beliefs.

A hypothetical example may be useful to illustrate and clarify how questions of this kind, which attempt to replicate the logic of controlled experiments, can contribute to making more refined and more valid causal interpretations in single case anlysis.

In our hypothetical example, independent variable XX (but not YY or ZZ)[12] has been found to be consistent with option A, which the decision-maker has chosen. The investigator now asks whether XX can explain and predict *only* option A. Or would options B, C, and D—not chosen by the decision-maker in this situation—also have been consistent with XX? If so, while XX may be part of the explanation, its explanatory (and predictive) power is diminished vis-à-vis other explanatory variables that are needed to round out the explanation as to why option A (and not B, C, or D) was chosen by the decision-maker.

The investigator now asks whether there are any other conceivable options in that situation that would not be consistent with XX. Let us assume that he finds evidence that options G, H, and I were proposed and favored by others, perhaps by some of the decision-maker's advisers or by persons outside of his administration, but that these options were not consistent with his beliefs and were not given sympathetic attention by him. In this event, important explanatory and predictive power can be attributed to XX on the grounds that its presence tended to exclude adoption of other policy options (G, H, or I) that might otherwise have been chosen (by other decision-makers having operational code belief YY rather than XX) in that situation.[13]

These interpretations of the explanatory power of operational

FIGURE 1

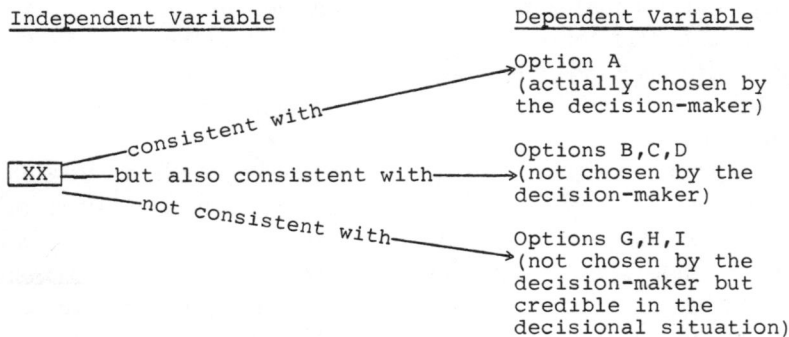

code belief *XX* in our hypothetical example are summarized in Figure 1.

A more refined analysis is possible. Suppose that although option *A* (as postulated here) differs in interesting respects from options *B, C,* and *D,* nonetheless all four options share a certain characteristic in common—namely, that all are "conciliatory" responses to an opponent's behavior (though the precise nature of the conciliatory response varies). Suppose further that, in contrast, options *G, H,* and *I* are all "hard, refractory" responses to the opponent's behavior. If so, then operational code belief *XX* acquires added explanatory and predictive power of a quite useful kind, for it does discriminate between conciliatory and refractory responses (though not by itself between variants of a conciliatory response). In this sense, as noted earlier, operational code beliefs introduce choice propensities into an actor's decision-making. In other words, the actor's adherence to belief *XX* does not determine in a linear, specific way his decision choice, but it does bound and delimit the general range or type of response he is likely to make in a given situation. That operational code beliefs will have this type of impact on information processing, it will be recalled, is consistent with our theoretical premises regarding the role that such general, fundamental cognitive variables can be expected to play in decision-making.

To extend our hypothetical example further, let us assume that *XX* is a particular image of the opponent that views him as a limited adversary who is interested in moderating conflict and in striving for accommodations (the first philosophical belief). In certain types of situations, this type of image of the opponent encourages the decision-maker to choose a conciliatory response of some kind. Now what type of conciliatory response he chooses may be influenced by other beliefs that further refine his general propensity for making a conciliatory response. For example, the actor's belief regarding the utility and role of different means for advancing one's interest (instrumental belief number five) may come into play, influencing him to prefer option A rather than option B, C, or D. In other words, a combination of several beliefs may further narrow his choice propensities, thereby increasing the explanatory-predictive power of the belief system as a whole. (Other combinations, of course, are also possible.)

Before concluding this discussion of the congruence procedure for assessing the causal role of operational code beliefs, we should note that this hypothetical example calls attention to the point made earlier regarding the critical importance of correctly deducing from an operational code what its implications should be for a decision. The investigator must describe the characteristics of the decision in terms of categories that are appropriate for catching the implications of the operational code beliefs in question. This is an essentially qualitative judgment that requires careful attention and justification. Failure in this respect can result either in an erroneous claim that the actual decision was consistent with the belief or in a failure to identify genuine consistency.

The Process-Tracing Procedure

Thus far we have considered ways in which consistency between an actor's beliefs and his choice of action might be utilized to develop causal interpretations. A more direct and potentially more satisfactory approach to causal interpretation in single case analysis takes the form of an attempt to trace the process—the intervening steps—by which beliefs influence behavior. Process-tracing seeks to establish the ways in which the actor's beliefs influenced his receptivity to and assessment of incoming information about the situation, his definition of the situation, his identification and evaluation of options, as well as, finally, his choice of a course of action.

The process-tracing procedure may be used by itself or as a means of assessing causal interpretations that were initially suggested by the congruency procedure. However, data requirements for employing the process-tracing procedure are substantially greater than those for the congruence procedure. Good data on information processing that preceded the policy maker's choice of action often are not available to the investigator; when this is the case it limits application of the process-tracing procedure. (This kind of information is not needed, on the other hand, for the congruency procedure.)

The task of introducing the functional equivalent of a controlled experiment into the interpretation of a single case is made easier, of course, if two or more appropriately selected cases are studied together in a "controlled comparison."[14] The importance of operational code beliefs in decision-making is likely to emerge in a more striking and plausible way when two or more leaders are compared. This is to be expected, since controlled comparison is a familiar (and recommended) way of compensating to some extent for inability to utilize experimental or quasi-experimental research designs or to undertake statistical analysis of a large sample.

Ideally, we would like to identify two leaders who are matched in every important respect and differ only in their operational code beliefs. The two leaders would be approximately the same age and (except for their beliefs) have similar personalities; they would have lived in the same sociohistorical epoch and undergone similar political socialization experiences; they would embrace the same ideology and occupy similar political roles—that is, they would be members of the same political elite occupying comparable positions at a given decision-making level. Further, they would receive the same informational inputs about emergent situations and have similar responsibilities for decision-making or, at least, for formulating responsible judgments and advice regarding the preferred option or strategy to pursue.

Such an ideal matching of two subjects in a comparative study would enable the investigator to ascertain with greater confidence the role that differences in their beliefs played in their information processing, their policy preferences, or recommendations for action. However, comparisons seldom achieve this degree of variable matching. One must usually work with less well-matched and, hence, less well-controlled comparisons.

Several studies have employed the comparative method in an effort to ascertain the importance of differences in operational codes. In an unpublished study, which can only be briefly summarized here, Gordon White (1969) found evidence of a longstanding difference in beliefs about the nature of political life and image of the opponent between Mao Tse-tung and Liu Shao-ch'i. These differences were inconsequential for all practical purposes for many years, encouraging Sinologists in the West to feel comfortable with the assumption that, unlike other elites, the Chinese

Communist elite was remarkably homogeneous in ideology and outlook. Yet although they started from a similar orthodox Marxist conception of the nature of the class enemy in internal and international affairs, Mao and Liu eventually diverged in their diagnosis of the location and danger of the enemy. As the Chinese revolution passed through different stages—in particular with respect to the crucial transitional period of socialism prior to the final establishment of a communist society—certain latent differences in the beliefs of these two leaders regarding the nature of the political conflict and the nature of the enemy were brought to the fore, resulting in an eventual incompatibility of their roles and policy preferences that hithertofore had proven to be complementary. Mao and Liu came to disagree in their view of the residual danger of the class enemy in the era of socialism. Liu felt that the internal enemy had declined in importance and, hence, that the intensity and pervasiveness of the policy of "struggle," could be moderated. Mao, however, lay greater emphasis on the persistence of contradictions and the continued necessity of "struggle."

White calls attention to these relationships between the two men's beliefs, their divergent diagnoses of the emergent historical situation, and their policy disagreement. He also enriches his analysis by suggesting that additional differences between the two men in personality, role, and socialization experiences may be important in the explanation of their emergent policy disagreement.

Another study (Ashby 1969) attempted to account for striking differences in policy preferences between Kurt Schumacher, leader of the Social Democratic Party (SPD) in Western Germany in the period after World War II, and Willy Brandt, then a young party leader of the SPD in West Berlin. The two men differed emphatically on all of the eight major policy issues on which the SPD, the minority party, had to take a position during those years. The task, therefore, was to explain these policy differences between the two men. Ashby's comparison of the operational code beliefs of the two SPD leaders revealed dramatic differences. The comparison could control only several of the possibly relevant variables: (1) both men were responding to the same historical situation that confronted occupied Germany and the SPD; (2) in addition, Schumacher and Brandt subscribed to virtually the identical socialist ideology: the primary goals for both were the democratization of West German society and, in the international arena, equal and fair treatment; (3) similarly, the two men agreed on the necessity for European cooperation as a long-range goal.

Schumacher and Brandt differed, however, in their personalities, their political socialization, and their political roles (although with respect to the latter variable, Ashby found little indication that it accounted for the policy differences between the two men). Since personality and political socialization and not just operational codes[15] could possibly account for the policy differences between the two men, the study does not afford a clear-cut opportunity for tracing the influence that these beliefs had on information processing and policy preferences. Schumacher's personality (insightfully analyzed by Edinger 1965) seems of particular importance for understanding his political behavior. At the same time, though on an impressionistic basis, Ashby found considerable consistency between each man's beliefs and the positions he took on policy issues. But he did not attempt to apply the alternative procedure of process-tracing to identify how each man's operational codes influenced the formulation of his policy preferences. Therefore, while this comparative study is highly suggestive, it remains undeveloped as a demonstration of the importance of operational code beliefs in policy making.

U.S. policy making in the Berlin crisis of 1961 may provide a better-controlled comparison for demonstrating the special role that the operational code—in particular, the image of the opponent—can play in information processing. Available historical materials indicate that two groups of policy advisers to Kennedy interpreted Khrushchev's statements and demands regarding Berlin differently, and that this difference in assessment of Khrushchev's intentions (the threat assessment) reflected a fundamental disagreement in the more basic image of the Soviet opponent.

One group of advisers, the "soft-line" school, included ambassadors Harriman and Thompson, Bohlen, and other political appointees in the State Department, Adlai Stevenson, staffers Rostow, Sorensen, and Schlesinger in the White House. This group believed that the expansionist dynamic of Soviet foreign policy, if indeed it had ever been as virulent as had been feared in the West, was becoming more moderate, and that the Kremlin leaders were now acting and would continue to act out of "nationalist," "consolidationist," and "defensive" motives—a trend that should be encouraged by flexibility on the part of the West.

In contrast to this soft-line school of advisers, another group, the "hard-line" school, included Dean Acheson (a special adviser to Kennedy), Paul Nitze (chairman of the State Department policy planning staff), General Maxwell Taylor, the joint chiefs of staff, many Pentagon civilians, and the German desk in the State Department. These advisers subscribed to the fundamental belief that the Kremlin, though it may have softened its tactics, retained essentially the same cold war objectives as ever.

From this fundamental difference over the "correct" image of the Soviet opponent emerged two different diagnoses of the situation. Both groups of advisers were operating in the same situation; both, presumably, had access to the same incoming information about Khrushchev's intimations of renewed pressure on West Berlin; both shared the role of advisers to the president. Their different images of the Soviet opponent led them to evaluate the available information and the emerging situation differently. Thus, the threat assessment made by the hard-line advisers was that Khrushchev was pursuing an offensive, expansionist strategy in Berlin that would pose serious dangers to the West. In contrast, the assessment of the soft-line advisers was that Khrushchev was engaged in an essentially defensive operation in Berlin aimed at consolidating Soviet control over the East European satellites by attempting to close off the "escape hatch" of West Berlin, through which many thousands of East Germans were fleeing to the West.

This difference in threat perception and evaluation led, in turn, to distinctly different preferred strategies for the U.S. response to the situation, resulting in contradictory advice to Kennedy. The hard-line advisers felt that the serious threat posed by an expansionist, offensive Soviet strategy could be contained only with a vigorous deterrence and defense effort by the United States. An unmistakable commitment to hold fast in Berlin was needed, in their view, and this should be backed by strengthening U.S. military capabilities. Negotiations should *not* be offered, for this would encourage the Soviets to press their demands and eventually increase the danger of war. The soft-line advisers, on the other hand, urged active negotiations without delay as an alternative to confrontation and as a means of communicating to the Soviets that the West would be responsive to the Soviet need in ways consonant with protection of basic Western rights in West Berlin. Only by opening negotiations promptly, the soft-liners felt, could the United States convince the Soviets that their legitimate minimum security interests would be respected, thereby minimizing the risk of war; they felt that intransigence of the kind advocated by the hard-liners could generate war by leading the Soviet rulers to undertake desperate moves. The role of operational code (the first

FIGURE 2

	Operational Code image of opponent	→	Diagnosis of threat	→	Preferred (recommended) U.S. policy response
"Hard-line" advisors	USSR rulers act out of ideological expansionist motives	→	USSR pursuing offensive objectives in Berlin	→	Vigorous deterrence & defense effort; defer negotiations until later
"Soft-line" advisors	USSR rulers act out of nationalist, consolidationist motives	→	USSR pursuing defensive objectives	→	Open negotiations immediately; some strengthening of U.S. capabilities

philosophical belief regarding image of opponent) in information processing may be depicted and summarized as in Figure 2.[16]

This account of the Berlin situation relies on published sources (as summarized in George and Smoke 1974:431-37). Additional research on this case, utilizing primary sources, is under way (George, forthcoming). Hopefully, it will enable us to trace the process depicted here in greater detail and to document it more thoroughly.[17]

In addition, studies of Kennedy's operational code beliefs (Hoagland 1978; Hoagland and Walker 1979; and Stuart, forthcoming) should permit a more refined interpretation of his response to the conflicting advice from these two groups of advisers. It should help us to answer the following questions: What was Kennedy's own image of the Soviet opponent at the time? Was it closer to that of his hard-line or soft-line advisers? On the face of it, Kennedy's policy response to the emerging crisis seems to have combined elements from both the hard and soft advisers. Was Kennedy's response, therefore, a policy compromise or did it differ from the recommendations of his two groups of advisers because he had a somewhat different, more complex image of the Soviets that led him to assess the situation and its requirements differently?

Notes

1. Less useful for decison-making analysis, in my judgment, are other types of units of analysis borrowed from cognitive psychology, such as attributes, traits, psychological "dimensions," and various structural cognitive categories like Rokeach's "open- and closed-mindness." (For discussion, see George and Holsti 1974).

2. It is significant that not only specialists on foreign policy decision-making but also those in comparative politics who study political elites have expressed dissatisfaction with the earlier preoccupation with temporally bound, relatively object-specific attitudes and are now giving more attention to the more central beliefs and fundamental belief-systems of political leaders. See, for example, Robert Putnam's interest in elite political orientations and his distinction between a "conflictful" and a "non-conflictful" image of politics, which is similar to the first philosophical belief dimension of the operational code (Putnam 1973). See also Donald Searing (1969:495): "We have found that expressed specific political attitudes ... may have little relationship to elite behavior patterns over time in any event. Underlying orientations on the other hand—which probably hold more relevance for elite

behavior patterns—may perhaps be more easily forecast among elite populations."

3. For present purposes and given space constraints, it is not possible to present all the reasons for rejecting these three conclusions. With regard to the differential stability over time of different hierarchical components of one's cognitive belief structure, see Rokeach (1960, 1972) and Bem (1970). On the role of cognitive variables in behavior, see Mischel (1973, 1977).

4. For assistance in monitoring these developments I am indebted to my Ph.D. student Deborah Larson (1976), whose forthcoming dissertation on the origins of the cold war utilizes recent developments in attribution theory.

5. The relevance and utility of the operational code construct in Soviet studies is noted and discussed by Hoffmann and Fleron (1971).

6. As noted some years ago (George 1969:220), the term "operational code" is somewhat of a misnomer insofar as it implies a set of recipes for action.

7. I would like to gratefully acknowledge the assistance of Vinod Aggarwal, a Ph.D. student in political science at Stanford University, in formulating the distinction between these two procedures. Aggarwal has also explored in a perceptive manner the relevance of general systems theory for operational code research (1977).

8. As yet these conditions do not appear to be well identified. It should be noted that as empirical findings bearing on the consistency hypothesis have accumulated it has become clear that consistency-striving and consistency-achievement admit many exceptions. Many individuals "tolerate" lack of perfect consistency among their beliefs and between beliefs and actions. Even when the drive to make actions consistent with beliefs is strong, it may be dominated or bypassed, as for example when an individual acts on the basis of strong ideological preferences instead of his cognitive beliefs or when an individual's choice of actions is controlled by personal ambition, a strong need for approval from significant others, or by ego defenses.

9. Thus, Walker traced the relation between (a) Kissinger's major instrumental beliefs about the use of force coupled wtih diplomatic initiatives of a conciliatory kind and (b) American bargaining moves vis-à-vis North Vietnam over a period of four years, from 1969 to 1973. Some sixteen U.S.–North Vietnam interaction sequences were identified as having occurred during this period. American bargaining behavior in fourteen of the sixteen cases was found to be consistent with Kissinger's operational code principles. (One of the two "deviations" may be more apparent than real, depending on what data sources are utilized. The other deviation is plausibly explained by Walker as an instance in which other variables in the decision process displaced Kissinger's approach to bargaining.) The coding rules employed in Walker's study were not included in the published article, but were kindly made available to me by the author.

10. It is, of course, possible in principle for an operational code belief to be a "sufficient" condition in some instances without being a necessary con-

dition for that type of decision, but it is seldom if ever likely to be the case in practice.

11. On the use of mental experiments in historical explanation as a means of replicating the logic of experiment, see Parsons (1949:612). On the frequent use and utility of "thought experiment" (*Gedankenexperiment*) in the work of creative natural scientists, see Kaplan (1964).

12. In other words, there is reason to believe that XX may be a "necessary" condition.

13. We have to recognize that policy option G, H, or I might still be chosen by the decision-maker, despite inconsistency with his beliefs (XX) if other variables such as the weight of domestic opinion or Congress constrained his choices severely.

14. The logic and rationale of "controlled comparison" are discussed, for example, in Arend Lijphart (1971 and 1975); see also Eckstein (1975). For a detailed explication of the design tasks and implementation procedures for effective controlled comparisons, see George (1979).

15. We defer discussion of the important relationships between personality development and political socialization and their impact, in turn, on the formation of operational code beliefs.

16. A similar use of the "process-tracing" procedure is evident in Abraham Ben-Zvi's research on the role that competing U.S. elite images of the Japanese opponent played in policy disagreements over how to deter the Japanese in the period before Pearl Harbor. See particularly his "American Preconceptions and Policies Toward Japan, 1940-1941: A Case Study in Misperception," *International Studies Quarterly*, June 1975; and "The Outbreak and Termination of the Pacific War: A Juxtaposition of American Preconceptions," *Journal of Peace Research*, 15, no. 1 (1978).

17. It should be noted that my forthcoming study of the Berlin crisis of 1961 will employ the process-tracing procedure, whereas the study by Hoagland and Walker reported in this volume employs the congruence procedure. Comparison of the two studies should provide useful insights into how these two procedures for assessing the impact of operational code beliefs on decision-making can complement each other.

References

Abelson, Robert. "Script Processing in Attitude Formation and Decision-making." In *Cognition and Social Behavior*, edited by J. S. Carroll and J. W. Payne. New York: Halstead Press, 1976.

Aggarwal, Vinod K. "The Use of Systems Theory in Analyzing the Operational Code." Paper presented to annual meeting of the International Studies Association, St. Louis, Mo., 1977.

Ashby, Ned. "Schumacher and Brandt: The Divergent 'Operational Codes' of Two German Socialist Leaders," mimeographed. Stanford University, 1969.

Bandura, Albert. "Behavior Theory and the Models of Man." *American Psychologist* (Dec. 1974).

Bem, Daryl J. *Beliefs, Attitudes, and Human Affairs.* Belmont, Ca.: Brooks/Cole Publishing Company, 1970.

Bem, Daryl J., and Andrea Allen. "On Predicting Some of the People Some of the Time." *Psychological Review* 81, no. 6. (1974).

Bowers, Kenneth. "Situationism in Psychology." *Psychological Review.* (Sept. 1973).

Brown, Steven. "Intensive Analysis in Political Research." *Political Methodology* (Winter 1974).

Campbell, Donald T. " 'Degrees of Freedom' and the Case Study." *Comparative Political Studies* (July 1975).

——. "Qualitative Knowing in Action Research." Paper presented to the American Psychological Association, New Orleans, Sept. 1974.

Campbell, Donald T., and Julian C. Stanley. *Experimental and Quasi-Experimental Designs for Research.* Chicago: Rand McNally, 1963.

Converse, Phillip E. "The Nature of Belief Systems in Mass Publics," in *Ideology and Discontent*, edited by David Apter. New York: The Free Press, 1964.

Cronbach, Lee. "Beyond the Two Scientific Disciplines of Scientific Psychology." *American Psychologist* 30, no. 2 (February 1975).

Diesing, Paul. *Patterns of Discovery in the Social Sciences.* Chicago and New York: Aldine-Atherton, 1971.

Eckstein, Harry. "Case Study and Theory in Political Science." Ch. 3, vol. 7 of *Handbook of Political Science*, edited by F. I. Greenstein and N. W. Polsby. New York: Addison Wesley, 1975.

Edinger, Lewis J. *Kurt Schumacher: A Study in Personality and Political Behavior.* Stanford University Press, 1965.

Gamson, William A., and Andre Modigliani. *Untangling the Cold War.* Boston: Little, Brown, 1971.

George, Alexander L. "The 'Operational Code': A Neglected Approach to the Study of Political Leaders and Decision-Making." *International Studies Quarterly* (June 1969).

——. "Case Studies and Theory Development: The Method of Structured, Focussed Comparison." In *Diplomatic History: New Approaches*, edited by Paul Gordon Lauren. New York: The Free Press, 1979.

——. "The Role of Operational Code Beliefs in U.S. Policy-Making in the Berlin 1961 Crisis," forthcoming.

George, Alexander L., D. K. Hall, and W. E. Simons. *The Limits of Coercive Diplomacy.* Boston: Little, Brown, 1971.

George, Alexander L., and Richard Smoke. *Deterrence in American Foreign Policy: Theory and Practice.* New York: Columbia University, 1974.

George, Alexander L., and Ole R. Holsti. "Operational Code Belief Systems and Foreign Policy Decision-Making." Research proposal submitted to and funded by the National Science Foundation, 1974.

Greenstein, Fred I. *Personality and Politics*. Chicago: Markham, 1969.
Heradtsveit, Daniel. "Decision-Making in the Middle East: Testing the Operational Code Approach" Norwegian Institute of International Affairs, 1977.
Hoagland, Steven W. "Operational Codes and the Analyses of International Crises: A Comparison of the Berlin Wall and Cuban Missile Crises." Tempe, Arizona: Arizona State University, 1978.
Hoagland, Steven W., and Stephen G. Walker. "Operational Codes and Crisis Outcomes." In *Psychological Models in International Politics*, edited by Lawrence Falkowski. Boulder, Co.: Westview Press, 1979.
Hoffmann, Erik P., and Frederick J. Fleron, eds. *The Conduct of Soviet Foreign Policy*. Chicago: Aldine-Atherton, 1971.
Holsti, Ole R. "The 'Operational Code' As an Approach to the Analysis of Belief Systems: Final Report to the National Science Foundation, Grant No. SOC 75-15368." Duke University, 1977.
———. "Foreign Policy Formation Viewed Cognitively." Chap. 2 in *Structure of Decision*, edited by Robert Axelrod. Princeton University Press, 1976.
———. "Cognitive Dynamics and Images of the Enemy: Dulles and Russia." In *Enemies in Politics*, edited by D. J. Finlay, O. R. Holsti, and R. R. Fagen. Chicago: Rand McNally, 1967.
Jervis, Robert. *Perception and Misperception in International Politics*. Princeton University Press, 1976.
Kaplan, Abraham. *The Conduct of Inquiry*. San Francisco: Chandler Company, 1964.
Larson, Deborah. "Cognitive Processes and Foreign Policy Decision-Making: An Information Processing Model," mimeographed. Stanford University, 1976.
Lazarus, Richard S. "The Self-Regulation of Emotions," mimeographed. Berkeley, Calif., n.d.
Leites, Nathan. *A Study of Bolshevism*. New York: The Free Press, 1953.
Lijphart, Arend. "Comparative Politics and the Comparative Method." *American Political Science Review* (September 1971).
———. "The Comparable-Cases Strategy in Comparative Research." *Comparative Political Studies* (July 1975).
Mischel, Walter. *Personality and Assessment*. New York: John Wiley, 1968.
———. "Toward a Cognitive Social Learning Reconceptualization of Personality." *Psychological Review* 80, no. 4 (1973).
———. "On the Future of Personality Assessment." *American Psychologist* (April 1977).
Parsons, Talcott. *The Structure of Social Action*. 2nd edition. Glencoe, Illinois: The Free Press, 1949.
Putnam, Robert D. *The Beliefs of Politicians*. New Haven, Conn.: Yale University Press, 1973.
Rokeach, Milton. *The Open and Closed Mind*. New York: Basic Books, 1960.
Ross, Lee. "The Intuitive Psychologist and His Shortcomings: Distortions in the Attribution Process." In *Advances in Experimental Social Psychology*,

edited by L. Berkowitz. New York: Academic Press, 1977.

Russett, Bruce M. "International Behavior Research: Case Studies and Cumulation." In *Approaches to the Study of Political Science*, edited by M. Haas and H. S. Kariel. New York: Chandler, 1970.

Searing, Donald D. "The Comparative Study of Elite Socialization." *Comparative Political Studies* (January 1969).

Stuart, Douglas. "The Operational Code of John F. Kennedy," Ph.D. dissertation, University of Southern California.

Verba, Sidney. "Some Dilemmas in Comparative Research." *World Politics* (October 1967).

Walker, Stephen G. "The Interface between Beliefs and Behavior: Henry Kissinger's Operational Code and the Vietnam War." *Journal of Conflict Resolution* (March 1977).

White, Gordon. "A Comparison of the 'Operational Codes' of Mao Tse-tung and Liu Shao-ch'i," mimeographed. Stanford University, 1969.

Yergin, Daniel. *Shattered Peace*. Boston: Houghton Mifflin, 1977. See especially Chapter 1, "The Breach: The Riga Axioms"; and Chapter 2, "The Yalta Maxims: Roosevelt's Grand Design."

Zajonc, Robert A. "Cognitive Theories in Social Psychology." In *Handbook of Social Psychology*, edited by G. Lindzey and E. Aronson. 2nd edition, vol. I. New York: Addison-Wesley, 1968.

6
Operational Codes and Crisis Outcomes

Steven W. Hoagland
Stephen G. Walker

Introduction

For almost twenty-five years, the study of international crises has been a major focus for exploring the strengths and weakness of a variety of foreign policy decision-making models. Beginning with the pioneering work of Snyder (1954, 1958) on the Korean War and followed by the Stanford studies of the 1914 crisis (Zinnes 1961; Holsti 1965; Hilton 1969) Allison's (1969, 1971) research on the Cuban missile crisis, Tanter's study of the Berlin crises (1974), and the replication of Tanter's research design in the analysis of the Arab-Israeli confrontations by McCormick (1975), successive waves of scholars have attacked and severely questioned the utility of the "unitary rational actor"[1] model in understanding crisis decision-making. During the same period, the rational actor model also went into eclipse as a popular approach among many students of comparative foreign policy and "routine" (non-crisis) foreign policy decisions.

In fact, as Ole Holsti has argued persuasively (1976, 1977), until quite recently cognitive and psychological approaches of all kinds have made relatively little impact on quantitative, data-based

---

The authors are listed alphabetically; each made a necessary contribution to the completion of the study. Hoagland did the initial research on the operational codes of Khrushchev and Kennedy; as part of his doctoral dissertation he formulated the elements of each man's code that appear here. Walker reorganized the OPCODE beliefs into axioms and theorems and then derived the hypotheses regarding the crisis behavior prescribed by these operational codes. He also conducted the data analysis of the two Berlin crises. The indices for crisis tactics and outcomes were developed as part of the Comparative International Crisis Analysis Project (CINCAP) at Arizona State University, for which Walker is the principal investigator. Hoagland's dissertation is based on data collected for CINCAP. This is a revised version of a paper prepared for delivery at the 1977 Annual Meeting of the Peace Science Society Conference (Southern Section) at Florida Atlantic University (Boca Raton), April 6-7, 1978.

efforts to formulate empirical theories of international politics and foreign policy. Among nonquantitative analysts of foreign policy decision, however, the assumptions of the rational actor model have remained important criteria for describing, explaining, and evaluating foreign policy behavior. Although these analysts do include nonrational elements—such as organizational constraints, bureaucratic infighting, and incomplete or imperfect information in their explanations of foreign policy decisions—they maintain that at least a model of "bounded rationality"[2] is of central importance and utility in understanding foreign policy behavior. (See, for example, Schelling 1960, 1966; Art 1973; Snyder 1971, 1976; Snyder and Diesing 1977; Jervis 1970, 1976; George 1969; George et al. 1971; George and Smoke 1974.)

Cognitive models of foreign policy have also experienced a renaissance among some quantitative theorists of international behavior. Their support for a cognitive approach is subject to several qualifications. The most systematic and articulate exposition of these limitations is provided by Holsti (1976:29), who argues that there is a growing body of empirical research that indicates that a cognitive approach may prove rewarding when one or more of the following conditions exist: innovative decision-making situations; long-range policy planning situations; decisions under highly complex, ambiguous, or unanticipated circumstances; decisions under stress; and decisions made by individuals at the top of an organization's hierarchy (Holsti 1976:30). One example that meets some of these conditions is the recent research focusing on international bargaining (Axelrod 1977; Hopmann and Smith 1977; Ramberg 1977; Walker 1977b; Zagare 1977). Other examples occur in the international crisis literature, already cited. Some of the analyses in this literature stem from cognitively based models of crisis decision-making, but those cognitive models that deal with crisis bargaining are not usually tested with quantitative data (Walker 1977a:4-14, 25).

In this essay we intend to apply one type of cognitive approach (the analysis of operational codes) to one type of foreign policy situation (international crisis) and link them with the aid of concepts from the international bargaining literature. These links are to be tested empirically for the 1948 and 1961 Berlin crises with quantitative data collected by Corson (1970) and reported by Tanter (1974). The major objectives in this analysis are: (a) to assess the congruence between descriptions of Soviet and U.S. operational codes and their crisis behavior; (b) to test the generalizability of the operational code construct from an individual to an aggregate (national) level of analysis; (c) to relate the dispositional traits of decision-makers to systemic (dyadic) outcomes.

The Analysis of Operational Codes

The analysis of operational codes as a cognitive approach to the study of political behavior was developed by Leites (1951) and later refined by George (1969) and Holsti (1977). Leites initially used the concept of operational code to refer to those instrumental aspects of Bolshevik beliefs that expressed prescriptions regarding the strategy and tactics of political action and thereby influenced Soviet decision-making. He subsequently investigated the philosophical components of the Bolshevik code and attempted to trace the origins of both kinds of beliefs to the personalities and historical experiences that shaped the Bolshevik approach to politics (Leites 1953). George (1969) has refined the principal themes from the Leites analyses of bolshevism into a series of questions to guide inquiries into the operational codes of other decision-makers.

According to George (1969:198), the analysis of operational codes is a "bounded rationality" approach to the study of political decision-making. A decision-maker's operational code consists of his beliefs regarding the issues presented in the following questions (George:201-16):

Philosophical Questions

1. What is the "essential" nature of political life? Is the political universe essentially one of harmony or conflict? What is the fundamental character of one's political opponents?
2. What are the prospects for the eventual realization of one's fundamental political values and aspirations? Can one be optimistic or must one be pessimistic on this score, and in what respects the one or the other?
3. Is the political future predictable? In what sense and to what extent?
4. How much "control" or "mastery" can one have over historical development? What is one's role in "moving" and "shaping" history in the desired direction?
5. What is the role of "chance" in human affairs and in historical development?

Instrumental Questions

1. What is the best approach for selecting goals or objectives for political action?
2. How are the goals of action pursued most effectively?
3. How are the risks of political action calculated, controlled, and accepted?
4. What is the best "timing" of action to advance one's interests?
5. What is the utility and role of different means for advancing one's interests?

Taken collectively, these beliefs constitute the rules which the decision-maker uses to cope with limitations or boundaries placed on his attempts at rational political decision-making. These limitations include the following types of constraints often associated with political decisions: (1) information about the decision-making situation is incomplete; (2) knowledge of ends-means relationships is not adequate enough to reliably predict the consequences of choosing one or another course of action; (3) there is considerable difficulty in formulating a single criterion for choosing which alternative course of action is the optimum one (George 1969:197-98). Aided by the results of operational code analyses from other scholars, George and Holsti (1974) and Holsti (1977) have begun to develop a typology of operational codes which they plan to employ in an investigation of the foreign policy decisions of selected U.S. policy makers during the post-1945 period.

The decision to apply the operational code approach to the study of foreign policy raises two interrelated major methodological issues in addition to the usual array of reliability and validity questions that accompanies any empirical analysis. The first issue is the imputation of a causal relationship between foreign policy and operational code elements. The second one is the problem of attributing foreign policy and operational code elements to the appropriate unit of analysis—i.e., to an individual, group, or organization. A detailed discussion of these problems as methodological issues per se is beyond the scope of this investigation, but we do need to acknowledge their existence and indicate our strategy for coping with them in the research design for this study of the two Berlin crises.

Advocates of the operational code approach have cautioned against positing a simple causal relationship between the behavior of a government and the dispositions or decisions of its policy makers. Holsti (1976:34-35) maintains that "It is not very fruitful to assume direct linkages between beliefs and foreign policy action ... [and] it is important to recognize the distinction between decisions and foreign policy actions. The literature on bureaucratic politics has illustrated the many potential sources of slippage between executive decisions and the implementation of policy in the form of foreign policy actions." George (1969:196-97) has argued against the conception of an operational code as "a set of rules and recipes to be applied mechanically to the choice of action." An individual's operational code beliefs may be consistent with several alternative decisions (George 1978:19). Moreover, even though the actual choice is consistent with an individual's operational code, it may in fact have been selected by other actors in the government (Walker 1977b:153-56).

These comments articulate specific aspects of the causal linkage and unit (level) of analysis problems associated with the operational code approach to the analysis of political decision-making. Our research strategy for coping with these difficulties involves the following steps. First, our exposition of the elements in the Soviet and U.S. operational codes is formulated precisely enough to be falsifiable; that is, they are stated specifically enough so it is possible to determine when actions are consistent with these beliefs and when they are not. Concurrently, we have developed measures of each actor's crisis behavior that permit us to discriminate between actions that are congruent with these beliefs and actions that do not correspond to the operational code elements. Second, our research design relies on evidence collected and interpreted by other scholars. This indicates the degree of homogeneity among the operational codes of the key decision-makers within each government. With the aid of these sources, we are in a better position to be sensitive to alternative interpretations of Soviet and American behavior within and across the Berlin crises.

Previous analyses of Soviet operational codes indicate a good deal of continuity among the beliefs of Lenin, Stalin, and Khrushchev (Leites 1951, 1964; George 1969). The differences between the OPCODES of Stalin and Khrushchev, the central Soviet decision-makers during the first and second Berlin crises, respectively, are differences in degree rather than kind. After a comparative examination of statements by Soviet leaders from the Stalinist and Khrushchevian eras, Leites cautiously concludes that "contemporary Soviet [i.e., Khrushchevian] leaders probably feel less constrained to push forward ... [and] may even have gained for themselves some slight liberty to concede without an immediate concession in return" (Leites 1964:196, 211, cited in George 1969:218). Our own analysis of Khrushchev's operational code qualifies this conclusion: we noted that it is questionable whether his beliefs about appropriate bargaining tactics in a crisis context mellowed. Instead, both he and Stalin apparently shared the same beliefs regarding crisis management and risk-taking.[3]

Analyses of the operational code belief systems for individuals in the U.S. government show that they are much less homogeneous. Important differences exist among individuals within and across the legislative and executive branches of the government.[4] However, this variety is unimportant unless more than one type of individual was able to consistently influence the behavior of our government during the two Berlin crises. In 1948, there were two major sets of operational code beliefs within the executive branch of the U.S. government. However, the most recent and thorough interpretation of the available evidence clearly indicates that just one set dominated the decisions and actions of the Truman administration during the first Berlin crisis. Moreover, our own analysis of Kennedy's operational code in 1961 reveals that it is virtually identical to the belief system that guided Truman and his key advisors during the 1948 crisis. Kennedy's code appears to be a synthesis of "hard" and "soft" beliefs held by other members of the U.S. government, just as Truman's orientations were shaped by advisors whose beliefs were located along a hard-soft continuum.[5]

There is also evidence to indicate that a government's decision-making process in a crisis situation is likely to become centralized under the control of its principal leader.[6] Taking this into consideration, we realize that the beliefs of Stalin and Khrushchev were more likely to influence the actions of the Soviet government in crisis than the beliefs of any other individual leader or any other actor in the government. Similarly, within the U.S. government the centralization of the decision-making process probably increased the influence of Truman's and Kennedy's beliefs on the crisis behavior of our government.

Allison (1969, 1971) has demonstrated that standard operating procedures and bureaucratic infighting within organizations—such as the collection of information or the timing and implementation of actions toward other governments—may affect pre- and post-decisional aspects of a government's crisis behavior. However, it is our contention that within the boundaries imposed by these constraints, decision-makers do attempt to behave rationally. It is still an empirical question whether the influence of nonrational variables is consistently more significant than the influence of premises compatible with a rational actor model.

The Analysis of Crisis Bargaining

In this analysis of the two Berlin crises our major rational assumption is that the actions of governments during international crises represent attempts by their leaders to engage in bargaining behavior toward one another. That is, the mixture of coercive and accommodative behavior that each government directs toward its opponent is intended to influence the actions of the target. These actions rest on the presumption that "most conflict situations are essentially *bargaining* situations ... in which the ability of one participant to gain his ends is dependent to an important degree on the choices or decisions that the other participant will make" (Schelling 1960:3-5; see also Snyder 1972). The central proposition to be tested in the following analysis of the Berlin crises, therefore, is that certain operational code beliefs of Soviet and U.S. leaders shaped the coercive and accommodative bargaining behavior of their governments toward each other.

The data necessary to test this proposition include the pertinent beliefs about effective bargaining tactics from the operational codes of Soviet and U.S. decision-makers, plus an inventory of the bargaining moves that each government implemented during the two crises. These two sets of variables are linked by means of a mediated stimulus-response relationship over time as shown in Figure 1. Other variables, such as the goals and capabilities of each actor, are postulated as constants within each crisis and as exogenous variables across the two crises. Although goals and relative military capabilities are important variables that structure the broad parameters of a conflict situation, within these constraints the variety and sequence of behaviors by the participants are a function of their mutual interactions as mediated by their beliefs about effective crisis behavior. For the two Berlin crises, the respective goals of the U.S. and the USSR included the maintenance versus the removal of a Western presence in Berlin. Both governments also wished to avoid a war over this issue. The distribution of military capabilities was essentially identical for both crises: the United States dominated the military balance at the nuclear force level, while the Soviets possessed superiority at the

FIGURE 1

Mediated Stimulus-Response Link Between
Bargaining Moves and Operational Codes

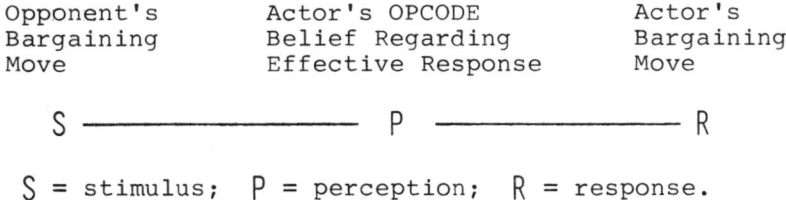

S = stimulus;   P = perception;   R = response.

level of local conventional forces. Our research design excludes the possible effects of these factors.[7]

Although it is permissible and even desirable to focus on the stimulus-perception-response relationships for the Berlin crises without including a capability or goal-oriented perspective, there are still some conceptual problems in the application of bargaining models to stimulus-response data. The most important ones appear to be how to operationalize with stimulus-response data three analytically important components in bargaining models: strategies, tactics, and outcomes. Each of these concepts poses its own set of analytical problems. Among qualitative crisis analysts the most creative treatment of these concepts is in the volume by Snyder and Diesing (1977). They argue that most international crises resemble one of several versions of a 2 x 2 mixed-motive game with two theoretical strategies available to each actor: conflict or cooperation. They identify strategies empirically as conflict, cooperation, or mixed conflict-cooperation in a series of historical cases by examining the overall sequence of behaviors by the actors in these crises. The dominant behavior by each actor during different phases of each crisis becomes that actor's strategy for the crisis phase under investigation, while tactics are the individual behaviors adopted by an actor at each successive point in time. The relationship between tactics and strategies becomes definitional: a strategy is a series of tactics. Outcomes are the results of a set of interacting strategies in which: (a) both actors pursue cooperative strategies and produce a cooperative outcome; (b) each side pursues a different strategy (cooperation versus conflict) resulting in a domination outcome; or (c) both sides pursue conflict strategies in which a war results (Snyder and Diesing 1977).

Within the framework of the 2 x 2 mixed-motive game, Snyder and Diesing focus primarily on the overall outcome at the end of a crisis rather than on the outcome (effect) of a particular set of behaviors within a crisis. Their empirical concern is primarily with cross-crisis variations and comparisons, rather than iterative, within-crisis variations and comparisons. They argue that it is possible to reduce the interval utility schedules in most game theory matrices to a series of ordinal preferences for each player. For example, if one actor's payoffs in each of four cells are +10, +5, -5, and -10, then his preference ordering for these payoffs from highest to lowest is 4 (+10), 3 (+5), 2 (-5), 1 (-10). These payoffs are a function of both the strategies selected by the actor and by his opponent, who has a similarly reducible interval utility schedule for the cells in the game matrix.

Snyder and Diesing argue that these preference orderings usually determine the game's structure as either Prisoner's Dilemma or Chicken. If the game is the former, then both parties may initially choose a conflict strategy that will result in war, unless each side recognizes the game as a prisoner's dilemma and moves toward mutual cooperation strategies. If the game is Chicken, then both sides may pursue conflict strategies until they collide in war or one side loses nerve and backs down.

Asymmetrical combinations of these games are also an important part of Snyder's and Diesing's framework. A game's payoffs may structure one side's preferences as Prisoner's Dilemma and the other side's as Chicken. According to Snyder and Diesing, conflicts escalate to crises (military confrontations) because, initially, there are some discrepancies in the perceptions by each actor of the preference ordering for each actor. Escalation occurs and (hopefully) de-escalation follows as each actor removes these discrepancies by producing a strategy of responses from the other actor with his own strategy (series of behaviors).

An asymmetrical game in which one actor's preferences are Prisoner's Dilemma and the other actor's preferences are Chicken, resulting in a game known as Called Bluff, appears in Figure 2. Snyder characterizes the Cuban Missile Crisis as a game of this type and explains the U.S. domination of this crisis as a function of each side's ultimate acknowledgement of this structure and the rational selection of strategies flowing from these preference orderings (Snyder 1971; Snyder and Diesing 1977).

Just as interval utility schedules can be reduced to ordinal preference orderings and described as crisis outcomes, these preference

FIGURE 2

Interval Utility and Ordinal Preference
Schedules for "Called Bluff"* Game

		B	
		COOP	CONF
A	COOP	+5, 0	−10, +10
	CONF	+10, −10	−5, −20

Interval Utility

		B	
		COOP	CONF
A	COOP	3, 3	1, 4
	CONF	4, 2	2, 1

Ordinal Preference

* A's preferences are "prisoner's dilemma" and B's preferences are "chicken."

FIGURE 3

Nominal Descriptions of Strategic and Tactical
Stimulus-Response Combinations
for an International Crisis

		B	
		COOP	CONF
A	COOP	CP, CP	CP, CF
	CONF	CF, CP	CF, CF

Strategic Matrix

		B	
		DE-ES	ESCAL
A	DE-ES	D, D	D, E
	ESCAL	E, D	E, E

Tactical Matrix

DE-ES = De-escalate; ESCAL = Escalate

orderings can also be taken out of the game matrix, and the two types of strategies inserted as paired nominal descriptions of crisis outcomes: cooperation, cooperation; conflict, cooperation; cooperation, conflict; conflict, conflict (See Figure 3).

Moreover, these pairs of behavioral strategies are also the logically possible pairs of tactics for an S-R relationship at a given point in time. By simultaneously reducing the entries in the game matrix from an interval to a nominal level of measurement and reducing the focus of analysis from a discussion of strategies and crisis outcomes to an examination of tactics and within-crisis outcomes, it is possible to extend the logic of Snyder's and Diesing's bargaining model from an analysis of strategy to an analysis of tactics. The only other modification that is required involves the relaxation of the simultaneous moves assumption associated with game theory. Snyder and Diesing get around this assumption

FIGURE 4

Data Matrix for Escalatory and De-Escalatory
S - R Relationships

		STIMULUS — A's TACTIC					
		DE-ESCALATION			ESCALATION		
		Complete	Partial	No Beh∆	Partial	Complete
R E S P O N S E	B's TACTIC	Complete					
		DE-ES Partial					
		No Beh∆					
		Partial					
		ESCAL Complete					

DE-ES = De-Escalate;   ESCAL = Escalate

by examining simultaneously (in retrospect) whole sets of behaviors (strategies) and outcomes associated with historically completed international crises.

The following analysis of the two Berlin crises will treat each S-R combination of moves by the U.S. and the USSR as a series of iterative games within each crisis in which each actor's goals and capabilities are held constant within the time period covered in the analysis of each crisis. The tactical bargaining propositions that are tested within this framework come from the operational codes of Soviet and U.S. decision-makers.

The data matrix necessary to test the effectiveness of escalatory and de-escalatory tactics during international crises appears in Figure 4. At least unidimensional ordinal measurement is required for both the stimulus and the response variables. The Tanter-Corson data (Corson 1970; Tanter 1974) are recoded into ordinal categories that constitute the columns and rows of the matrix. Each actor's behavior is "double-coded" (i.e., as both a stimulus and a response, since it is both a response to the other actor's previous behavior and a stimulus that precedes the other actor's subsequent behavior). With these categories it is possible to classify all but two of the behaviors in the Tanter-Corson data set. All of the events in this data set are scaled by Corson as conflict rather than cooperative acts, with the exception of these two behaviors, which are excluded from the data matrix.[8]

The logical structure of the data matrix is similar to the structure of Snyder's and Diesing's 2 x 2 game matrix. The latter provided each actor (A and B) with two options, cooperate or conflict. Because the Berlin data do not contain cooperative events, the data matrix in Figure 4 is simply a subdivision of the conflict option for each actor into five ordinal categories. It is possible to expand this matrix from a 5 x 5 conflict matrix to a 10 x 10 matrix with five cooperative ordinal categories for each actor that correspond logically to the five conflict categories for each actor. However, the linking together of conflict and cooperation categories along a single dimension may not be theoretically valid. The concepts of cooperation and conflict may be located on different dimensions that are not bridgeable by a zero point.

The escalation and de-escalation variables in Figure 4 are measured by the following definitions of each variable's values, where A = actor A; B = actor B; Beh_t = present behavior; Beh_{t+1} = behavior immediately following Beh_t.

Stimulus

1) If $_A Beh_t < {_A Beh_{t-1}}$ and $_A Beh_t < {_B Beh_t}$, then Complete De-Escalation.
2) If $_A Beh_t < {_A Beh_{t-1}}$ and $_A Beh_t \geq {_B Beh_t}$, then Partial De-Escalation.
3) If $_A Beh_t = {_A Beh_{t-1}}$, then No Change.
4) If $_A Beh_t > {_A Beh_{t-1}}$ and $_A Beh_t \leq {_B Beh_t}$, then Partial Escalation.
5) If $_A Beh_t > {_A Beh_{t-1}}$ and $_A Beh_t > {_B Beh_t}$, then Complete Escalation.

Response

1) If $_B Beh_{t+1} < {_B Beh_t}$ and $_B Beh_{t+1} < {_A Beh_t}$, then Complete De-Escalation.
2) If $_B Beh_{t+1} < {_B Beh_t}$ and $_B Beh_{t+1} \geq {_A Beh_t}$, then Partial De-Escalation.
3) If $_B Beh_{t+1} = {_B Beh_t}$, then No Change.
4) If $_B Beh_{t+1} > {_B Beh_t}$ and $_B Beh_{t+1} \leq {_A Beh_t}$, then Partial Escalation.
5) If $_B Beh_{t+1} > {_B Beh_t}$ and $_B Beh_{t+1} > {_A Beh_t}$, then Complete Escalation.

Although the definitions for these variables are expressed according to logical symbols, they are based on commonsensical notions of escalation and de-escalation. Escalation and de-escalation both denote movement, either an increase or a decrease, respectively, in A's present behavior compared to his immediately preceding behavior. The distinction between partial and complete escalation or de-escalation depends on whether the present behavior that A selects is greater or less than B's existing behavior at the time that A selects his behavior. If A not only increases his behavior but also increases it above B's behavior, then A has selected complete escalation. If A's escalation is less than or equal to B's behavior, then A has selected partial escalation. Similarly, the distinction between partial and complete de-escalation is derived from a comparison of A's behavior with both his own previous behavior and B's present behavior.[9]

The crisis bargaining literature provides some concepts that help to identify the circumstances under which decision-makers may select escalatory or de-escalatory behavior. Three key concepts are the notions of commitment, credibility, and risk. Commitment refers to the ability of a decision-maker to communicate to the opponent the intensity of his intention to pursue or maintain his objectives. Credibility alludes to the ability of the decision-maker to communicate this intensity in a clear and believable way. Risk taps the probability of an undesirable outcome associated with a particular action.[10] It is possible to measure aspects of these concepts with the scales from the data matrix in Figure 4 by employing the following operational definitions of credibility, commitment, and risk. In these definitions, A = actor A; B = actor B; Beh_t = present behavior; Beh_{t-1} = behavior immediately preceding Beh_t; Beh_{t-2} = behavior just prior to Beh_{t-1}; Beh_{t+1} = behavior immediately following Beh_t.

De-Escalation Credibility by Actor A (DESCRED)

1) If $_ABeh_t < {_A}Beh_{t-1}$ and $_ABeh_{t-1} > {_A}Beh_{t-2}$, then Least Credible.

2) If $_ABeh_t < {_A}Beh_{t-1}$ and $_ABeh_{t-1} = {_A}Beh_{t-2}$, then More Credible.

3) If $_ABeh_t = {_A}Beh_{t-1}$ and $_ABeh_{t-1} < {_A}Beh_{t-2}$, then Even More Credible.

4) If $_ABeh_t < {_A}Beh_{t-1}$ and $_ABeh_{t-1} < {_A}Beh_{t-2}$, then Most Credible.

Escalation Credibility by Actor A (ESCRED)

1) If $_A Beh_t > {_A}Beh_{t-1}$ and $_A Beh_{t-1} < {_A}Beh_{t-2}$, then Least Credible.

2) If $_A Beh_t > {_A}Beh_{t-1}$ and $_A Beh_{t-1} = {_A}Beh_{t-2}$, then More Credible.

3) If $_A Beh_t = {_A}Beh_{t-1}$ and $_A Beh_{t-1} > {_A}Beh_{t-2}$, then Even More Credible.

4) If $_A Beh_t > {_A}Beh_{t-1}$ and $_A Beh_{t-1} > {_A}Beh_{t-2}$, then Most Credible.

Commitment to De-Escalate By Actor A (COMDESC)

1) If $_A Beh_{t-1} > {_B}Beh_t$, then A's Commitment to De-Escalate is lower than B's.

2) If $_A Beh_{t-1} = {_B}Beh_t$, then A's Commitment to De-Escalate equals B's.

3) If $_A Beh_{t-1} < {_B}Beh_t$, then A's Commitment to De-Escalate is higher than B's.

Commitment to Escalate By Actor A (COMESC)

1) If $_A Beh_{t-1} < {_B}Beh_t$, then A's Commitment to Escalate is lower than B's.

2) If $_A Beh_{t-1} = {_B}Beh_t$, then A's Commitment to Escalate equals B's.

3) If $_A Beh_{t-1} > {_B}Beh_t$, then A's Commitment to Escalate is higher than B's.

Risk

1) $VBeh_t$ = the variety of A's present behavior.

2) If $_A Beh_t > {_A}Beh_{t-1}$ or $_A Beh_t < {_A}Beh_{t-1}$ and $_A VBeh_t = {_A}Beh_t$, then Risk (least ambiguous) Behavior

3) If $_A Beh_t > {_A}Beh_{t-1}$ or $_A Beh_t < {_A}Beh_{t-1}$ and $_A VBeh_t$ is from $_A Beh_{t-1}$ to $_A Beh_t$, then Medium Risk (more ambiguous) behavior.

4) If $_A Beh_t > {_A}Beh_{t-1}$ and $_A Beh_t < {_A}Beh_{t-1}$, then the range of $VBeh_t$ is both > and < Beh_{t-1} and is Low Risk (most ambiguous) behavior.

The credibility concept is measured by the consistency of A's present escalatory or de-escalatory behavior compared to his two most recent preceding behaviors. The two least credible behavior patterns are an escalation preceded by a de-escalation, and vice versa. The two most credible behavior patterns are two escalations in a row and two de-escalations in a row. The two intermediate types are ranked according to the chronological position of the behavior (Beh_t or Beh_{t-1}) that represents a change from the preceding behavior (Beh_{t-1} or Beh_{t-2}). A change in behavior from Beh_{t-2} to Beh_{t-1}, followed by a repetition of Beh_{t-1} at time$_t$, is ranked higher in credibility than a pattern in which there is not change from Beh_{t-2} to Beh_{t-1}, followed by a change from Beh_{t-1}

to Beh_t. The rationale for this ranking is that a repeated signal is more credible than a new signal. Commitment is measured by comparing A's previous behavior with B's previous behavior. If the behavior of A and B is symmetrical, then their commitment to escalate or de-escalate is equal. If their behavior is asymmetrical in favor of A, then A's commitment to escalate or de-escalate is greater than B's.

Risk is measured by the ambiguity of A's behavior. If A does only one type of action at one level of intensity prior to B's response, then it is least ambiguous, most easily interpreted, and consequently the most risky behavior. If A engages in more than one type of behavior prior to B's response, but they are either all more intense than A's previous tactic or all less intense than A's previous tactic, then it is more ambiguous, less easily interpreted by B, and less risky behavior. If A employs more than one type of behavior prior to B's response, and if this variety ranges in intensity both above and below A's previous behavior, then it's the most ambiguous, least easily interpreted, and least risky behavior.[11]

Soviet Crisis Bargaining Propositions

Not only are these credibility, commitment, and risk variables among the central concerns of crisis bargaining theorists, they are also relevant to the examination of the instrumental beliefs that are a part of Soviet and U.S. operational codes. George (1969: 205-14) has formulated two key questions that deal with these concepts in his synopsis of Leites's (1951, 1953, 1964) analyses of the Bolshevik code. They are: How are the goals of action pursued most effectively? How are the risks of political action calculated, controlled, and accepted? George summarizes the Leites analysis of the Bolshevik beliefs regarding the first question as follows: "The classical Bolshevik answer to this question can be summarized in three maxims: 'push to the limit,' 'engage in pursuit' of an opponent who begins to retreat or make concessions, *but* 'know when to stop' " (George 1969:211). These rules guide Bolshevik offensive tactics. Three other maxims prescribe Bolshevik actions when they are on the defensive " 'resist from the start' any encroachment by the opponent, no matter how slight it appears to be; *but* 'don't yield to enemy provocations' and 'retreat before superior force.' " (George 1969:212).

The Bolshevik approach to the calculation and control of risks is characterized by a limiting of the means which they initially select in the pursuit of ambitious objectives. They thereby keep an undesirable outcome several moves away in a probable temporal sequence. This approach projects a sequence of moves in a conflict situation and requires the a priori identification of possible Soviet moves to redirect or de-escalate the conflict as an undesirable outcome becomes more imminent (George 1969:212-15).

Our reexamination of the Leites research, the George synopsis, and several other sources that have analyzed Khrushchev's rhetoric prior to and during the 1961 crisis period show no significant departure from the Bolshevik beliefs of Khrushchev. During a crisis situation, Khrushchev's operational code called for him to initiate the crisis on his schedule, to continue as long as he had a chance of winning, to retreat when he was no longer willing or able to match the raises of his opponents (Horelick and Rush 1965:169; Slusser 1973:1; Spier 1961:140-41; Dulles 1972:22). There is little evidence prior to the 1961 Berlin crisis to indicate that Khrushchev had either significantly modified or rejected the Bolshevik tactical and risk-taking maxims (Hoagland 1978:78-113). Consequently, we will base the following propositions about Soviet bargaining behavior on the Bolshevik operational code.

These propositions are organized as axioms, theorems, and hypotheses to reflect a descending order of abstraction and a corresponding increase in operational meaning. The sequence of hypotheses, 1., 2., 3., etc., for each theorem is ordered according to their increasing complexity; the number of variables and/or the number of values for each variable tends to increase in each successive hypothesis for a given theorem.

Axiom I. (Tactics) Push to the limit/Engage in pursuit/Know when to stop.

> ***Theorem A.*** Even if the opponent initially shows no signs of yielding, the Soviets believe that one should always exert maximum energy to attain one's objectives and that one should keep pressure on an opponent (George 1969:211). Therefore:
>
> > *H1.* Soviet escalation behavior will tend to be high in credibility.
> >
> > *H2.* Soviet escalation behavior will tend to be high in commitment.
> >
> > *H3.* If the credibility of U.S. escalation is less than maximum, the Soviets will escalate.

H4. If the commitment of U.S. escalation is less than maximum, the Soviets will escalate.

Theorem B. If the opponent begins to yield, the Soviets believe that additional gains may be possible, and one should not relax pressure when the opponent begins to yield (George 1969:211). Therefore:

H1. If the Americans de-escalate, then the Soviets will escalate.

H2. The more credible the U.S. de-escalation, the greater the tendency for the USSR to escalate.

H3. The more committed the U.S. de-escalation, the greater the tendency for the USSR to escalate.

H4. If the Soviets de-escalate in response to U.S. de-escalation, the Soviet de-escalation will tend to be partial rather than complete.

Theorem C. If the opponent continues to stand firm and if rational analysis indicates that the costs of pushing forward are likely to be high, then the Soviets believe that one should stop pushing and even retreat (George 1969:211-12). Therefore:

H1. As the credibility of U.S. escalatory behavior increases, Soviet behavior will tend toward partial escalation, partial de-escalation, and even complete de-escalation.

H2. As the commitment of U.S. escalatory behavior increases, Soviet behavior will tend toward partial escalation, partial de-escalation, and even complete de-escalation.

Axiom II. (Tactics) Resist from the start/Avoid yielding.

Theorem A. If an opponent attempts to pressure the USSR, the Soviets believe that one must resist with as much strength as the situation will allow (George 1969:212). Therefore:

H1. Soviet de-escalatory behavior will tend to be low in credibility.

H2. Soviet de-escalatory behavior will tend to be low in commitment.

Theorem B. One should avoid yielding except in the face of clear superiority and determination (George 1969:212). Therefore:

H1. Unless U.S. escalatory behavior is accompanied by high credibility, Soviet escalatory behavior will tend to match or better U.S. escalation.

H2. Unless U.S. escalatory behavior is accompanied by high commitment, Soviet escalatory behavior will tend to match or better U.S. escalation.

H3. If U.S. escalatory behavior is high in credibility, then the Soviets will tend to de-escalate.

H4. If U.S. escalatory behavior is high in commitment, then the Soviets will tend to de-escalate.

Axiom III. (Risk-Taking) A conflict situation that requires several intermediate events prior to the onset of war is a low-risk situation.

Theorem A. In a crisis situation, control the level of risk by using limited means to pursue one's goals (George 1969:213). Therefore:

H1. The Soviets will tend to select low-risk escalatory behavior.

H2. The Soviets will tend to select partial rather than complete escalatory behavior.

Theorem B. In a crisis situation, risks can be controlled by adopting a risk-reducing, follow-on strategy (George 1969: 214-15; Triska and Finlay 1968:322, 329-30, 345-57; Hoagland 1978:94).

H1. The greater the level of risk associated with U.S. escalatory behavior, the lower the level of risk associated with the Soviet escalatory response.

H2. The greater the risk associated with U.S. escalatory behavior, the more likely that the Soviets will de-escalate or only partially escalate.

Axiom IV. (Risk-Taking) Caution is especially necessary in high-risk situations.

Theorem A. Caution is necessary in situations that can easily escalate (George 1969:214-15). Therefore:

H1. The greater the credibility of U.S. escalatory behavior, the less risky will be the Soviet escalatory response.

H2. The greater the commitment of U.S. escalatory behavior, the more risky will be the Soviet de-escalatory response.

H3. The greater the credibility of U.S. escalatory behavior, the more risky will be the Soviet de-escalatory response.

H4. The greater the commitment of U.S. escalatory behavior, the more risky will be the Soviet de-escalatory response.

U.S. Crisis Bargaining Propositions

The U.S. operational code that guided the selection of bargaining tactics toward the Soviet Union during the two Berlin crises represents a synthesis of competing images of the Soviet Union. In 1945, U.S. foreign policy makers were divided over the answer to the OPCODE philosophical question formulated by George (1969:201): "What is the fundamental character of one's political opponents?" According to Yergin (1977:11), there were two sets of beliefs regarding the character of the Soviet Union within the U.S. decision-making elite in the 1940s:

> At the heart of the first set was an image of the Soviet Union as a world revolutionary state, denying the possibilities of coexistence, committed to unrelenting ideological warfare, powered by a messianic drive for world mastery. The second set downplayed the role of ideology and the foreign policy consequences of authoritarian domestic practices and, instead, saw the Soviet Union behaving like a traditional great power within the international system, rather than trying to overthrow it.

Yergin argues persuasively (with extensive documentation) that the first image had become the dominant set of beliefs within the U.S. government by 1948. The dominant period for the alternative view ended with the death of President Roosevelt, although these beliefs maintained some influence over President Truman during the first two years after FDR passed away.

The bargaining tactics that were associated with these two images varied primarily in their respective assessments of the role of negotiations and the utility of negative sanctions. Proponents of the hard image of the USSR prescribed a strategy of containment implemented by negative sanctions against acts of recalcitrance or expansion by the Soviet Union. They were not optimistic about the possibilities for a negotiated settlement of the postwar issues between the United States and the Soviet Union.

The advocates of the soft image of the USSR believed that a strategy of compromise implemented by negotiations was the best approach. Truman initially subscribed to a hard image and negative tactics, then oscillated for two years between this perspective and a synthetic approach which combined a willingness to negotiate with negative sanctions of an economic nature (Yergin 1977:69-105, 220-301). By 1948, however, Truman and his advisors had become committed to a containment strategy, a policy of non-cooperation with the Soviets in the implementation of the Potsdam reparations schedules for Germany, and a goal of political unification for the Allied occupation zones in West Germany.

Thirteen years later, the bargaining tactics in John F. Kennedy's operational code closely resembled the prescriptions associated with the tactics adopted by the Truman administration. Moreover, they appear to rest on a synthesis of the hard and soft images of the Soviet Union that existed within the United States government at the end of World War II. Like Truman, Kennedy was surrounded by advisors with different beliefs—some advocating the hard image position and others the soft view—and he had to choose among competing tactical recommendations during the 1961 Berlin Crisis (George and Smoke 1974:431-37). Our analysis of JFK's instrumental OPCODE beliefs indicates that he thought negotiations should never be ruled out as an option; however, one should also avoid any show of weakness toward the Soviet Union (Hoagland 1978:118-20).

Kennedy's tactical assessment appears to have been a modification of his more general beliefs to fit an image of his opponent, one which seemed to indicate the need for firmness. His general predisposition to emphasize negotiations as the best method for dealing with conflicts is more compatible with the tactics associated with a soft image of the Soviet Union. The emphasis on firmness in addition to flexibility is based on a belief about the specific character of his adversary and not necessarily on more general convictions about his essential nature of political life. This tactical perspective is very close to Truman's synthesis of the bargaining prescriptions he knew. Kennedy rested his instrumental beliefs on an image of Nikita Khrushchev which incorporated most of the important elements of the Soviet leader's operational code, including an awareness of his preference for committal bargaining tactics and his likely response to flexibility by an opponent. Kennedy was also aware of the existing, though limited, possibilities of negotiated settlements in conflicts with Khrushchev, and he realized that Khrushchev was impressed with firmness by an opponent, as long as it was not too provocative (Hoagland 1978:124-28).

The uneasy coexistence of competing bargaining prescriptions and images of the Soviet Union among U.S. foreign policy makers could influence the crisis bargaining tactics of the U.S. government in several ways. There could be an alternation of committal and conciliatory initiatives by the United States in which an uncertain president with divided advisors experiments with a variety of tactics. A more likely pattern, based on our analysis of Kennedy's code and Yergin's interpretation of the Truman administration's belief system, would be that the American response to Soviet committal tactics in both Berlin crises would be a firm one.

Predicting the American response pattern to conciliatory Soviet moves across both crises is more problematical. Formal negotiations often do not play a significant role during the crisis phase of a conflict. Since they are not important in either of these crises, the significance of Kennedy's greater emphasis on negotiations (in comparison to the Truman administration's) appears to be low. Instead, the more crucial consideration would appear to be whether they differed significantly in their sensitivities and responses to tacit bargaining overtures, such as de-escalatory moves by the opponent. Truman and Kennedy shared a concern that U.S. flexibility might be interpreted as weakness or appeasement, but neither they nor their advisors appear to have been predisposed against a de-escalation of the crisis. The U.S. commitment to the status quo in Berlin made them able to answer Soviet de-escalatory moves with similar responses, as long as the Western presence in Berlin was not jeopardized. In contrast, any Soviet de-escalatory move prior to the removal of the Allied presence from Berlin was a prima facie concession to the continuation of the status quo. This common asymmetry in the tactical positions of the superpowers existed across both crises. Offset by the common concern of both Truman and Kennedy that U.S. flexibility might be misconstrued, it is plausible to hypothesize that the two U.S. presidents and their advisors were approximately identical in their responsiveness to Soviet de-escalatory tactics.

Consequently, the following propositions about U.S. crisis bargaining tactics make no distinctions between the behavior of the Truman and the Kennedy administrations. The actual data base for these propositions, however, is the qualitative content analysis of Kennedy's operational code by Hoagland (1978). This research focuses on the instrumental beliefs in JFK's code, plus his image of Khrushchev. Although it certainly appears plausible that Kennedy's instrumental beliefs were virtually identical with the views of Truman and his advisors regarding the management of

Soviet-American confrontations, this assumption can only be tested indirectly by comparing the congruence between U.S. tactics across both crises and between Kennedy's beliefs and our government's tactics during the second Berlin crisis.

Axiom I. (Tactics) One should make every effort to be flexible in the interest of peace, yet one should avoid actions that could be interpreted as a show of weakness.

Theorem A. In a crisis, the most effective approach is one balanced with elements of both force and diplomacy; one must show resolve and yet be willing to negotiate (Hoagland 1978: 119, 123). Therefore:

H1. If the Soviet Union de-escalates, then the United States will de-escalate.

H2. If the Soviet Union escalates, then the United States will escalate.

H3. The greater the credibility of Soviet de-escalatory behavior, the greater the tendency of the United States to select a de-escalatory response.

Theorem B. In a crisis, respond to the opponent's challenge with a carefully limited action designed to offer the opponent the same poor choice that he offered you: escalation or retreat (Hoagland 1978:123). Therefore:

H1. If the Soviet Union escalates, the United States will escalate or de-escalate in a symmetrical fashion, i.e., (a) a Soviet complete escalation will elicit a U.S. complete escalation; or (b) a Soviet partial escalation will elicit a U.S. partial de-escalation.

H2. The greater the credibility of Soviet escalatory behavior, the greater the credibility of the U.S. escalatory response.

H3. The greater the credibility of Soviet escalatory behavior, the greater the commitment of the U.S. escalatory response.

Axiom II. (Risk-taking) It is very important to reduce the risks associated with the opponent's miscalculation.

Theorem A. In a crisis, one must be careful to insure that the opponent does not miscalculate the firmness of your resolve (Hoagland 1978:120-30). Therefore:

H1. U.S. escalatory behavior will tend to be low-risk behavior that is high in credibility.

H2. U.S. escalatory behavior will tend to be low-risk behavior that is high in commitment.

Theorem B. In a crisis, one must be careful that the opponent does not misinterpret flexibility for weakness (Hoagland 1978: 120, 129-30). Therefore:

H1. U.S. de-escalatory behavior will tend to be low-risk behavior.

H2. U.S. de-escalatory behavior will tend to be low in credibility, unless it is preceded by a highly credible Soviet de-escalatory behavior.

H3. U.S. de-escalatory behavior will tend to be low in commitment, unless it is preceded by a Soviet de-escalatory behavior with high commitment.

Data Analysis

The analysis of the relatioships between the OPCODE hypotheses and the crisis behavior of the Soviet and U.S. governments during the two Berlin crises involves the following steps. Initially, the congruence between the beliefs and the behavior of each actor will be assessed and the most important relationships between these variables will be identified. Once these links are identified, the relationships among beliefs, actions, and systemic outcomes will be explored. Although the OPCODE beliefs of the actors are stated as universal axioms and theorems, the test of congruence for the hypotheses is the degree of fit between the hypothesized and the actual relationships.

For univariate hypotheses, a comparison of the hypothesized and actual distributions of the variable's values is the test of congruence. The existence and degree of congruence are a function of the degree to which 50 percent or more of the actual distribution of cases conforms to the hypothesized distribution. For bivariate hypotheses, the criteria for "goodness of fit" (i.e., congruence) are the sign and magnitude of two measures of association, Gamma (G) and Somer's D. These two statistics vary between -1.0 and $+1.0$, so their signs indicate the direction of the relationship between two variables, while their magnitudes indicate the degree of association between two variables. Somer's D is the more stringent measure of association, because it requires perfect linear correlation to achieve a 1.0 value. It is possible for Gamma to achieve a 1.0 value when the data are not linearly distributed along the diagonals of a table.[12] Congruence exists between an actor's OPCODE belief and crisis behavior when the hypothesized and actual signs for the relationships between two variables are identical; the degree of congruence increases as the magnitude of this signed relationship increases.

The findings for the Soviet univariate hypotheses are presented in Table 1. Two of the univariate propositions are confirmed for both Berlin crises and within the upswing and downswing phases of the two crises.[13] They are the hypotheses associated with the Soviet Axiom (II) "Resist from the start/Avoid yielding," and the Theorem (IIA) "If an opponent attempts to pressure the USSR, the Soviets believe that one must resist with as much strength as the situation will allow." The first hypothesis (IIA-H1) states that (therefore), "Soviet de-escalatory behavior will tend to be low in credibility," and the second hypothesis (IIA-H2) specifies that (therefore), "Soviet de-escalatory behavior will tend to be low in commitment." As the distributions in columns three and four of Table 1 reveal, a majority of Soviet de-escalatory moves are low in credibility and commitment.

In Figure 5 are the results of the tests of congruence for the Soviet bivariate hypotheses across both Berlin crises. The Soviet responses to different aspects of U.S. *escalatory* behavior are partially consistent with the actions prescribed by Soviet OPCODE beliefs. The major exceptions are Soviet tactics and risk-taking in response to variations in the commitment and credibility of U.S. escalatory behavior. The Soviet response pattern for different aspects of U.S. *de-escalatory* behavior is generally incongruent with the maxims of the Soviet operational code. The small number of cases makes it difficult to profitably disaggregate these results by crisis or phase. The low Ns also make it impractical to control for the simultaneous effects of several aspects of U.S. behavior and Soviet OPCODE beliefs on Soviet tactics and risk-taking. The results of disaggregation for Soviet tactics are included on heuristic grounds; the Ns are simply too small for the disaggregation of Soviet risk-taking.

The results for the disaggregation of Soviet tactics by crisis and phase are in Figures 6 and 7. Soviet responses to U.S. escalatory behavior are similar in both crises, with the exception of the relationship between Soviet tactics and the credibility of U.S. escalation.

TABLE 1

Findings for Soviet Univariate OPCODE Hypotheses

			Both Crises	1948 Crisis	1961 Crisis	Upswing Phases	Downswing Phases
(F) IA-1 SOV ESCRED	Low	F %	21 67.7	11 61.1	10 76.9	12 75.0	9 60.0
	More	F %	1 3.2	1 5.6	0 0.0	0 0.0	1 0.0
	Even More	F %	0 0.0	0 0.0	0 0.0	0 0.0	0 0.0
	Most	F %	9 29.0	6 33.3	3 23.1	4 25.0	5 33.3
(F) IA-2 SOV COMESC	Low	F %	21 67.7	14 77.8	7 53.8	10 62.5	11 73.3
	Equal	F %	1 3.2	1 5.6	0 0.0	1 6.3	0 0.0
	High	F %	9 29.0	3 16.7	6 46.2	5 31.3	4 26.7
(T) IIA-1 SOV DESCRED	Low	F %	20 80.0	11 84.6	9 75.0	10 76.9	10 83.3
	More	F %	0 0.0	0 0.0	0 0.0	0 0.0	0 0.0
	Even More	F %	0 0.0	0 0.0	0 0.0	0 0.0	0 0.0
	Most	F %	5 20.0	2 15.4	3 25.0	3 23.1	4 16.7
(T) IIA-2 SOV COMDESC	Low	F %	15 57.7	7 53.8	8 61.5	8 57.1	7 58.3
	Medium	F %	3 11.5	3 23.1	0 0.0	1 7.1	2 16.7
	High	F %	8 30.8	3 23.1	5 38.5	5 35.7	3 25.0
(F) IIA-1 SOV ESCRISK	Low	F %	8 25.8	5 27.4	3 23.1	6 37.5	2 13.3
	Medium	F %	8 25.8	5 27.8	3 23.1	4 25.0	4 26.7
	High	F %	15 48.4	8 44.4	7 53.8	6 37.5	9 60.0
(F) IIIA-2 SOV ESCLEV	Partial	F %	12 38.7	7 38.9	5 38.5	5 31.3	7 46.7
	Complete	F %	19 61.3	11 61.1	8 61.5	11 68.8	8 53.3

(F) = Falsified; (T) = True.

FIGURE 5

Actual and Hypothesized Relationships Between
Soviet Crisis Behavior and Soviet OPCODE
Beliefs Across Both Berlin Crises

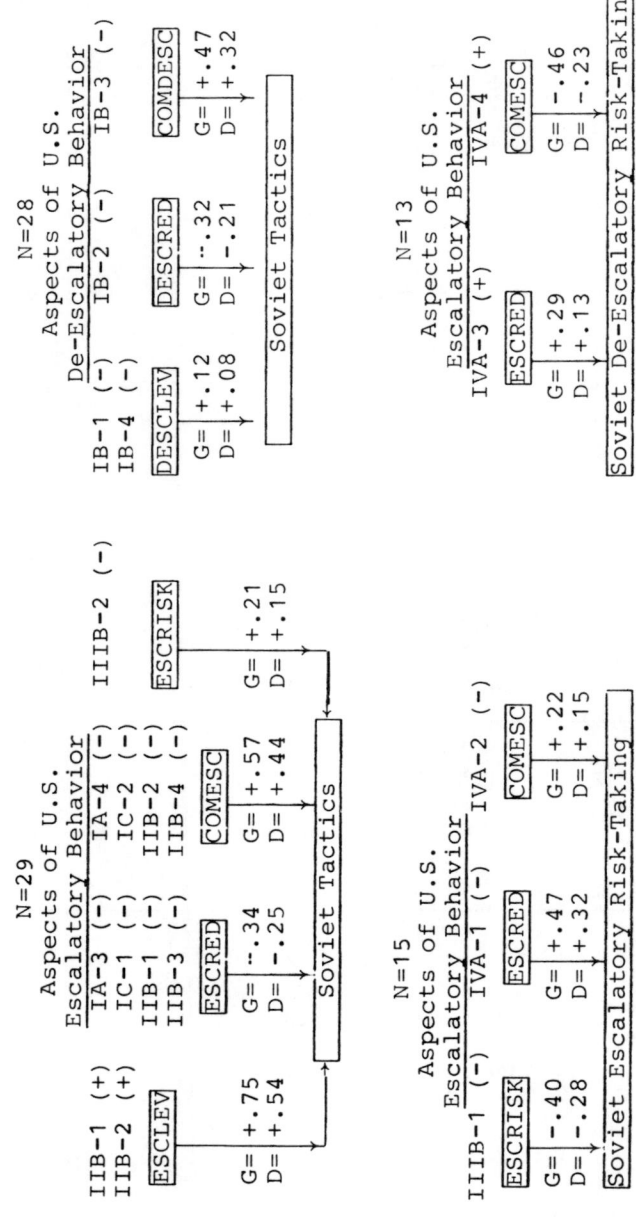

FIGURE 6

A Comparison of Soviet Tactics During the 1948 and 1961 Berlin Crises

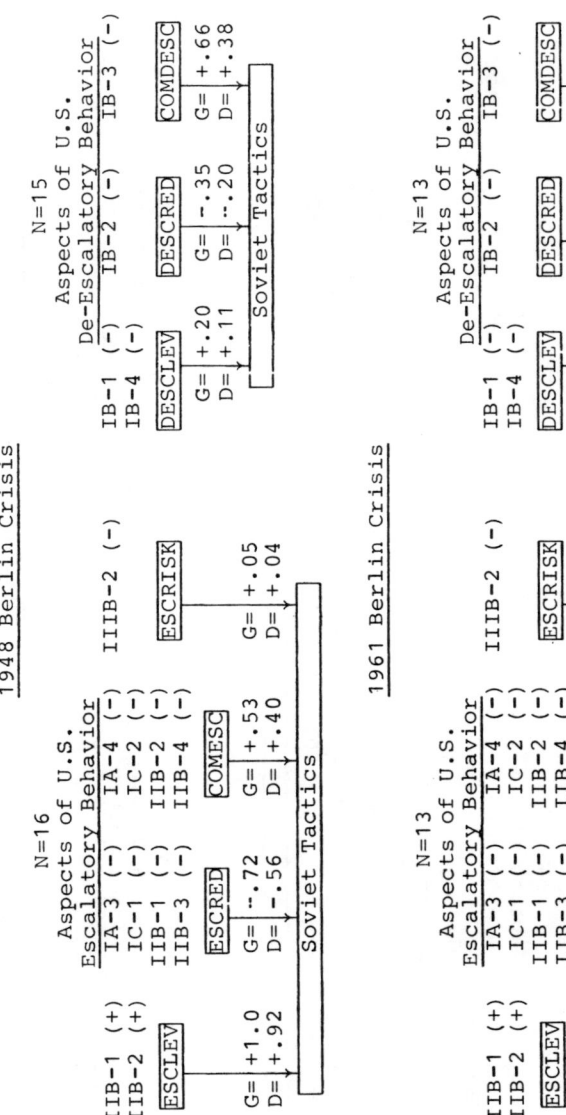

FIGURE 7

A Comparison of Soviet Tactics During the Upswing
and Downswing Phases of the Berlin Crises

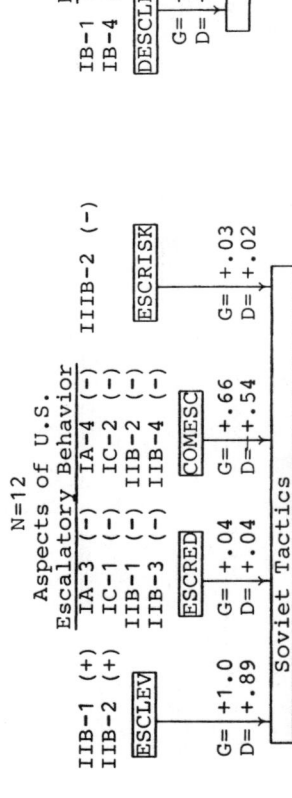

The USSR was very sensitive to the credibility of U.S. escalation during the 1948 crisis—in a manner consistent with the Bolshevik OPCODE beliefs. However, during the 1961 crisis, the USSR tended to violate these beliefs and engaged in high-risk, counterescalatory tactics in response to increases in the credibility of U.S. escalatory behavior. The disaggregation of Soviet tactics in response to U.S. de-escalatory behavior indicates that the Soviet deviation from Bolshevik beliefs regarding the appropriate response to an increase in U.S. de-escalatory commitment occurred primarily during the 1948 crisis.

A comparison of Soviet tactics during the upswing and downswing phases of the Berlin crises shows that the USSR's response to the credibility of U.S. escalatory behavior tended to be congruent with the Bolshevik OPCODE during the upswing phase. The lack of congruence for the downswing phase is also reasonable if one weights the plausible contextual effects of the downswing phase. Soviet escalation during this phase would appear to be less likely to elicit a dramatic counterescalation by the United States. A similar argument may be advanced to explain the positive Soviet response to the credibility and commitment of U.S. de-escalatory behavior during the downswing phase.

The findings for the U.S. univariate hypotheses appear in Table 2. With the exception of the distribution of behaviors for the COMESC variable in the 1948 crisis, all of these hypotheses are completely falsified at every level of aggregation. During the 1948 Berlin crisis, the United States did tend to select escalatory behavior that was high in commitment; however, the riskiness of that behavior was randomly distributed across the risk categories. There was also essentially a random relationship between RISK and COMESC for these cases ($G = -.11; D = -.08; N = 16$).

In Figure 8 are the results of the tests of congruence for the U.S. bivariate hypotheses across both crises. The U.S. responses to Soviet de-escalatory behavior are congruent with American OPCODE beliefs; there also tends to be a congruent response pattern to Soviet escalatory behavior. When U.S. responses to Soviet de-escalatory behavior are disaggregated by crisis and phase, the pattern of congruency is maintained. The only significant exception is the inverse relationship between U.S. tactics and Soviet de-escalatory behavior during the upswing phase. ($G = -1.0; D = -.69; N = 14$). Then the U.S. response to Soviet de-escalation is to escalate, which partly contradicts the U.S. OPCODE belief (IA-H1) that one "should be flexible in the interests of peace and be

TABLE 2

Findings for American Univariate OPCODE Hypotheses

			Both Crises	1948 Crisis	1961 Crisis	Upswing Phases	Downswing Phases
(F)	Low	F %	19 67.9	11 68.8	8 66.7	10 62.5	9 75.0
IIA-1	More	F %	0 0.0	0 0.0	0 0.0	0 0.0	0 0.0
AM ESCRED	Even More	F %	0 0.0	0 0.0	0 0.0	0 0.0	0 0.0
	Most	F %	9 32.1	5 31.3	4 33.3	6 37.5	3 25.0
(F)	Low	F %	17 58.6	7 43.8	10 76.9	10 58.8	7 58.3
IIA-2 AM	Medium	F %	0 0.0	0 0.0	0 0.0	0 0.0	0 0.0
COMESC	High	F %	12 41.4	9 56.3	3 23.1	7 41.2	5 41.7
(F)	Low	F %	8 27.6	5 31.3	3 23.1	6 35.3	2 16.7
IIA-1&2 AM	Medium	F %	10 34.5	5 31.3	5 38.5	5 29.4	5 41.7
ESCRISK	High	F %	11 37.9	6 37.5	5 38.5	6 35.3	5 41.7
(F)	Low	F %	5 17.9	2 13.3	3 23.1	2 14.3	3 21.4
IIB-1 AM	Medium	F %	10 35.7	8 53.3	2 15.4	5 35.7	5 35.7
DESCRISK	High	F %	13 46.4	5 33.3	8 61.5	7 50.0	6 42.9

(F) = Falsified

FIGURE 8

Actual And Hypothesized Relationships Between American Crisis Behavior and American OPCODE Beliefs Across Both Berlin Crises

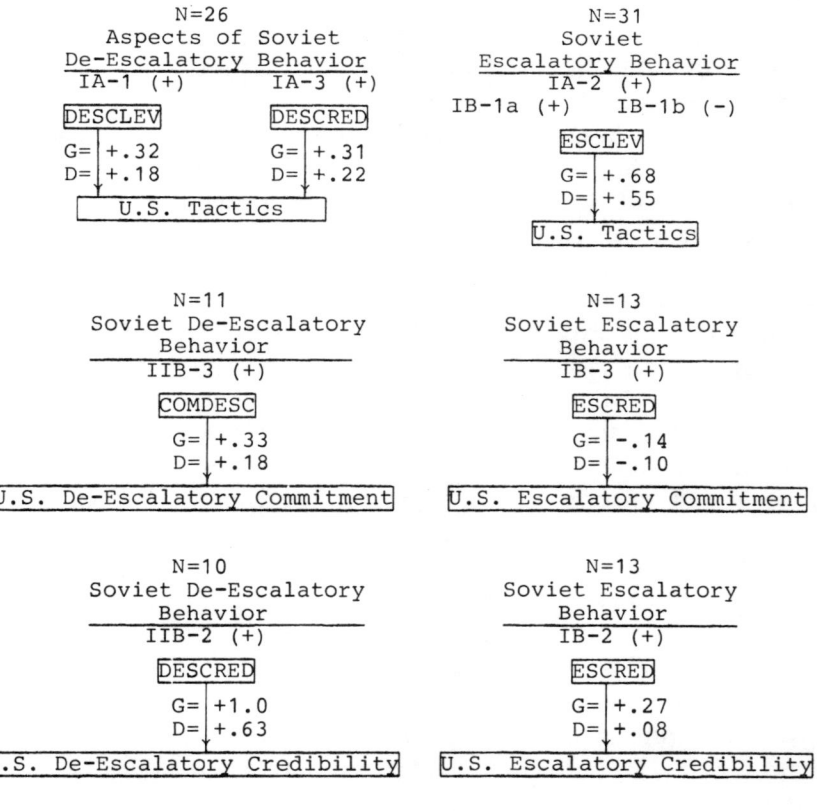

willing to negotiate." The contextual effects of the upswing phase, however, may have activated the corollary to this belief: that one "should show resolve and avoid actions that could be interpreted as a show of weakness" (IA-H1). Although there are some other minor deviations between U.S. crisis behavior and the American OPCODE, they are based on such a small number of cases ($N \leqslant 10$) that they are virtually useless even for heuristic purposes. Consequently, they are not reported in this analysis.

Operational Codes and Crisis Outcomes

An examination of the relationships between OPCODE beliefs and crisis outcomes involves bridging three levels of analysis: individual, national, and systemic (dyadic). We have argued that the differences in OPCODE beliefs among Soviet decision-makers were insignificant during the two Berlin crises, which permits us to attribute both Soviet beliefs and behavior to the same collectivity, i.e., the Soviet government. We have made the same argument with respect to the Truman and Kennedy administrations. Differences between the operational codes of Soviet and U.S. decision-makers make it difficult to attribute actions by these two collectivities to the same OPCODE beliefs. Yet it is their sequence of actions that is the immediate cause of the outcomes of their interactions for any given period of time. Earlier (see Figure 3), we argued that these tactical outcomes can be reduced to four types: mutual de-escalation (D, D), two mixed outcomes, in which one actor escalates while the other de-escalates (D, E and E, D), and mutual escalation (E, E). Although these outcomes are derived from game theory and its accompanying assumption of simultaneous moves by the two actors, it is possible to relax this assumption and conceptualize tactical outcomes as the state of dyadic relations between two actors, A and B, at any given point in time. This conceptualization is diagrammed in Figure 9, which shows that for any given time t_n, the tactical outcome for dyad (A, B) or (B, A) is an immediate function of their current Stimulus-Response (S-R) interaction pattern, which is defined by their most recent moves.

But our preceding analysis of the determinants of these moves at the national level has rested on hypotheses that attribute them to features of the opponents' previous moves and the actor's own operational code beliefs (see Figure 1). Therefore, to the extent that our analysis of these moves is valid, it would appear that the

FIGURE 9

Tactical Outcomes Defined With S - R Data

Dyad (B, A):	Outcome$_{t_2}$
Time Sequence (S - R):	S - R — S - R
Dyad (A, B):	Outcome$_{t_1}$ Outcome$_{t_3}$

FIGURE 10

The Theoretical Relationship Among OPCODE Beliefs, Crisis Moves, and Dyadic Outcomes

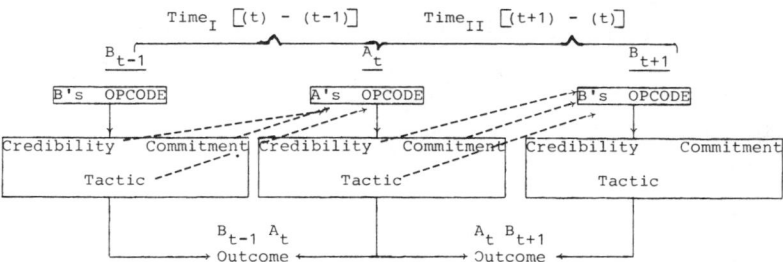

relationships among beliefs, actions, and outcomes should follow the patterns diagrammed in Figure 10.

To test the model in Figure 10 completely is beyond the scope of this paper. We lack, in particular, the necessary knowledge pertaining to the U.S. operational code. For example, our delineation of Kennedy's OPCODE has not provided us with a belief that specifies when it is appropriate for the United States to de-escalate in response to a Soviet escalation (E_{Sov}). Without this knowledge it is virtually impossible to link an (E_{Sov}, D_{US}) tactical outcome to the U.S. operational code. However, the analysis of the Soviet operational code by Leites and George, together with our analysis of Khrushchev's OPCODE, is sufficiently detailed to specify the conditions under which the Soviets believe it is appropriate to respond to a U.S. escalation (E_{US}) or de-escalation (D_{US}) with an escalation (E_{Sov}) or de-escalation (D_{Sov}) of their own. These conditions are specified by the Gamma and Somer's D coefficients in Figure 5. They indicate that the best predictor of a Soviet escalatory response (E_{Sov}) to an E_{US} is the level of escalation by the United States. The best predictor of a D_{Sov} response to an E_{US} is also ESCLEV$_{US}$. The corresponding predictors of an E_{Sov} response and a D_{Sov} response, respectively, to a D_{US} move are the commitment of D_{US} and the credibility of D_{US}. Although the commitment level of D_{US} is the best predictor, its relationship to Soviet action is incongruent with the Soviet OPCODE; consequently, we will use the credibility of D_{US} as our predictor of the Soviet response to D_{US}. The links between OPCODE beliefs and systemic outcomes, therefore, are established by the significance assigned to these predictor variables in the OPCODES of the decision-makers.

The test that we will use to establish the existence and strength of these links is the degree of association between the predictor variables and those systemic outcomes in which U.S. behavior is a given and Soviet behavior is the missing half of the dyadic outcome. Specifically, we will examine the distribution of outcomes (E_{US}, E_{Sov}) (E_{US}, D_{Sov}) (D_{US}, E_{Sov}) (D_{US}, D_{Sov}) and hypothesize the following relationships. The results of each test are summarized next to each hypothesis.

Fit	Mode	Lambda	N		
Yes	14	.46	28	H1:	Given E_{US}, if the predictor variable ESCLEV$_{US}$ takes a high value, then the modal outcome will be (E_{US}, E_{Sov}).
Yes	7	.46	28	H2:	Given E_{US}, if the predictor variable ESCLEV$_{US}$ takes a low value, then the modal outcome will be (E_{US}, D_{Sov}).
Yes	10	.14	28	H3:	Given D_{US}, if the predictor variable DESCRED$_{US}$ takes a low value, then the modal outcome will be (D_{US}, D_{Sov}).
Yes	5	.14	28	H4:	Given D_{US}, if the predictor variable DESCRED$_{US}$ takes a high value, then the modal outcome will be (D_{US}, D_{Sov}).

These tests are for Soviet tactics across crises and phases. When the data are disaggregated by crisis and phase, the following hypotheses are the appropriate tests to assess the link between Soviet OPCODE beliefs and tactical outcomes. The predictor variables are taken from Figures 6 and 7.

1949 Berlin, Crisis

Fit	Mode	Lambda	N		
Yes	11	.75	15	H1:	Given E_{US}, if the predictor variable ESCLEV$_{US}$ takes a high value, then the modal outcome will be (E_{US}, E_{Sov}).
Yes	3	.75	15	H2:	Given E_{US}, if the predictor variable ESCLEV$_{US}$ takes a low value, then the modal outcome will be (E_{US}, D_{Sov}).

Fit	Mode	Lambda	N		
Yes	7	.17	15	H3:	Given D_{US}, if the predictor variable DESCRED$_{US}$ takes a low value, then the modal outcome will be (D_{US}, D_{Sov}).
Yes	2	.17	15	H4:	Given D_{US}, If the predictor variable DESCRED$_{US}$ takes a high value, then the modal outcome will be (D_{US}, E_{Sov}).

1961 Berlin Crisis

Fit	Mode	Lambda	N		
No	5	.00	13	H1:	Given E_{US}, if the predictor variable ESCLEV$_{US}$ takes a high value, then the modal outcome will be (E_{US}, E_{Sov}).
Yes	4	.00	13	H2:	Given E_{US}, if the predictor variable ESCLEV$_{US}$ takes a low value, then the modal outcome will be (E_{US}, D_{Sov}).
No	5	.20	13	H3:	Given D_{US}, if the predictor variable DESCRED$_{US}$ takes a low value, then the modal outcome will be (D_{US}, D_{Sov}).
Yes	3	.20	13	H4:	Given D_{US}, if the predictor variable DESCRED$_{US}$ takes a high value, then the modal outcome will be (D_{US}, E_{Sov}).

Crisis Upswing Phase

Fit	Mode	Lambda	N		
Yes	4	.25	16	H1:	Given E_{US}, if the predictor variable ESCRED$_{US}$ takes a high value, then the modal outcome will be (E_{US}, D_{Sov}).
Yes	6	.25	16	H2:	Given E_{US}, if the predictor variable ESCRED$_{US}$ takes a low value, then the modal outcome will be (E_{US}, E_{Sov}).
Yes	6	.33	14	H3:	Given D_{US}, if the predictor variable DESCRED$_{US}$ takes a low value, then the modal outcome will be (D_{US}, D_{Sov}).
Yes	3	.33	14	H4:	Given D_{US}, if the predictor variable DESCRED$_{US}$ takes a high value, then the modal outcome will be (D_{US}, E_{Sov}).

Crisis Downswing Phase

Fit	Mode	Lambda	N		
Yes	3	.75	11	H1:	Given E_{US}, if the predictor variable DESCLEV$_{US}$ takes a low value, then the modal outcome will be (E_{US}, D_{Sov}).
Yes	7	.75	11	H2:	Given E_{US}, if the predictor variable DESCLEV$_{US}$ takes a high value, then the modal outcome will be (E_{US}, E_{Sov}).
---	--	---	--		(There are no congruent relationships between Soviet OPCODE beliefs and Soviet tactics in response to U.S. de-escalation during the downswing phase.)

With the exception of the 1961 Berlin crisis, there appears to be a consistent pattern of fairly strong linkages between selected Soviet OPCODE beliefs and those tactical crisis outcomes for which we have sufficient information to make a prediction. Lambda, which is calculated in this paper as an asymmetric statistic with outcome as the dependent variable, is a measure of association between the predictor variable and the outcome variable for each hypothesis. It is based on the modal frequency for a bivariate realtionship and varies between 0 and 1.0 (Garson 1971:163-65; Nie et al. 1975:225-26; McGaw and Watson 1976:268-71). Lambda increases as the predictive power of the predictor variable increases, although the predictions may not correspond to the ones that were hypothesized when the predictor variable was selected. If the Lambda value also predicts the hypothesized predictions, then the fit in the margin next to the hypothesis is "Yes." If the prediction is either random ($\lambda = .00$) or different from the hypothesized distribution, then the fit is "No." The modes in the margin next to the hypotheses are the modal outcome values for the hypothesized values of the predictor variables. If the mode falls into the hypothesized categories for the predictor variable, then the fit is "Yes." If not, then the fit is "No."[14]

Conclusion

Our analysis of the relationships among operational codes, crisis behavior, and crisis outcomes has yielded mixed results. The findings presented here are based on a relatively small number of cases and are consequently heuristic in nature. The congruence between OPCODE beliefs and crisis behavior is fairly high for the USSR, although there are some discrepancies when the data are disaggregated by crisis and phase. A similar pattern results from the analysis of congruence between U.S. OPCODE beliefs and crisis behavior. The linkages between OPCODE beliefs and crisis outcomes appear to be fairly strong for those cases where sufficient data are available to test these relationships. Perhaps the two main contributions of our analysis have been: (a) to demonstrate the feasibility of utilizing the operational code construct in the formulation and testing of falsifiable hypotheses with quantitative data; (b) to show how it may be possible to aggregate findings across several levels of analysis by linking OPCODE beliefs with systemic (dyadic) outcomes.

Some deviations in Soviet behavior from the precepts of the Bolshevik operational code, however, call into question the advisability of generalizing from individuals to groups. There are some potentially significant differences in the responsiveness of Stalin and Khrushchev to credible U.S. escalatory tactics. While Stalin responded cautiously in a manner consistent with the Bolshevik beliefs, Khrushchev tended to engage in high-risk, counterescalatory tactics. Perhaps the two leaders did not internalize the

Bolshevik belief system in an identical fashion, or maybe their image of the opponent differed significantly. There is some evidence to indicate that Khrushchev believed Kennedy's desire for peace, and his efforts to reach a settlement of the Berlin question during earlier negotiations made the president very susceptible to Soviet diplomatic and military pressure in Berlin (Hoagland 1978: 90; Slusser 1973:8, 129, 270; Dulles 1972:9, 13; Horelick and Rush 1965:xiv, 163, 167, 171, 186, 193).

Other deviations in Soviet and American behavior at different points within the Berlin crises may be attributable to the contextual effects of the crisis phase. The operational codes of both protagonists stress the necessity for firmness in dealing with one another, but the patterns for the two Berlin crises suggest that firmness and committal bargaining tactics are more typical behavior during the upswing phases. Some tendency for reciprocal de-escalation appears in the downswing phases. This conforms to the American belief system but violates the Bolshevik OPCODE. An examination of Soviet responses to those American tactics that demonstrate a commitment to de-escalate shows that Stalin was likely to reciprocate with a de-escalatory response, while Khrushchev was equally likely to escalate or de-escalate. The small number of cases makes it infeasible to control for the simultaneous effects of crisis, actor, and phase; however, the more bellicose response by Khrushchev to de-escalatory tactics is consistent with the evidence that he may have viewed Kennedy as "soft" on the Berlin question.

Finally, the escalatory U.S. responses to Soviet de-escalatory tactics during the upswing phases of the Berlin crises indicate that the crisis phase and a "hard" image of the opponent may be influential intervening variables in the belief systems of decision-makers who would otherwise prefer conciliatory tactics. This pattern and Khrushchev's aggressive behavior toward Kennedy reinforce the contention by George and Holsti (1974:49) that an actor's view of the nature of political life and especially his image of the opponent is likely to be a "master belief" in his operational code. In other words, this belief "is likely to constrain, if not dominate, other elements of the actor's belief system" (Holsti 1977:156). The belief by Kennedy and Truman that Soviet decision-makers would "push to the limit" perhaps realigned their instrumental OPCODE beliefs from a preference for conciliatory tactics to a committal approach to crisis management. Conversely, the belief that Kennedy was soft may have exaggerated the tendency by

Khrushchev to "push to the limit."

The trend noted by Leites (1964:196, 211) that Khrushchev and his Kremlin colleagues felt less constrained to push forward and even developed some propensity to make concessions is inconsistent with Khrushchev's tactics during the 1961 Berlin crisis. That trend may have developed somewhat later, perhaps in the aftermath of the Cuban missile crisis, due to a change in Khrushchev's image of Kennedy as a result of their confrontation in the Caribbean (Allison 1971:221-230). In any event, the tactics of Soviet and U.S. decision-makers during the Berlin crises suggest that the image of the opponent may qualify the impact on crisis behavior of more general beliefs about the nature of political life. It is possible that this variable may exacerbate the importance of certain already existing instrumental beliefs or perhaps even temporarily redefine the actor's instrumental beliefs regarding effective political tactics.

Notes

1. The defining assumptions of this model are: (a) the decision-maker(s) have complete information upon which to base their action (choice); (b) this information is not only complete but also perfect (accurate); (c) the decision-maker's information includes a consistent ordering of goals and objectives, plus the costs and benefits associated with all possible options with respect to these goals and objectives; (d) the decision-maker will select the alternative that maximizes his benefits and minimizes his costs; (e) if there is more than one decision-maker, i.e., the decision-making unit is a group, then they are identical (like-minded) with respect to conditions a, b, c, and d (see Holsti 1977:1; Allison 1971:28-38).

2. This model assumes that although the conditions associated with the rational actor model do not exist, a decision-maker will still try to maximize benefits and minimize costs within the limitations imposed by imperfect and incomplete information (see George 1969:197-98).

3. The sources for this inference include Leites (1951, 1953, 1964), George (1969), and other analyses. See Hoagland (1978:71-104).

4. This literature is reviewed by Holsti (1977) and reworked into a typology of operational codes.

5. The existence of these competing belief systems among JFK's advisors is noted by George and Smoke (1974:431-37); Yergin (1977) documents a similar distribution of views among key members of the Truman administration. There also exist some attempts on the cold war literature to formalize these beliefs into models for research purposes. See Welch (1970) and Gamson and Modigliani (1971).

6. For a discussion of this evidence, see Hermann (1972:286-91). The applicability of this assumption to the Soviet government is documented by Hoagland (1978:71). Paige (1968) and Allison (1971) document its applicability to the U.S. government. For our purposes, a crisis situation is defined to be one in which the threat to the goals of the participants is high and the possibilities for the use of military force are imminent. For a discussion of the existing definitions of crisis in the international politics literature, see Hermann (1972:3-17) and Walker (1977a:1-4). The extent to which operational codes can be attributed to groups and organizations as well as individuals is explored by Merton (1940), Tillema (1973), and Barnet (1973), who argue that members of bureaucracies often acquire similar world views, values, and response repertoires as they become socialized into their organizations.

7. The potential influence of other variables, such as perceptions of hostility by the participants within each crisis and variations in the structure of the international system across crises, is also omitted. For a review of the impact of hostile perceptions, see Sullivan (1976:53-57) and Hilton (1969). Snyder (1976) and Snyder and Diesing (1977) explore the impact of systemic structure, military capabilities, and goals on crisis behavior.

8. The two cooperative acts occurred in June 1948 and consisted of the U.S. release of the USSR commander after arresting him for speeding; the United States accompanied his release with an apology. Both the release and the apology were scaled by Corson as cooperative actions. In addition to these omissions, some conflict acts are omitted from this analysis of the Tanter-Corson data set. The pre-crisis and post-crisis events from the 1948 case were eliminated, since the focus of this research is on behavior during the crisis phases of international conflict. Operationally, this decision means that only events between June 7, 1948 and August 1, 1948 are included in the data for this paper. To obtain a comparable time period for the 1961 crisis, the data for this case cover the period between June 10, 1961 and September 12, 1961. Although this time-frame is slightly longer than the one for the 1948 case, its ending point corresponds to Tanter's cutpoint between the crisis and post-crises phases of the conflict. Its starting point also shares a characteristic with the starting point for the 1948 crisis. Each one marks a dramatic event or series of events. The 1961 date is when the USSR published their latest six-month ultimatum on Berlin. In 1948, the Soviets began the blockade of Berlin in early June, shortly after the West announced, on May 31, 1948, their agreement to unite West Germany. Finally, these time-frames encompass roughly the same number of coded moves, which make them statistically comparable: the 1948 case has 64 moves, 31 by West and 33 by East; the 1961 case has 54 moves, 27 by each bloc.

In coding these moves, a few events were discarded as unattributable to either actor or as meetings and not behaviors. The actors were West and East, defined as follows: West = the governments of USA, UK, FR, FRG, or West Berlin, plus their joint actions; East = the governments of USSR, POL, DRG, or East Berlin, plus their joint actions. We also decided to include actions by the allies of the U.S. and the USSR in calculating the behavioral indices presented here, although their decision-makers may not share the same OPCODE beliefs as their bloc leaders. The rationale for this decision is based on the existence of a small number of such actions in the Corson data set and the assumption that the bloc leaders exerted significant influence over the behavior of their allies during the crisis phases of the Berlin conflicts.

9. Where one actor (A) engaged in more than one type of behavior at more than one level of intensity on the Corson scale prior to the other actor's (B's) response, the following coding rules were applied to classify A's behavior on the ordinal scales in Figure 4. (1) If A engages in more than one type of behavior prior to B's response, but they are all either more intense than A's previous tactic or all less intense than B's previous tactic, then A's behavior is ranked by either the most intense or least intense behavior in its range of variety. If A's range of behavior is more intense than A's previous tactic, then A's most intense behavior is used to rank the entire range of behavior. If A's range of behavior is less intense than A's previous tactic, then A's least intense behavior is used for ranking purposes. (2) If A employs more than one type of behavior prior to B's response, and if this variety ranges in intensity both above and below A's previous tactic, then A's behavior is ranked by calculating a composite interval scale value for the range of A's behavior. The formula for the composite value of A's behavior is: (Highest $A^{Beh}{}_t - A^{Tactic}{}_{t-1}) - (A^{Tactic}{}_{t-1} -$ Lowest $A^{Beh}{}_t$) + Tactic $A^{Beh}{}_{t-1}$.

10. These nominal definitions of commitment, credibility, and risk do not exhaust the complexities suggested by these concepts. They do verbalize the assumptions associated with the operational definitions for the indices of commitment, credibility, and risk used in this chapter. For an extended discussion of these concepts, see Schelling (1960, 1966), Snyder and Diesing (1977), Milburn and Billings (1976), and Kirkpatrick et al. (1976).

11. Risk in this analysis is not equivalent to uncertainty. Rather, it refers to the probability of an undesirable outcome associated with a particular action. For a discussion of alternative definitions of risk in terms of uncertain and/or undesirable outcomes, see Milburn and Billings (1976); Kirkpatrick et al. (1976).

12. See Garson (1971:161-62), Nie et al. (1975:228-29), and Buchanan (1969:221-26) for brief discussions of the calculation and properties of Gamma and Somer's D. For a general discussion of the various criteria for selecting a statistical measure of association, see Galtung (1967:207-14) and Weisberg (1974).

13. The division of the two Berlin crises into phases follows Tanter (1974: 84-91) and McClelland (1972). The upswing phase corresponds to the chronological period within each crisis when the trend of conflict behaviors exchanged by the participants increases to peak intensity, while the downswing phase encompasses the chronological period when the exchange of conflict exhibits a downward trend. The turning point from upswing to downswing is

July 1, 1948 for the first Berlin crisis and August 15, 1961 for the second Berlin crisis (Tanter 1974:86-91).

14. For H2 in the 1961 Berlin crisis although λ = .00, the mode falls into the hypothesized category for the predictor variable. Consequently, we have assigned a "Yes" value to the fit between OPCODE beliefs and outcome.

References

Allison, G. "Conceptual Models and the Cuban Missile Crisis." *APSR* (September 1969), pp. 689-718.

———. *Essence of Decision*. Boston: Little, Brown, 1971.

Art, R. "Bureaucratic Politics and American Foreign Policy." *Policy Sciences* 4 (1973).

Axelrod, R. "Argumentation in Foreign Policy Settings: Britain in 1918, Munich in 1938, and Japan in 1970." *Journal of Conflict Resolution* (December 1977), pp. 727-744.

Barnet, R. *Roots of War*. New York: Atheneum, 1972.

Buchanan, W. *Understanding Political Variables*. New York: Charles Scribner's, 1969.

Corson, W. "Conflict and Cooperation in East-West Relations: Measurement and Explanation." Prepared for the Sixty-Sixth Annual Meeting of the American Political Science Association, Los Angeles, Calif., 1970.

Dulles, E. *The Wall: A Tragedy in Three Acts*. Columbia, S.C.: University of South Carolina Press, 1972.

Galtung, J. *Theory and Methods of Social Research*. New York: Columbia University Press, 1967.

Gamson, W., and A. Modigliani. *Untangling the Cold War*. Boston: Little, Brown, 1971.

Garson, G. *Handbook of Political Science Methods*. Boston: Holbrook Press, 1971.

George, A. "The Operational Code." *International Studies Quarterly* (June 1969).

———. "The Causal Nexus Between 'Operational Code' Beliefs and Decision-Making Behavior." Paper presented to the Annual Meeting of the International Studies Association. Washington, D.C., 1978.

George, A., and O. Holsti. Application for NSF Grant to Study Operational Codes of American Decision-Makers, 1974.

George, A., and R. Smoke. *Deterrence in American Foreign Policy*. New York: Columbia University Press, 1974.

George, A., D. Hall, and W. Simons. *The Limits of Coercive Diplomacy*. Boston: Little, Brown, and Company, 1971.

Hermann, C., ed. *International Crises*. New York: Free Press, 1972.

Hilton, G. "The 1914 Studies: A Re-assessment of the Evidence and Some Further Thoughts." *Peace Research Society (International) Papers* (1969).

Hoagland, S. "Operational Codes and the Analyses of International Crises: A Comparison of the Berlin Wall and Cuban Missile Crises." Tempe: Arizona State University, 1978.

Holsti, O. "The 1914 Case." *APSR* (June 1965).

———. "Foreign Policy Formation Viewed Cognitively." In *The Structure of Decision*, edited by R. Axelrod. Princeton University Press, 1976.

———. "The 'Operational Code' As an Approach to the Analysis of Belief Systems." Final NSF Report, Grant No. SOC 75-15-368. Durham: Duke University, 1977.

Hopmann, P. T., and T. C. Smith. "An Application of a Richardson Process Model: Soviet-American Interactions in the Test Ban Negotiations, 1962-1963." *Journal of Conflict Resolution* (December 1977), pp. 701-726.

Horelick, A., and M. Rush. *Strategic Power and Soviet Foreign Policy*. Santa Monica, Calif.: Rand Corp., 1965.

Jervis, R. *The Logic of Images in International Relations*. Princeton University Press, 1970.

———. *Perception and Misperception in International Politics*. Princeton University Press, 1976.

Kirkpatrick, S., D. Davis, and R. Peterson. "The Process of Political Decision-Making in Groups: Search Behavior and Choice Shifts." *American Behavioral Scientist* (September-October 1976).

Leites, N. *The Operational Code of the Politburo*. New York: McGraw-Hill, 1951.

———. *A Study of Bolshevism*. New York: Free Press, 1953.

———. "Kremlin Moods." *RM-3535-ISA* (January). Santa Monica, Calif.: Rand Corp., 1964.

McClelland, "The Beginning, Duration, and Abatement of International Crises." In *International Crises*, edited by C. Hermann. New York, Free Press, 1972.

McCormick, J. "Evaluating Models of Crisis Behavior: Some Evidence from the Middle East." *International Studies Quarterly* (March 1975).

McGaw, D., and G. Watson. *Political and Social Inquiry*. New York: John Wiley, 1976.

Merton, R. "Bureaucratic Structure and Personality." In *Reader in Bureaucracy*, edited by R. Merton. New York: Free Press, 1940.

Milburn, T., and R. Billings. "Decision-Making Perspectives from Psychology: Dealing with Risk and Uncertainty." *American Behavioral Scientist* (September-October 1976).

Nie, N., C. H. Hall, J. Jenkins, K. Steinbrenner, D. Bent. *SPSS*. 2nd ed. New York: McGraw-Hill, 1975.

Paige, *The Korean Decision*. New York: Free Press, 1968.

Ramberg, B. "Tactical Advantages of Opening Positioning Strategies: Lessons from the Seabed Arms Control Talks, 1967-1970." *Journal of Conflict Resolution* (December 1977), pp. 685-700.

Schelling, T. *The Strategy of Conflict.* Cambridge, Mass.: Harvard University Press, 1960.

———. *Arms and Influence.* New Haven, Conn.: Yale University Press, 1966.

Slusser, R. *The Berlin Crisis of 1961.* Baltimore: John Hopkins University Press, 1973.

Snyder, G. "Prisoner's Dilemma and Chicken Models of International Politics." *International Studies Quarterly* (March 1971).

———. "Crisis Bargaining." In *International Crises,* edited by C. Hermann. New York: Free Press, 1972.

———. "Conflict and Crisis in the International System." In *World Politics,* edited by J. Rosenau. New York: Free Press, 1976.

Snyder, R. et al. *Foreign Policy Decision Making.* New York: Free Press, 1962.

Snyder, R., and G. Paige. "The United States Decision to Resist Aggression in Korea." *Administrative Science Quarterly* 3 (1958).

Snyder, G., and P. Diesing. *Conflict Among Nations.* Princeton University Press, 1977.

Spier, H. *Divided Berlin.* London: Thames and Hudson, 1961.

Sullivan, M. *International Relations: Theories and Evidence.* Englewood Cliffs, N.J.: Prentice-Hall, 1976.

Tanter, R. *Modelling and Managing International Crises.* Beverly Hills, Calif.: Sage, 1974.

Tillema, H. *Appeal to Force.* New York: Thomas Y. Crowell, 1973.

Triska, J., and D. Finlay. *Soviet Foreign Policy.* New York: Macmillan Co., 1968.

Walker, S. "Comparative International Crisis Project Outline (CINCAP)," mimeographed. Arizona State University, 1976.

———. (1977a). "Committal and Conciliatory Tactics during the First and Second Berlin Crises." Prepared for the Annual Meeting of the International Studies Association, St. Louis, Mo., 1977.

———. (1977b). "The Interface Between Beliefs and Behavior; Henry A. Kissinger's Operational Code and the Vietnam War." *Journal of Conflict Resolution* (March 1977).

Weisberg, H. "Models of Statistical Relationship." *American Political Science Review* (December 1974).

Welch, W. *American Images of Soviet Foreign Policy.* New Haven, Conn.: Yale University Press, 1970.

Yergin, D. *Shattered Peace.* Boston: Houghton-Mifflin, 1977.

Zagare, F. "A Game–Theoretic Analysis of the Vietnam Negotiations." *Journal of Conflict Resolution* (December 1977), pp. 663-684.

Zinnes, D., R. North, and H. Koch. "Capability, Threat, and the Outbreak of War." In J. Rosenau (ed.) *International Politics and Foreign Policy,* edited by J. Rosenau. 1st ed. New York: Free Press, 1961.

7
National Role Conceptions and Systemic Outcomes

Stephen G. Walker

Introduction

A dominant theme in the post-behavioral era of scientific international relations research is the emphasis on policy-relevant subjects. For example, there is concern with topics of "global importance" such as international crises (Young 1977), resource scarcity (Pirages 1977), and ecological problems (Meadows et al. 1972); a preoccupation with forecasting as a research objective (Choucri 1976; O'Leary and Coplin 1975); an explicit reintroduction of normative goals in the research process (Snyder et al. 1976; Gillespie 1976). These developments are part of a larger movement whose dynamics can be observed in most of the fields of political science (Haas and Kariel 1970; Easton 1970).

Whatever its origins, there now exists a clear demand for policy-relevant theory as a product of scientific international relations research (George 1976; Smoke 1976). The distinguishing feature of this type of theory should be the incorporation of variables that can be controlled by policy makers in a productive fashion. Otherwise, the theory yields relatively sparse policy prescriptions. Unless the policy maker can control the political process, its vicissitudes become problematical in the same way that the weather is. One simply adapts to forces that are beyond one's immediate control, although they may be diagnosed, anticipated, and explained in a comprehensible fashion. Much of the scientific international relations theory (IR theory) that preceded the current emphasis on policy-relevant research yielded these insights.

This is a revised version of a paper prepared for delivery at the 1978 Annual Meeting of the International Studies Association, Washington, D.C., February 22-25, 1978.

These analyses focused on broad variations in national attributes, dyadic combinations of national traits, and the structural characteristics of different international systems (Sullivan 1976). With the exception of study of international crises, which has focused on the perceptions and behaviors of decision-makers within a mediated stimulus-response design (Holsti 1972) or a bureaucratic framework (Allison and 1971), there is relatively little in the scientific IR theory literature that deals with the analysis of short-run problems or the "routine" international behavior of nations.[1]

What policy makers could use is a theory of short-range political influence in the conduct of foreign policy and a scheme for monitoring the implementation of policy and the assessment of its results. There have been some attempts to provide such a theory. They have focused primarily on the interactions of diplomats and politicians in a bargaining or coalition-building context (George and Smoke 1974; Morgan 1977; Jervis 1970; Fisher 1969; Coplin, Mills, and O'Leary 1973; Allison and Halperin 1972; Franck and Weisband 1971). These efforts have generally been heuristic in nature, however, and have not been systematically applied to a large number of historical cases. Efforts to construct a scheme for monitoring the implementation of policy and the assessment of its results are virtually nonexistent. Without such a scheme, it is difficult to test those few theories of political influence that do exist in the IR literature in order to see if they are effective guides to productive political action.

In Figure 1 the outline of a foreign policy monitoring and assessment scheme is shown. It depicts three major levels of decision in the conduct of foreign policy, plus the range of systemic outcomes that flows from these levels in relationships between nations. The scheme encompasses what one analyst has identified as three conceptions of foreign policy: a cluster of orientations, a set of commitments and plans for action, and a form of behavior (Rosenau 1976:16-17). Various decision-making theories have focused on these three types of foreign policy decisions and attempted to identify their determinants. Foreign policy rhetoric has been scrutinized with the aid of various cognitive process approaches, including the operational code construct, psychoanalytical assessments, personality inventories, cognitive maps, and cybernetic concepts (George 1969; Holsti 1976; Axelrod 1976; Steinbrunner 1974). The use of organizational process and bureaucratic politics models has characterized the analysis of foreign policy programs (Allison and Halperin 1972). The study of foreign

FIGURE 1

A Levels-of-Decision Scheme for Monitoring and Assesing Foreign Policy

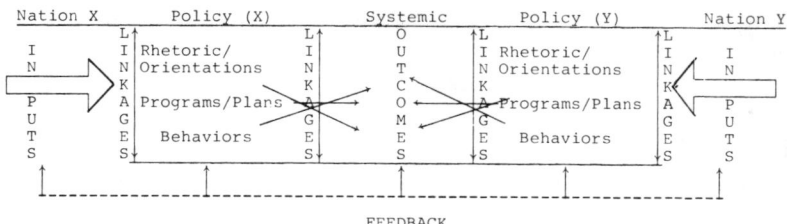

FEEDBACK

policy as behavior has occurred primarily within the framework of national attribute models (Sullivan 1976:102-42).

Although some IR theorists clearly recognize that the linkages among these various aspects of foreign policy are important, relatively little systematic research has been undertaken to explore their relationships—for a variety of reasons. These include theoretical or methodological reservations about previous efforts to identify linkages and the conclusion that the bureaucratic politics literature "has illustrated the many potential sources of slippage between executive decisions and the implementation of policy in the form of foreign policy actions" (Holsti 1976:22-33, 35). This conclusion is a more self-consciously theoretical restatement of the traditional IR scholar's contention that "the majority of foreign policy decisions are like Topsy—they just grow. They grow out of past policies, are molded somewhat in the bureaucratic (or other) machine, are heavily circumscribed by the logic of events" (Miller 1969:61; see also Hartmann 1973). As a result, the tendency is for each scholar to focus on one of these three levels of decision and trace its determinants to (a) societal inputs in the case of foreign policy as behavior; (b) organizational constraints in the case of foreign policy as programs; and (c) cognitive processes in the case of foreign policy as rhetoric.

Some attention has been given to the systematic analysis of the linkages between the levels of foreign policy decisions and international systemic outcomes in a theoretical context. The emphasis of the major new research in this direction is on forecasting, which is an outgrowth, methodologically, of the gaming and simulation literature (Alker and Brunner 1969), and on the development of deterministic mathematical models (Zinnes and Gillespie 1976). These studies are somewhat speculative, since they are either projections of trends for the future or solutions to equations whose parameters are set by the analyst. Their validity is therefore problematical until it is confirmed by events. Moreover, unless these research efforts reveal crucial variables under the control of policy makers, the results are not optimally useful for the conduct of foreign policy.

Although each theorist may tend to focus on one level of decision in the analysis of foreign policy, the policy maker tends to adopt a cross-level perspective. Diplomats and intelligence analysts in one nation record the rhetoric, programs, and behavior of another nation and attempt to compare these levels so their own government can adopt an appropriate policy. When a foreign policy is adopted, its authors try to make congruent the linkages among its rhetoric, programs, and behavior. There is also a periodic concern with assessing the effectiveness of the policy at various levels by focusing on policy (systemic) outcomes.

Consequently, it seems relevant to ask whether IR theorists have available a set of interrelated concepts that might aid the policy maker in monitoring and assessing the conduct of foreign policy. Since the process of policy making takes place in both an operational and a psychological environment (i.e., under both the actually existing circumstances of the moment and the circumstances perceived by the policymaker(s)), it would be desirable to employ a conceptual framework that bridges these analytical perspectives. Other desirable traits of such a network would include an analytical scope that encompasses systemic outcomes and lends itself to normative analysis as well as description and explanation.

At least four sets of candidates for this task already exist in the IR literature. They include the decision-making frameworks outlined by Snyder and Paige (1958) and Brecher et al. (1969) and developed by Paige (1968), Allison (1971), and Steinbrunner (1974), plus the linkage politics analyses of Rosenau (1969, 1970) and a somewhat similar type of framework developed by Hanrieder (1967a, 1967b). The international systems frameworks pioneered by Kaplan (1957) and Rosecrance (1963) and extended by Hopkins and Mansbach (1973: Chaps. 6 and 7) and Lampert et al. (1978) are a third set of candidates. The first two sets of approaches are amenable to normative analysis as well as description and explanation, and all three have the scope to encompass systemic outcomes as well as the decision-maker's psychological and operational environments. A fourth set of concepts are the ones associated with role theory, which has received relatively little attention from IR theorists (Holsti 1970; Wilkinson 1969; Wish 1977).

Role Theory and the Analysis of Foreign Policy[2]

The concept of role entered the social science literature from the theatre, where it referred to certain characters in a story rather than to the actors who played them. The utility of the role concept and its connotations for understanding "real" world behavior as well as behavior on the theatrical stage depends on the resemblance between the two arenas. In the discipline of social psychology, the focus is on the enactment of roles by persons in social settings. This focus includes a concern for the contribution of other actors to the enactment of the role. For example, do other individuals, groups, or organizations supply reinforcements for the role or do they deliver cues that elicit the enactment of another role (Sarbin and Allen 1968:489)?

There is also a definite normative component to role theory as it has been employed by social psychologists. They are interested in the answers to the following questions (Sarbin and Allen 1968: 490):

1. Is the conduct appropriate to the social position granted to or attained by the actor? That is, do his performances indicate that the actor has taken into account the ecological context in which the behavior occurs? In short, has he selected the correct role?
2. Is the enactment proper? That is, does the overt behavior meet the normative standards that serve as valuational criteria for the observer? Is the performance to be evaluated as good or bad?
3. Is the enactment convincing? That is, does the enactment lead the observer to declare unequivocally that the incumbent is legitimately occupying the position?

Finally, social psychologists and other scholars have adapted the role concept for use in the analysis of organizations. In an organization, programs are identified as a cluster of activities, premises, and constraints. The set of programs associated with the behavior of a particular individual in an organization is a role (Cyert and MacCrimmon 1968:576, 585).

The appropriateness of the role concept in policy analysis as a metaphor for "policy" is striking. A political actor's behavior in the political arena is supposed to complement his policy, just as a dramatic actor's behavior on the stage is intended to complement his role. More importantly, the development by social psychologists of role theory as a set of interrelated dimensions implicit in the concept of role is relevant to several dimensions of policy analysis. The incorporation of the contributions of other actors in role theory parallels those aspects of policy formation and implementation that are oriented toward the target of the policy. The normative component of role theory is applicable to the process of policy assessment. The adaptation of the role concept for the analysis of organizations is consistent with the focus on programs in policy analysis.

The application of role concepts to the description of foreign policy involves the following distinctions. The rhetorical component of foreign policy defines the normative criteria for the enactment of the role. This rhetoric articulates the goals, identifies the target nation, and delineates a cooperative or conflictual direction. Depending on the content of the issue area that the policy addresses, programs in several different government agencies may become engaged in the enactment of the role. The day-to-day execution of these programs is reflected in the stream of cooperative and conflictual behavior directed toward the target nation.

A particularly explicit example of this type of analysis appears in President Nixon's 1971 Report to the Congress, *U.S. Foreign Policy for the 1970's: Building for Peace*. Under the heading "The New American Role," the author(s) of this document introduce the Nixon Doctrine as the rhetorical expression of U.S. foreign policy for the 1970s. The Nixon Doctrine seeks "to place America's international commitments on a sustainable, long-term basis, to encourage local and regional initiatives, to foster national independence and self-sufficiency, and by so doing to strengthen the total fabric of peace" (Nixon 1969, cited in Nixon 1971:10). This statement represents the rhetorical expression of foreign policy at the most general level. The implication of this policy for individual nations occupies the remainder of the Nixon report to Congress. In the section "The Process of Implementation," the architects of the Nixon Doctrine recognize that, "Policy becomes clearer only in the process of translation into programs and actions." The bulk of the report and its successor, *U.S. Foreign Policy for the 1970's: The Emerging Structure of Peace* (1972), is devoted to documenting the Nixon Doctrine's implementation in the form of different programs and actions toward various nations and regions.

This example of the Nixon Doctrine illustrates and supports three important points that have already been asserted in this chapter. First, the scheme in Figure 1 for monitoring and assessing foreign policy does incorporate distinctions in the levels of foreign policy decisions that are recognized by policy makers themselves. Second, in their analyses, policy makers tend to adopt a cross-level perspective of foreign policy that extends from the rhetorical level through the relevant programs and behaviors that implement the policy as rhetoric. Third, the analogy between policy analysis and role analysis has face validity, which is recognized even by the author(s) of the Nixon reports to the Congress. Further evidence of the aptness of this analogy is supplied by comparing the normative questions from the role analysis literature with the tests of appropriateness applied to the Nixon Doctrine by its architects:

Question 1: Is the conduct appropriate to the social position granted to or attained by the actor? That is, do his performances indicate that the actor has taken into account the ecological context in which the behavior occurs? In short, has he selected the correct role?

Answer: Perception of the growing imbalance between the scope of America's role and the potential of America's partners thus prompted the Nixon Doctrine. It is the key to understanding what we have done during the past two years, why we have done it, and where we are going (Nixon 1971:10-11).

Question 2: Is the enactment proper? That is, does the overt behavior meet the normative standards that serve as valuational criteria for the observer? Is the performance to be evaluated as good or bad?

Answer: This [1972] Report is an accounting of ... [the reshaping of] American foreign policy. It is beyond dispute that we have made signal progress. Taken together, the initiatives of 1971 constitute a profound change in America's world role (Nixon 1972: 4).

Question 3: Is the enactment convincing? That is, does the enactment lead the observer to declare unequivocably that the incumbent is legitimately occupying the position?

Answer: Policy becomes clearer only in the process of translation into programs and actions. In this process the Nixon Doctrine seeks to reflect the need for continuity as well as the mandate for change. There are two concurrent challenges:

- to carry out our new policy so as to maintain confidence abroad.
- to define our new policy to the American people and to elicit their support.

This transition from bearing the principal burdens to invoking and supporting the efforts of others is difficult and delicate ... the method is crucial.... The challenge is not merely to reduce our presence, or redistribute our burden, or change our approach, but to do so in a way that does not call into question our very objectives. Others judge us—and set their own course—by the steadiness of our performance as well as the merit of our ideas (Nixon 1971:15).

The descriptive and normative characteristics of role theory appear to lend themselves to foreign policy analysis, but does role theory provide a scientific explanation of foreign policy? The answer to this question must remain tentative until further research provides more evidence. So too must the judgments regarding the descriptive and normative utility of role theory in the analysis of foreign policy. However, it is possible to sketch a preliminary outline of the explanation offered by role theory. In addition, there are some studies that have already explored this problem and yielded some data that can be used for a crude test of the explanatory power of role theory (Holsti 1970; Backman 1970).

As a scientific explanation of social phenomena, role theory tends to be conceptually rich and methodologically poor. It consists of a fairly elaborate set of concepts, but there is lacking a set of axiomatic "if ... then" propositions and operational definitions which would make it a paradigmatic theory in the Kuhnian sense. Consequently, it has served more as a conceptual framework within which scholars from various disciplines have conducted research using a variety of methodologies. Its explanatory value for the analysis of foreign policy is likely to take two forms. First, its concepts may perform the umbrella function of subsuming several middle-range research hypotheses about foreign policy under more general propositions, created by linking various concepts associated with role theory in a way that is consistent with these research hypotheses. Second, it may be possible to operationalize the concepts of role theory with a relatively rigorous methodology. If so, role theory may perform the heuristic function of generating testable explanatory hypotheses about various aspects of foreign policy (Backman 1970:310-11).

The diagram in Figure 2 outlines the explanation of foreign policy suggested by role theory. Variations in the conduct of foreign policy are a function of what role theorists would call the process of "role location." In the social psychology literature, the concept of role location is an inference process having to do with finding which role is appropriate in a particular situation (Sarbin and Allen 1968:489-90). Such inferences are determined by the actor from his repertoire of roles, which he has acquired from previous experience in similar situations. If it is a novel situation, then the actor may have to learn a new role or "muddle through" with one in his existing repertoire that is not completely appropriate. The matching of role with situation can be a rather complex inference process, in which the expectations associated with the various role in the actor's repertoire are compared with the cues and demands in the existing situation.

Role expectations, role cues, and role demands are the three sets of independent variables in role theory that determine an actor's selection and enactment of a role. The role theory literature provides fairly explicit distinctions among these variables. Role expectations refer to a set of cognitions pertaining to performance by any occupant of a social position in relation to occupants of other positions (complementary roles) in a social structure (Sarbin and Allen 1968:497-98, 506). These cognitions are formed as a result of an interaction between prescriptions previously communicated to the actor from other actors and the actor's own perceptions, values, and attitudes. Unless the prescriptions from others are highly authoritative and very specific, there is hardly ever a one-to-one correspondence between an actor's conception of his or her role and the expectations of other actors in complementary roles.

Role cues and role demands are variables in the actor's immediate situation which influence the selection and maintenance of a role. Cues are actions performed by others in the situation which either reinforce or discriminate against the enactment behavior

FIGURE 2
The Role Location Process

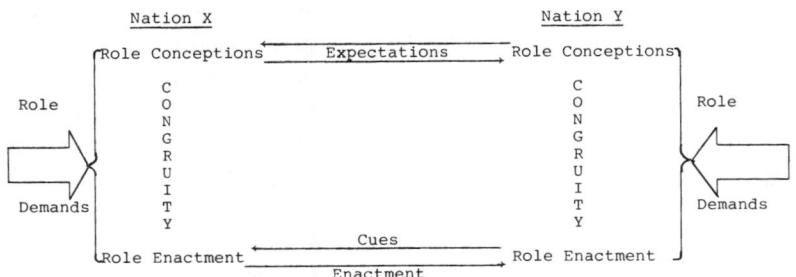

associated with a role initially selected by an actor.[3] Demands (such as the composition of the audience) are additional features of the situation that influence an actor's role selection and enactment. For two actors operating within a common culture, demands may be other cultural norms than the ones specifically associated with the role being selected or enacted, but ones which nevertheless modify the enactment of the role in a significant fashion. For example, face-saving norms or reciprocity norms may influence the actor to select one role rather than another or modify the enactment of a particular role (Sarbin and Allen 1968:510-11).

There may be competing demands in the environment. Cues may be ambiguous or contradictory, and expectations may be imperfectly understood or modified by the actor. Consequently, the process of role location is an uncertain one. As Sarbin and Allen (1968:491) point out, under such conditions:

> The actor must maintain a semblance of flexibility and be ready to take into account the probabilistic nature of interaction. . . . This is contrary to the unwarranted belief that role theorists regard human beings as operating on the basis of a pseudohomeostatic principle, seeking a perfect fit between role expectations and enactment. . . . Although the fiction may approach the reality in small, closed societies—for example, in a cloister of nuns—there are no instances where it can be seen as an accurate representation of the actual happenings within social organizations.

The uncertain complexity of role theory appears to account for both its conceptual richness and its lack of methodological rigor in comparison to other theories with simpler and perhaps more parsimonious sets of concepts.

Nevertheless, the conceptual complexity of role theory lends itself to the umbrella function of subsuming middle-range research hypotheses under the more general propositions that can be formulated with role concepts. For example, the distinctions between cues and demands could be used to organize research finding regarding the relative influence on policy of behavior by other actors versus other attributes of the situation. After distinguishing between domestic and international sources of cues and demands, it might be possible to make some useful generalizations about the relative potency of domestic versus international cues and demands on foreign policy at different levels of decision. This task would entail a systematic review of the existing literature, which deals separately with foreign policy as rhetoric, program, and behavior.

An alternative approach would be to formulate and test a general proposition from role theory—e.g., that there should be a congruent relationship between role conceptions and role enactments.[4] This task would involve the development of indices at least for role conceptions and role enactments, and perhaps also for role expectations, cues, and demands, Variations in the latter three sets of variables might explain deviations in the congruity between role conceptions and role enactments. In Figure 3 fifteen congruity and cue relationships available for monitoring and assessing the three levels of foreign policy decisions between two nations are presented. The congruity relationships within each nation link the various levels of decision in the foreign policy process. The cue relationships between the nations may be treated as a reciprocal stimulus-response process. Or the various cross-national relationships may be aggregated and treated as systemic (dyadic) outcomes.

There is congruity between an actor's role conception and his role enactment when the latter is judged as appropriate and convincing according to the norms provided by the former. In the role theory literature, this judgment is based on a qualitative analysis of the evidence available regarding role conceptions and role enactments. This analysis is more or less complicated, depending on whether more than one role is activated in the actor's repertoire of roles by the cues and demands in a social situation. If more than one role is evoked, there are three patterns of simultaneous enactment of multiple roles within a given time-frame (Sarbin and Allen 1968:538):

FIGURE 3

Fifteen Sets of Cross-Level Relationships for Monitoring and Assessing Foreign Policy

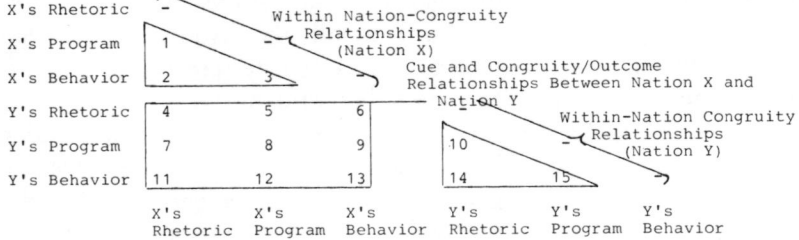

1. the alternation of two or more roles within the period of observation;
2. the merging of two or more roles so they are indistinguishable in terms of role enactment behavior within the period of observation;
3. the interpenetration of roles without their merger in behavioral terms within the period of observation.

These complicated patterns can make the congruity between multiple role conceptions and multiple role enactments difficult to judge.

Congruity in the cognitive dynamics literature has been operationalized in a quantitative fashion and demonstrated to be a special case of the principle of cognitive balance (Zajonc 1968: 354). Congruity exists between two elements when they correspond in direction and magnitude regarding a common trait; balance exists when they correspond in direction, that is, they have the same sign (+ or -) regarding a common trait.[5] The cognitive dynamics literature in social psychology has focused almost exclusively on the congruent relationships within an actor's cognitive structure (e.g., his repertoire of role conceptions). However, there may be an isomorphic relationship among elements of an actor's cognitive structure, elements of his behavioral structure, and elements of the social structure in which the actor is a member. In fact, these congruent relationships are the ones hypothesized by role theory to occur among role conceptions, role enactment, and the role expectations shared by the members of a social situation.[6]

Perhaps it is possible to adapt the operational methods for assessing congruence among elements of an actor's cognitive structure and use them to assess congruence among the cognitive, behavioral, and systemic components of role theory. There do exist some data, collected by IR theorists, which can test in a crude way the feasibility of this idea. Holsti (1970) has done a content analysis of the speeches by leaders from seventy-one nations. The results identify seventeen types of role conceptions which these leaders articulated during the period January 1965 to December 1967. Six of these types are cold war role conceptions, including faithful ally, antiimperialist agent, defender of the faith, bastion of the revolution, regional protector, and protectee. A few others reveal an unaligned orientation toward both regional and global politics: independent, active-independent, mediator-integrator, bridge, and isolate role conceptions fall into this category. In addition, there are some other role conceptions that are regionally directed or domestically oriented.[7]

The World Events Interaction Survey (WEIS) provides an inventory of the behaviors which the nations in the Holsti study directed toward one another between January 1966 and August 1969. From these two data sources we can extrapolate a set of nations with role conceptions and behaviors that can be used to test congruity among role conceptions, role expectations, and role enactments at two levels of analysis.[8] At the national level, the focus is on the correspondence between each nation's role conceptions in the Holsti study, the role enactment revealed by each nation's behaviors in the WEIS data, and the role expectations communicated to each nation as cues in the form of behavior received from other nations. At the systemic (dyadic) level, we can compare a dyad's "role set" and the interaction patterns created by the enactment of these roles in terms of their symmetry, stability, and congruity.[9]

The difficulties of combining the data from these two sources, plus the somewhat uneven coverage of all the nations in the world within each data set, make it necessary to extrapolate a relatively small number of cases for analysis. The criteria for selection are:

1. the inclusion of each nation in both data sets;
2. evidence that each nation participated in at least one exchange of behavior with both the United States and the Soviet Union;
3. the manifestation by each nation of either "cold war" or "unaligned" global role conceptions.

These criteria are intended to identify those nations in the data sets who expressed a rhetorical policy regarding their role in the cold war and who interacted with the leader of each block in that conflict. The number of nations which meet all of these criteria is forty-five, not counting the United States and the Soviet Union. Consequently, the total number of dyads for analysis is ninety: forty-five U.S./Nth nation dyads and forty-five USSR/Nth nation pairs.[10]

The cognitive dynamics literature has identified several properties of cognitive structures with regard to a given empirical referent. These include differentiation, complexity, unity, organization, prominence, and valence (Zajonc 1968:328). Of these attributes, valence—the overall orientation toward the referent generated by the cognitive structure—is the one most easily operationalized with the role conception data in a manner consistent with the role enactment data. Both data sets contain items that can be coded as either pro–United States and anti–Soviet Union, or pro–Soviet Union and anti–United States. In addition, the role conception data include neutral items regarding these two referents. Consequently, the valence of each nation's cognitive orientation toward the superpowers depends on the distribution and frequency of its role conceptions, whether pro, neutral, or anti regarding each superpower. The valence of each nation's behavioral orientation toward the superpowers depends on the distribution and frequency of its cooperative (pro) and conflict (anti) behavior toward the United States and the Soviet Union.

The construction of indices from these items is a somewhat arbitrary process. The operational definition of a "general impression" (i.e., the valence for a set of cognitive elements) has taken two simple forms, averaging and summation, as well as a variety of more complex forms in the cognitive dynamics literature (Zajonc 1968:324). In this test of the congruity principle for role theory, the indices that appear in Figure 4 will be used. The direction and stability of the valence for each nation's cold war role conceptions are arrived at by taking the percentage difference between the frequency of cooperative (pro) and conflict (anti) role conceptions and dividing it by one plus the frequencey of unaligned role conceptions which a nation displays toward the United States and the Soviet Union.[11] This algorithm identifies the degree to which pro or anti role conceptions dominate foreign policy as rhetoric, which is discounted by the neutralist (unaligned) role conceptions. The direction and stability of the role enactment's valence are found in the percentage difference between the frequency of cooperative

FIGURE 4

Indices of National and Systemic Variables Derived from Role Theory

Indices	Range
$RCV = \left[\dfrac{COOP-CONF}{COOP+CONF}\right] \times \dfrac{1}{1+NEU} \times 100$	-100 to +100
$REV = \left[\dfrac{COOP-CONF}{COOP+CONF}\right] \times 100$	-100 to +100
$NEUT = \dfrac{NEU}{COOP+CONF+NEU} \times 100$	0 to 100 (Maximum NEUT)
$SYM_{RCV} = ABS\ (A\text{'s}\ RCV_{ABS} - B\text{'s}\ RCV_{ABS})$	0 to 100 (Maximum Asymmetry)
$STAB_{RCV} = \dfrac{RCV_A + RCV_B}{2}$	-100 to +100
$CONG_{RCV} = ABS \left[\dfrac{(RCV_A - RCV_B)}{2}\right]$	0 to 100 (Maximum Incongruity)
$SYM_{REV} = ABS\ (A\text{'s}\ REV_{ABS} - B\text{'s}\ REV_{ABS})$	0 to 100 (Maximum Asymmetry)
$STAB_{REV} = \dfrac{REV_A + REV_B}{2}$	-100 to +100
$CONG_{REV} = ABS \left[\dfrac{(REV_A - REV_B)}{2}\right]$	0 to 100 (Maximum Incongruity)

RCV = Role Conception Valence; REV = Role Enactment Valence; COOP = Frequency of cooperative role conceptions in RCV and NEUT indices and frequency of cooperative behavior in REV index; CONF = Frequency of conflict behavior in REV index; NEU = Frequency of neutral, unaligned role conceptions; Neut = Neutralist orientation; SYM = the symmetry of a dyadic relationship; STAB = The stability of a dyadic relationship; CONG = The congruity of a dyadic relationship; ABS = The absolute (unsigned) value of a variable or an expression; A = One member of a dyad; B = The other member of a dyad.

(pro) and conflict (anti) behavior directed to the United States and the USSR. This index is intended to estimate the degree to which pro or anti role enactment dominates foreign policy as behavior for each nation.

The role conceptions of the forty-five nations in this study are not coded explicitly with respect to targets. Consequently, it is necessary to develop some coding rules in order to infer the targets of the role conceptions. The author of the role conception data set identifies six cold war role conceptions (Holsti 1970). They are double-coded for the analyses in this paper. Each of the pro-U.S. role conceptions is assigned a plus (+) value equal to its frequency for the U.S./Nth nation analysis and a minus (−) value equal to its frequency for the USSR/Nth nation analysis. Each of the pro-USSR role conceptions is coded with a plus (+) value equal to its frequency for the USSR/Nth nation analysis and a minus (−) value equal to its frequency for the U.S./Nth nation analysis.

The cold war role conceptions of the United States and the USSR are coded as plus (+) frequencies toward their respective bloc members and as minus (−) frequencies toward the members of the other superpower's bloc. Toward members of the neutralist bloc each superpower's role conceptions are coded as plus or minus frequencies, depending on the target's role conceptions. For example, if a neutralist bloc member espouses a "bastion of the revolution" role conception, then U.S. cold war role conceptions are assigned minus frequencies toward that nation, and USSR cold war role conceptions toward that nation are given plus frequencies.[12]

In addition, "developer," "internal development," and "regional/subsystem collaborator" role conceptions are included in the calculation of each nation's valence. The "developer" role conceptions are included as plus frequencies in each superpower's valence toward those members of its own bloc that articulate "internal development" role conceptions and toward those members of the neutralist bloc that express "internal development" role conceptions. The "internal development" role conceptions of Eastern and Western bloc members are assigned plus frequencies toward their respective superpowers. The "internal development" role conceptions of neutralist bloc members are given plus frequencies toward both superpowers. The "regional/subsystem collaborator" role conceptions are included as plus frequencies in the calculation of the valences for each member of the dyads formed by each superpower and those nations from their respective regions who are also members of their blocs. For the United States the region is the Western Hemisphere. The relevant region for the Soviet Union is Eastern Europe. The inclusion of these three role conceptions is intended to adjust for events related to these role conceptions and included in the role enactment data. They cannot be removed, because the events are not coded according to issue (policy) area. Consequently, the role conception valences are calculated on the basis of intermingled "cold war, developer, internal development, and regional/subsystem collaborator" frequencies to compensate for role enactment valences based on similarly intermingled event frequencies.

Other indices in Figure 4 describe various aspects of the interaction relationships established by the U.S./Nth nation and USSR/Nth nation dyads. The *symmetry* of the role conceptions relationship is measured by the difference between the absolute values of the role conception scores for each Nth nation/superpower dyad. The symmetry of the role enactment relationship for each Nth nation/superpower dyad is estimated by the difference between the absolute values of their respective role enactment scores. The symmetry indices describe the distribution of the contributions by dyad members to the dyadic relationship. The *stability* of the interaction relationships for the dyad's role conceptions and role enactments is calculated by summing the role conception and role enactment scores, respectively. The sum of the role conception valences indicates the stability of the role expectations between the members of each dyad.

The sum of the role enactment valences for each pair of nations measures the stability of the cues exchanged between each member of the role set. These sums indicate stability by calculating how much change in policy one member of the dyad would have to initiate by calculating how much change in policy one member of the dyad would have to initiate in order to shift the direction of the relationship unilaterally. The index that measures the *congruity* of the dyad's role conception and role enactment valences is the absolute value of the differences in the valences. This value measures the distance between the roles as they are conceived and enacted by each of the dyads.

The proper operationalization of the concept of congruity is open to debate at both the national and systemic levels of analysis. It is possible to have cases where the combination of valence scores has congruent signs, e.g. (+ +) or (– –), even though the distance between the values of these valence scores may be very great. Similarly, although a (+ –) combination has incongruent signs, the distance between the valence scores may be less than the distance between the scores of two valences with the same sign. In the social psychology literature, this problem is handled by distinguishing between a balanced relationship (same signs) and a congruent relationship; the latter is a special case of balance in which the signs and the values of the dyadic relationship are identical.

Consequently, in the following hypotheses there is a distinction between "balance" and "congruity" as two forms of "correspondence" between role conception and role enactment at both the national and the dyadic levels of analysis. The hypotheses at the national level test the congruity between the valence of each nation's role conception and the valence of its role enactment toward each superpower. The hypotheses at the systemic (dyadic) level test the association between role conception and role enactment regarding the properties of symmetry, stability, and congruity. Finally, there are hypotheses at the national level regarding role enactment toward both superpowers simultaneously.

National Level Hypotheses

Axiom I. There tends to be a correspondence between a nation's foreign policy as rhetoric and a nation's foreign policy as behavior.

Theorem A. There tends to be a balanced relationship between the valence of a nation's role conception and the valence of a nation's role enactment.

H1. There tends to be a *balanced* relationship between the valence of a nation's role conception and the valence of a nation's role enactment toward the USA.

H2. There tends to be a *balanced* relationship between the valence of a nation's role conception and the valence of a nation's role enactment toward the USSR.

H3. There tends to be a *balanced* relationship between the valence of a nation's role enactment toward the USA and the valence of a nation's role enactment toward the USSR.

H4. There tends to be a *balanced* relationship between the valence of the U.S. role conception and the valence of the U.S. role enactment toward an Nth nation.

H5. There tends to be a *balanced* relationship between the valence of the USSR role conception and the valence of the USSR role enactment toward an Nth nation.

Theorem B. There tends to be a congruent relationship between the valence of a nation's role conception and the valence of a nation's role enactment.

H1. There tends to be a *congruent* relationship between the valence of a nation's role conception and the valence of a nation's role enactment toward the USA.

H2. There tends to be a *congruent* relationship between the valence of a nation's role conception and the valence of a nation's role enactment toward the USSR.

H3. There tends to be a *congruent* relationship between the valence of a nation's role enactment toward the USA and the valence of a nation's role enactment toward the USSR.

H4. There tends to be a *congruent* relationship between the valence of the U.S. role conception and the valence of the U.S. role enactment toward an Nth nation.

H5. There tends to be a *congruent* relationship between the valence of the USSR role conception and the valence of the USSR role enactment toward an Nth nation.

Systemic (Dyadic) Level Hypotheses

Axiom II. There tends to be a correspondence between the rhetorical and the behavioral levels of dyadic interaction.

Theorem A. The more symmetrical the dyad's role conception valence, the more symmetrical the dyad's role enactment valence.

H1. The greater the *symmetry* of the role conception valence for the USA/Nth nation dyad, the greater the *symmetry* of the role enactment valence for the USA/Nth nation dyad.

H2. The greater the *symmetry of the role conception* valence for the USSR/Nth nation dyad, the greater the *symmetry* of the role enactment valence for the USSR/Nth nation dyad.

Theorem B. The more stable the dyad's role conception valence, the more stable the dyad's role enactment valence.

H1. The greater the *stability* of the role conception valence for the USA/Nth nation dyad, the greater the *stability* of the role enactment valence for the USA/Nth nation dyad.

H2. The greater the *stability* of the role conception valence for the USSR/Nth nation dyad, the greater the *stability* of the role enactment valence for the USSR/Nth nation dyad.

Theorem C. The more congruent the dyad's role conception valence, the more congruent the dyad's role enactment valence.

H1. The greater the *congruity* of the role conception valence for the USA/Nth nation dyad, the greater the *congruity* of the role enactment valence for the USA/Nth nation dyad.

H2. The greater the *congruity* of the role conception valence for the USSR/Nth nation dyad, the greater the *congruity* of the role enactment valence for the USSR/Nth nation dyad.

Theorem D. There tends to be a balanced relationship between the stability of a dyad's role conception valence and the stability of a dyad's role enactment valence.

H1. There tends to be a *balanced* relationship between the stability of the role conception valence for the USA/Nth nation dyad and the stability of the role enactment valence for the USA/Nth nation dyad.

H2. There tends to be a *balanced* relationship between the stability of the role conception valence for the USSR/Nth nation dyad and the stability of the role enactment valence for the USSR/Nth nation dyad.

The definitions of balance and congruity in national-level hypotheses IA-H3 and IB-H3 are different from their definitions in the remaining balance and congruity hypotheses. These two hypotheses address triadic relationships among the USA, the USSR, and an Nth nation, whereas the other hypotheses focus on dyadic relationships either between an Nth nation and a superpower or between the role conception valence and the role enactment valence of a given set of nations. According to the rules of interpretation for cognitive theories of balance, a dyadic relationship is balanced if relations between the dyads are either all positive or all negative. However, a triad is balanced when all three relations are positive or when two relations are negative and one is positive (Zajonc 1968:339-45; see also Holsti 1966:346-48). For the cold war triads formed by the USA, the USSR, and the Nth nations in this study, the USA/USSR relationship is given as negative. Consequently, the signs of the Nth nation/superpower relationships must be mixed in order for the triads to be balanced. For these two relationships to be congruent, there should be an inverse relationship between the magnitude of their valences. These alternatives are diagrammed in Figure 5.[13]

In role theory, the concepts of role strain and role conflict account for incongruity between role conception and role enactment. Role strain is a cognitive property: the felt difficulty of fulfilling role expectations. The other concept, role conflict, refers to two sources of role strain. Role conflict occurs when honoring

FIGURE 5

Balanced Relationships Between Any Nation (N) and One or Both Super-Powers

Balanced Dyads   Balanced Triads

one expectation calls for behavior that violates another expectation. This latter expectation may be attributed to the same role as the former expectation, or it may be the property of another role in the actor's repertoire of roles. In the first case, there is *intrarole* conflict, and in the second instance, *interrole* conflict (Sarbin and Allen 1968:539-44; Backman 1970:314-15).[14] In the cognitive dynamics literature, congruity between the perceptions of two actors toward a third object assumes reciprocity in the attitudes of each actor toward the other. Investigations of this assumption to account for felt tension in role-playing experiments have found that balance assumes reciprocity for cases where the reciprocal bonds are positive as well as negative. Reciprocity, therefore, appears to be a necessary condition for balance and also a necessary condition for congruity, to the extent that the latter is a special case of balance (Zajonc 1968:351, 354).

The concepts of role strain and role conflict and the principle of reciprocity suggest some control variables that can be used in testing national balance and congruity hypotheses. These variables are the cues provided to the Nth nation by the role conception and role enactment valences of each superpower. Regarding the balance and congruity between an Nth nation's role conception and its role enactment toward a given superpower (IA-H1 and IA-H2; IB-H1 and IB-H2), a lack of balance and congruity may be a function of the cues provided by the rhetoric and the actions directed toward the Nth nation by that superpower. If such a relationship shows up in the data, it may indicate the presence of role strain experienced by the policy makers of the Nth nation. In this instance, role strain would result from interrole conflict. For example, if the valence of an Nth nation's role conceptions calls for a conflictual role enactment toward the United States, but the valence of U.S. behavior toward the Nth nation is predominately cooperative, then the policy makers of the Nth nation may instead implement cooperative behavior toward the United States. This response would violate the expectations associated with the Nth nation's role conception and make the role conception and role enactment incongruent.

From the perspective of the superpower, whose behavior is a source of cues, the selection of incongruent behavior by the Nth nation could be an example of successful "altercasting." This process can occur because of the reciprocal nature of role relations. Theoretically, one member of a role set can select a role and behave toward the other such that the latter has to adopt and enact a role which is advantageous to the former (Backman 1970: 313). In this case, the superpower's actions may be designed to elicit a cooperative response from the Nth nation by casting it in a cooperative role through the cues transmitted by the superpower's behavior. To test for the existence of altercasting directly, it would be necessary to have longitudinal data that contained changes in the superpower's role conception valence and role enactment valence, followed by changes in the Nth nation's role conception and role enactment valences. The data sets presented here do not lend themselves to longitudinal analysis. Therefore, the possibility of altercasting can only be hypothesized as an explanation for a superpower cue that is associated with imbalance and incongruity between the role conception and the role enactment valences of an Nth nation.

Regarding the hypotheses of balance and congruity (IA-H3 and IB-H3) with respect to an Nth nation's behavior toward both superpowers, the rhetoric and/or actions of each superpower toward the Nth nation are control variables that may account for the absence of balance and congruity. According to the principle of triadic balance, if the valence of each superpower toward the other is negative (conflictual), or at least perceived that way by the Nth nation's policy makers, then the valences of the Nth nation's behavior toward each superpower should be mixed—that is, positive toward one and negative toward the other. However, if the rhetoric and the actions of both superpowers toward the Nth nation are the same, then the Nth nation's behavior toward them cannot be simultaneously reciprocal toward each superpower and balanced (congruent) toward both of them. Here again is a situation in which cues are presented that could disrupt the congruent relationship between an Nth nation's role conceptions and its role enactment toward the superpowers. The exceptions would be where the Nth nation's role conceptions are neutral, positive, or negative toward both superpowers.

In this data set there are no instances in which an Nth nation has a positive role conception valence toward both superpowers and only two cases (China and Albania) that have negative role conception valences toward both the United States and the USSR. Consequently, there is a possibility for the remaining forty-three nations in this study to experience role strain if both superpowers behave identically toward any of them. The ability of each nation to cope with this contingency may be related to the strength of the neutralist orientations among its policy makers. In fact, regardless of each superpower's behavior toward an Nth nation, variations in the latter's neutralist orientations may affect the congruity of its role enactment valences towards the superpowers. If so, then it is reasonable to hypothesize that three types of variables, the neutralist orientations of the Nth nation, the rhetoric of each superpower, and the behavior of each superpower toward the Nth nation, may affect the congruity of the Nth nation's behavior toward the other two members of the triad.

To introduce these control variables in the analysis, it is necessary to create an index of the variation in neutralist orientations across the forty-five nations in this study. The neutralist index for each nation will be its frequency of unaligned role conceptions (independent, active-independent, mediator-integrator, bridge, and isolate) divided by its total number of cold war and unaligned role conceptions. The indicators of superpower rhetoric and behavior toward each nation will be the valences of each superpower's role conception and role enactment toward an Nth nation. At this point it is desirable to restate Axiom I's research hypotheses by incorporating one or more of these control variables. Whether the original or the reformulated versions of these propositions are more plausible will depend on the results of the data analysis and further testing by other scholars with other data.

Revised Hypotheses

> IA-H1. There tends to be a *balanced* relationship between the valence of a nation's role conception and the valence of a nation's role enactment toward the United States, unless that balance is undermined by cues from the U.S. role conception and role enactment valences.
>
> IA-H2. There tends to be a *balanced* relationship between the valence of a nation's role conception and the valence of a nation's role enactment toward the USSR, unless that balance is undermined by cues from the USSR role conception and role enactment valences.
>
> IA-H3. There tends to be a *balanced* relationship between the valence of a nation's role enactment toward the USA and the valence of a nation's role enactment toward the USSR, unless that balance is undermined by cues from the role conceptions and role enactments of the superpowers and/or unless the nation has a strong neutralist orientation.

IA-H4. There tends to be a *balanced* relationship between the valence of the U.S. role conception and the valence of the U.S. role enactment toward an Nth nation, unless that balance is undermined by cues from the Nth nation's role conception and role enactment valences.

IA-H5. There tends to be a *balanced* relationship between the valence of the USSR role conception and the valence of the USSR role enactment toward an Nth nation, unless that balance is undermined by cues from the Nth nation's role conception and role enactment valences.

IB-H1. There tends to be a *congruent* relationship between the valence of a nation's role conception and the valence of a nation's role enactment toward the United States, unless that congruence is weakened or reversed by cues from the U.S. role conception and role enactment valences.

IB-H2. There tends to be a *congruent* relationship between the valence of a nation's role conception and the valence of a nation's role enactment toward the USSR, unless that congruence is weakened or reversed by cues from the USSR role conception and role enactment valences.

IB-H3. There tends to be a *congruent* relationship between the valence of a nation's role enactment toward the United States and the valence of a nation's role enactment toward the USSR, unless that congruence is weakened or reversed by cues from the role conceptions and role enactments of the superpowers and/or unless the nation has a strong neutralist orientation.

IB-H4. There tends to be a *congruent* relationship between the valence of the U.S. role conception and the valence of the U.S. role enactment toward an Nth nation, unless that congruence is weakened or reversed by cues from the Nth nation's role conception and role enactment valences.

IB-H5. There tends to be a *congruent* relationship between the valence of the USSR role conception and the valence of the USSR role enactment toward an Nth nation, unless that congruence is weakened or reversed by cues from the Nth nation's role conception and role enactment valences.

Analytical Procedures and Findings

The procedures for testing the national and systemic-level propositions include the use of bivariate and multivariate Pearsonian correlation analysis for both the balance and the congruity hypotheses. The zero-order and partial correlation coefficients that summarize the results of this analytical procedure can vary between −1.0 and +1.0 as measures of association. The analysis involves the following steps. First, the bivariate and multivariate hypotheses regarding congruity, symmetry, and stability relationships will be tested with Pearsonian correlation analysis. Second, the bivariate and multivariate balance hypotheses will be tested with Pearsonian correlation analysis on the same data in trichotomized form (−1, 0, +1), so only the signs and not the magnitudes are correlated. Third, the national-level hypotheses will be tested on the range of cases identified as possessing balanced relationships from an inspection of their signs. These results will be compared with a similar analysis of imbalanced cases.

In the social psychology literature, the congruity principle has failed to achieve its potential for predicting the magnitude of a relationship, yet the balance principle has been relatively successful in attaining its more modest goal of predicting the direction of a relationship (Zajonc 1968:345-59). The implementation of the first two steps makes possible a comparison between the results of congruity and balance interpretations of the same data. The completion of all three steps in the data analysis permits a comparison of the empirical implications of two conceptualizations of congruity. In step one, congruity is defined as the absolute distance between two variables, regardless of their signs. In step three, congruity is defined as a special case of balance in which the magnitudes of two balanced variables are highly correlated.

Step 1. The relationships between role conception and role enactment valences for the two superpowers and the other forty-five nations are summarized in Table 1. These relationships are not particularly strong, but there are some interesting comparisons between the role congruity of the superpowers and the role congruity of the other nations. The superpowers tend to have greater congruence between rhetoric and behavior than the rest of the nations, whose role enactments tend to be influenced by the behavior of the superpowers as much or more than by their own role conceptions. However, the superpowers themselves tend to be rather sensitive to the expectations of the targets of their behavior. Even in the case of the United States, where the target's role conceptions are eliminated from the analysis due to multicollinearity, the collinearity is between U.S. role conceptions and the target's

TABLE 1

Congruity Relationships Between Role Conception and Role Enactment Valences for All Nations

N=45 Actor/Target	Pearson's Correlations Zero-Order r's* Congruity	Partial Correlations Controls for Cues/Expectations Target's Behavior/Target's Conception		Variance		
				Explained[a]	Revised[b]	(Exp – Rev)[c]
Nth/US	+.27	+.21	---**	.07	.04	.03
Nth/USSR	+.37	+.20	+.25	.14	.06	.08
US/Nth	+.50	+.48	---**	.25	.23	.02
USSR/Nth	+.44	+.35	+.29	.19	.10	.09

* If r ≥ .30, then p < .05 for both zero and partial r's.

** --- Multicolliniarity precludes use of this variable in either the analysis of the partials or the variance.

[a] The explained reduction in the variance measures the congruity between role conception and role enactment valences without taking the effects of cues (target's behavior) and expectations (target's conception) into account.

[b] The revised reduction in the variance measures the congruity between role conception and role enactment valences after the effects of cues (target's behavior) and expectations (target's conception) are removed. It is the square of the partial correlation when all eligible control variables are introduced into the analysis.

[c] (Explained minus Revised) variance is the reduction in the variance between role conception and role enactment valences that should be attributed to the target's cues and expectations ceteris paribus.

role conceptions.[15] It is, therefore, plausible to interpret U.S. role enactment as a response to the expectations associated with the target's role conceptions as well as to the expectations associated with U.S. role conceptions.

The congruity between role enactment valences toward both superpowers for all forty-five nations is basically random and not attributable to the masking effects of cues or expectations from either superpower. There is also no significant contribution to this relationship from variations in the neutralist orientations of these nations (see Table 2). At the systemic (dyadic) level, the pattern is essentially the same. Relatively little correspondence exists between the rhetorical and behavioral interaction patterns for the forty-five U.S./Nth nation dyads and the forty-five USSR/Nth nation dyads. The only exception is the correspondence between the stability of these two dyadic relationships, which tends to be relatively high compared to the correspondence of symmetrical and congruous properties for these dyads (see Table 3).

Step 2. The relationship between role conception and role enactment valences for the two superpowers and the other forty-five nations does not change substantially when the relationship is examined for balance rather than congruity. Although they do tend to be balanced, the relationships between the direction of rhetoric and behavior are actually weaker than the relationships between the magnitudes of rhetoric and behavior (see Tables 1 and 4).

The analysis of balance between the role enactment valences for these nations toward both superpowers appears in Table 5, while the balance between the rhetorical and behavioral interaction patterns for the U.S. and USSR dyads is reported in Table 6. The balance relationships in these two tables also follow the patterns of their counterparts in the earlier congruity analysis. There is a random pattern to the balance relationship between the role enactment valences of these nations toward the superpowers, just as there was earlier for the congruity relationship (see Tables 2 and 5). At the systemic (dyadic) level, balance between rhetorical and behavioral interaction is again more likely for the property of stability than for the properties of symmetry or congruity (see Tables 3 and 6).

Step 3. When congruity is defined as a special case of balance— i.e., when balance is postulated as a necessary but not sufficient condition for congruity to exist—the results are rather dramatic. The partition of the forty-five cases into two groups, balanced and imbalanced, reveals some striking differences in the congruity

TABLE 2

Congruity Relationship Between Role Enactment Valences For
All Nations Toward Both Superpowers

Nth/Superpowers Role Enactment Congruity	N = 45 Zero-Order Pearson's r*	Partial Correlations Controlling for Expectation, Cues and Dispositions				Variance**	
		Conceptions US	Enactments USSR US USSR		Neutralist Orientations	Explained	Revised (Exp − Rev)
Coefficents	+.19	+.22 +.17	+.23	+.09	+.19	.04 .01	.03

* If r ≥ .30, then p ≤ .05 for both zero-order and partial r's.

** See note in Table 7.1 for definition of explained and revised variance

TABLE 3

Congruity Between the Rhetorical and Behavioral Levels
of Dyadic Role Interaction for All Dyads

N = 45 Correspondence	US Dyads			USSR Dyads		
	Symmetry	Stability	Congruity	Symmetry	Stability	Congruity
Pearson's r*	+.21	+.46	−.29	−.03	+.43	−.01
Explained Variance (r^2)	.04	.21	.08	.00	.19	.00

* If r ≥ .30, then p < .05

TABLE 4

Congruity Relationships Between Role Conception and
Role Enactment Valences for All Nations

N = 45 Actor/Target	Pearson's Correlations Zero-Order r's* Congruity	Partial Correlations Controls for Cues/Expectations Target's Behavior/Target's Conception		Variance Explained	Variance Revised (Exp - Rev)
Nth/US	+.25	+.22	---**	.06	.05	.01
Nth/USSR	+.24	+.15	---**	.06	.02	.04
US/Nth	+.27	+.24	---**	.07	.08	.01
USSR/Nth	+.37	+.29	---**	.14	.08	.06

* If r ≥ .30, then p < .05 for both zero-order and partial r's.

** See notes in Table 7.1 for definitions of explained and revised variance.

** --- Multicollinearity precludes use of this variable in either the analysis of the partials or the variance.

TABLE 5

Congruity Relationship Between Role Enactment Valences
for All Nations Toward Both Superpowers

Nth/Superpowers N = 45 Role Enactment Zero-Order Congruity Pearson's r*	Partial Correlations* Controlling for				Neutralist Dispositions Orientations	Variance**		
	Expectations Conceptions†		Cues and Enactments			Explained	Revised	(Exp − Rev)
	U.S.	USSR	U.S.	USSR				
Coefficients −.08	−.07	−.05	−.10	−.04		.01	.00	.01

* If $r \geq .30$, then $p < .05$ for both zero-order and partial r's.

** See notes in Table 7.1 for definitions of explained and revised variance.

† The U.S. and USSR role conceptions are treated as one variable because of their multicollinearity. The −.07 correlation is calculated with the values for Soviet role conceptions because they are skewed in the same direction as the other variables in the analysis.

TABLE 6

Congruity Between the Rhetorical and Behavioral Levels
of Dyadic Role Interaction for All Dyads

N = 45 Correspondence	U.S. Dyads			USSR Dyads		
	Symmetry	Stability	Congruity	Symmetry	Stability	Congruity
Pearson's r*	+.18	+.37	−.13	+.03	+.40	+.06
Explained Variance (r^2)	.03	.14	.02	.00	.16	.00

* If $r \geq .30$, then $p < .05$

relationships and the influence of cues or expectations on the nations and dyads in each group. For those nations whose rhetoric and behavior are balanced toward a particular superpower, the congruity between rhetoric and behavior is very high and not influenced much by cues from that superpower. Similarly, in those instances where there is a balanced relationship between the role conception and role enactment of a superpower toward a target nation, the congruity of these two valences is also quite strong and is not influenced much by cues or expectations from the target (see Table 7). Congruity is also strong for nations with balanced role enactment valences toward both superpowers (see Table 8), and the correspondence betweeen rhetorical and behavioral interaction for dyads with balanced stability relationships is also very high (see Table 9).

For nations with an imbalanced relationship between role conception and role enactment valences toward a superpower, the accompanying incongruity is influenced by cues and expectations from the superpowers. The partial correlations in Table 10 imply that superpower behavior perhaps moderates the incongruity between role conception and role enactment valences for Nth-actor/superpower-target combinations, while superpower rhetoric tends to exacerbate the incongruity. In contrast, for those cases in Table 10 where an imbalanced relationship exists between a superpower's role conception and role enactment valences, the accompanying incongruity relationship is a random one that is not traceable to the influence of the target's cues or expectations. Nations with role enactment valences that do not balance toward both superpowers also possess role enactment valences whose magnitudes toward both superpowers are highly correlated in an incongruent way. This pattern is independent from the cues and expectations provided by the superpowers and from each nation's own neutralist orientations (Table 11). Finally, for imbalanced dyads, there is a weak inverse relationship between the stability of a dyad's rhetorical interaction pattern and the stability of its behavioral interaction pattern. The strength of this relationship for USSR dyads is understated, because for those cases the distributions of the role conception and role enactment valences are skewed in opposite directions (Table 12).

Conclusion

The results of this analysis should be viewed with some caution and even skepticism. The number of cases is small enough to make

TABLE 7

Congruity Relationships Between Role Conception and
Role Enactment Valences for Balanced Nations

		Pearson's Correlations Zero-Order r's	Partial Correlations		Variance*		
Actor/Target	N	Congruity	Controls for Cues/Expectations Target's Behavior/Target's Conception		Explained	Revised	(Exp - Rev)
Nth/US	(23)	+.78**	+.72**	---***	.61	.52	.09
Nth/USSR	(26)	+.73**	+.63**	---***	.53	.40	.13
US/Nth	(23)	+.94**	+.93**	---***	.88	.87	.01
USSR/Nth	(27)	+.83**	+.75**	+.79**	.69	.53	.16

* See notes in Table 7.1 for definitions of explained and revised variance

** p = .001

*** --- Multicollinearity precludes the use of this variable either in the analysis of the partials or the variance.

TABLE 8

Congruity Relationship Between Role Enactment Valences
Which Balance Toward Both Superpowers

Nth Superpowers Role Enactment Congruity	N = 19 Zero-Order Pearson's r**	Partial Correlations** Controlling for Expectations, Cues and Dispositions						Variance*	
		Conceptions		Enactments		Neutralist Orientations		Explained Revised	(Exp – Rev)
		US	USSR	US	USSR	US	USSR		
Coefficients	r = -.66	---***	-.70	-.69	-.64		-.61	.44 .53	.00

* See note in Table 7.1 for definitions of explained and revised variance.

** Both zero-order and partial r's have p < .01

*** --- Multicollinearity precludes the use of this variable in either the analysis of the partials or the variance.

TABLE 9

Correspondence of Rhetorical and Behavioral Stability
for Role Interaction Between Balanced Dyads

Correspondence	N = 25 Stability N = 28	
	US Dyads	USSR Dyads
Pearson's r	+.88*	+.80*
Explained Variance (r²)	.77	.64

*p = .001

TABLE 10

Incongruity Relationships Between Role Conception and
Role Enactment Valences for Imbalanced Nations

Actor/Target	N	Pearson's Correlations Zero-Order r's Congruity	Partial Correlations Controls for Cues/Expectations Target's Behavior/Target's Conception		Variance* Explained Revised		(Exp - Rev)
Nth/US	(22)	-.69***	-.70***	-.49***	.48	.29	.19
Nth/USSR	(19)	-.33	-.37	-.12	.11	.01	.10
US/Nth	(22)	+.17	+.17	+.19	.03	.06	.00
USSR/Nth	(18)	+.05	-.08	-.07	.00	.02	.00

* See notes in Table 7.1 for definitions of explained and revised variance

** p < .05

*** p = .001

203

TABLE 11

Incongruity Relationships Between Role Enactment Valences
Which Do Not Balance Toward Both Superpowers

Nth Superpowers	N = 23			Partial Correlations** Controlling for				
Role Enactment	Zero-Order			Expectations, Cues and Dispositions				Variance*
Congruity	Pearson's r**			Conceptions	Enactments	Neutralist		
				US USSR	US USSR	Orientations	Explained Revised	(Exp − Rev)
Coefficients	r = +.86			+.86 +.85	+.87 ---***	+.85	.74 .71	.03

* See note in Table 7.1 for definitions of explained and revised variance.

** Both zero-order and partial r's have p = .001

*** --- Multicollinearity precludes the use of this variable in either the analysis of the partials or the variance.

TABLE 12

Correspondence of Rhetorical and Behavioral Stability
for Role Interaction Between Imbalanced Dyads

Correspondence	N = 20 Stability N = 17	
	US Dyads	USSR Dyads
Pearson's r	−.31	−.16
Explained Variance (r^2)	.10	.03

*p > .10

the correlation coefficients very sensitive to measurement errors. There are also problems with evaluating the validity of the role conception valence scores for the superpowers. The coding rules for determining those scores involved inferences based partly on the content of the target's role conceptions, which no doubt contributed to the multicollinearity problems in some of the tables. This coding procedure also resulted in little variability in the distribution of valence scores for superpower role conceptions in some instances.[16]

In addition to these weaknesses there are some broader validity issues. These include the question of the impact of variables at the program level of foreign policy decisions that could intervene between the rhetoric of role conceptions and the behavior of role enactments to qualify or reverse these findings. There is also the question of whether the aggregation and correlation of rhetoric and behavior by means of an overall valence index obscures more than it reveals. The correlation of role conceptions and role enactment behaviors in a disaggregated form, by issue area, and longitudinally by nation and dyad, might be more enlightening.

Nevertheless, this exercise has demonstrated that some important foreign policy questions can be investigated by using a combination of concepts from role theory and methods inspired by the cognitive dynamics literature. By counterbalancing the normative notion of appropriate role behavior with the measurement of congruity from the cognitive dynamics literature we can identify two groups of nations: those nations with balanced, congruent foreign policies and those nations with imbalanced, incongruent foreign policies. In principle, the ability to make this distinction with aggregate data should also carry over to lower levels of aggregation, such as issue areas or individual nations. Unfortunately, limitations in the data sets for this analysis hinder the pursuit of these refinements using these data.

The ability to make a distinction between coherent and incoherent foreign policy across several levels of foreign policy decisions demonstrates the potential descriptive and normative utility of role theory in monitoring and assessing the conduct of foreign policy. Its explanatory utility and its potential for providing policy makers with a policy-relevant theory are less clear. The fact that role theory focuses on cues and expectations as sources of influence on a nation's foreign policy may eventually produce empirical generalizations that can be translated into short-term policy prescriptions.

Lastly, we must look at the value of role theory as an analytical tool for linking individual and systemic generalizations. Ideally, such linkages should be isomorphic conceptually and involve a minimum loss of information empirically. In this investigation, the concepts of valence and congruity have been used to aggregate and link the attitudes of policy makers with their behaviors and with selected triadic and dyadic relationships. The axioms and research hypotheses have been stated as congruent relationships in fairly isomorphic terms, within the limits imposed by shifts from national to international levels of analysis and across different levels of decision within each nation. The concept of valence has been operationalized at each of these levels so its indices could be used to represent aggregations of role conceptions, role enactments, and the outcomes of several sets of roles. If these analyses had been based on data sets collected explicitly for these purposes, it probably would have been possible to conduct them with little or no information loss—by retaining the capability to disaggregate and aggregate across several levels of generalization. Ultimately, the potential value of role theory as an analytical tool for linking individual and systemic generalizations is high.

Notes

1. Another exception may be the international/transnational integration and functionalist literature, which tends to focus on the "routine" or "low" politics of economic issues rather than the "high" politics of strategic issues. See Hoffman (1966) and Lindberg and Scheingold (1970).

2. The following exposition of role theory relies heavily on the summary and critique of the relevant literature in the discipline of social psychology by Sarbin and Allen (1968).

3. An important source of cues and expectations in addition to the target is the audience. Sarbin and Allen (1968:527) point out that, "Though the dyad is usually considered to be the unit of analysis of role theory—a role and its complementary role—more refined analysis would suggest a triad. Use of a triad would give explicit recognition to the importance of the audience in the formulation of the ongoing role-enactment process."

4. The nouns "congruity and congruence," and the adjectives "congruous and congruent" are used interchangeably to minimize the necessity of repetitious language. They all refer to "correspondence," denoting a "close fit" or "match-up" when two items are compared.

5. The calculation of balance is less straightforward when the number of

elements increases to the triadic level and beyond. However, the mathematics have been worked out in the form of graph theory (Zajonc 1968:342-45).

6. Research by social psychologists has not uncovered isomorphic relationships between a cognitive structure and the social structures that serve as referents in the formation of the cognitive structure (Zajonc 1968:327-39).

7. The identification of cold war roles and their relationships with other national roles are discussed by Holsti (1970:289-94).

8. There is some overlap between time-frames for the role conception data set and the events data set which, strictly speaking, violates the requirement of temporal precedence for making causal inferences between role conceptions and international behavior. Also, the source for the WEIS data is the aggregation of conflict and cooperative acts extrapolated from the WEIS data and reported by McGowan and O'Leary (1975).

9. The totality of complementary roles related to a given role is a *role set* (Sarbin and Allen 1968:498).

10. These nations include Canada, Cuba, Brazil, Britain, Holland, Belgium, France, Switzerland, West Germany, East Germany, Poland, Hungary, Czechoslovakia, Italy, Albania, Yugoslavia, Bulgaria, Rumania, Finland, Sweden, Guinea, Ghana, Congo (Kinshasha), Tanzania, Ethiopia, Morocco, Algeria, Tunisia, Iran, Turkey, Iraq, Egypt, Syria, Lebanon, Israel, Afghanistan, China (Peking), Japan, India, Pakistan, Ceylon, Cambodia, Malaysia, Indonesia, and Australia.

11. Each of these role conceptions is coded separately for the analysis of each nation's behavior toward the United States and the USSR, respectively. Cooperative role conceptions toward the United States are coded as conflictual ones toward the USSR, while cooperative role conceptions toward the USSR are coded as conflictual toward the United States.

12. Membership in the Western, Communist, and neutralist blocs is determined by Burton's (1965:214) classifications for the nations in this data set, which are based on military alliances with each superpower for Western and Communist bloc membership and participation in conferences of nonaligned states for neutralist bloc membership. See also McGowan and O'Leary (1975).

13. Although this calculation of balance is consistent with the mathematics of graph theory, it is interesting to note that initial studies of traidic relations by social psychologists assumed a completely negative triad to be balanced too. See Zajonc (1968:338-42).

14. See also Holsti (1970:301-04), who recognizes these concepts in a somewhat cursory fashion, lumping them together under the rubric of role incompatibility. Backman (1970:315) distinguishes between role conflict and role competition as sources of incongruity between role conceptions and role enactments. Role competition occurs when "actions taken to honor one expectation compete in time and resources with actions necessary to meet another expectation." This phenomenon may occur even when honoring one expectation does not violate another expectation, which is the distinguishing feature of role conflict.

15. The cutpoint for intolerable collinearity between independent variables in this paper is $r \geq .70$.

16. To minimize some of the possible distorting effects which this lack of variability and potential for multicollinearity can produce, the findings are reported with a two-tailed test of significance, rather than a one-tailed test, and a multicollinearity threshold of .70 rather than .80 is employed.

References

Alker, Hayward, and R. D. Brunner. "Simulating International Conflict: A Comparison of Three Approaches." *International Studies Quarterly* (March 1969), pp. 70-110.

Allison, Graham. *Essence of Decision.* Boston: Little, Brown, 1971.

Allison, Graham, and Morton Halperin. "Bureaucratic Politics: A Paradigm and Some Policy Implications," In *Theory and Policy in International Relations*, edited by Raymond Tanter and Richard Ullman, pp. 40-79. Princeton University Press, 1972.

Axelrod, Robert. *Structure of Decision.* Princeton University Press, 1972.

Backman, Carl. "Role Theory and International Relations." *International Studies Quarterly* (September 1970), pp. 310-319.

Brecher, Michael, M. A. Steinberg, and J. Stein. "A Framework for Research On Foreign Policy Behavior." *Journal of Conflict Resolution* (March 1969), pp. 75-101.

Burton, Charles. *International Relations: A General Theory.* London: Cambridge University Press, 1975.

Choucri, Nazli. "From Correlation Analysis to Computer Forecasting: Evolution of a Research Program." In *Search of Global Patterns*, edited by James Rosenau, pp. 81-90. New York: Free Press, 1976.

Coplin, William, Stephen Mills, and Michael O'Leary. "The PRINCE Concepts and the Study of Foreign Policy." In *Sage International Yearbook of Foreign Policy Studies*, vol. 1, edited by Patrick McGowan, pp. 1-85. Beverly Hills, Calif.: Sage, 1973.

Cyert, Richard, and Kenneth R. MacCrimmon. "Organizations." In *The Handbook of Social Psychology*, 2nd ed., vol. 1, edited by Gardner Lindsey and Eliot Aronson. Reading, Mass.: Addison-Wesley, 1968.

Easton, David. "The New Revolution in Political Science." In *Approaches to the Study of Political Science*, edited by Michael Haas and Henry Kariel, pp. 511-529. Scranton, Pa.: Chandler Publishing Company, 1970.

Fisher, Roger. *International Conflict for Beginners.* New York: Harper and Row, 1969.

Franck, Thomas, and Edward Weisband. *Verbal Strategy Among the Superpowers.* New York: Oxford University Press, 1971.

George Alexander. "Bridging the Gap between Theory and Practice." In *In Search of Global Patterns*, edited by James Rosenau, pp. 114-119. New York: Free Press, 1976.

———. "The Operational Code: A Neglected Approach to the Study of Political Decision-Making." *International Studies Quarterly* (June 1969), pp. 190-222.

George, Alexander, and Richard Smoke. *Deterrence in American Foreign Policy.* New York: Columbia University Press, 1974.

Gillespie, John. "Optimal Control Theory: A Promising Approach for Future Research." In *In Search of Global Patterns*, edited by James Rosenau, pp. 235-245. New York: Free Press, 1976.

Haas, Michael, and Henry Kariel. *Approaches to the Study of Political Science.* Scranton, Pa.: Chandler Publishing Company, 1970.

Hanrieder, Wolfram (1967a). "Compatibility and Consensus: A Proposal for the Conceptual Linkage of External and Internal Dimensions of Foreign Policy." *American Political Science Review* (September 1967).

———.(1967b). *West German Foreign Policy, 1949-1963.* Stanford University Press, 1967.

Hartmann, Frederick. *The Relations of Nations.* 4th ed. New York: Macmillan, 1973.

Hoffmann, Stanley. "Obstinate or Obsolete: The Fate of the Nation-State and the Case of Western Europe." *Daedelus* (Summer 1966), pp. 862-916.

Holsti, K. J. "National Role Conceptions in the Study of Foreign Policy." *International Studies Quarterly* (September 1970), pp. 233-309.

Holsti, Ole. "Foreign Policy Formation Viewed Cognitively." In *Structure of Decision,* edited by Robert Axelrod, pp. 18-54. Princeton University Press, 1976.

———. *Crisis, Escalation, War.* Montreal: McGill-Queens University Press, 1972.

———. "External Conflict and Internal Consensus: The Sino-Soviet Case." In *The General Inquirer: A Computer Approach to Content Analysis*, edited by Phillip J. Stone et al., pp. 343-358. Cambridge, Mass: The M.I.T. Press, 1966.

Hopkins, Raymond, and Richard Mansbach. *Structure and Process in International Politics.* New York: Harper and Row, 1973.

Jervis, Robert. *The Logic of Images in International Relations.* Princeton University Press, 1970.

Kaplan, Morton. *System and Process in International Politics.* New York: John Wiley, 1957.

Lampert, Donald, Lawrence Falkowski, and Richard Mansbach. "Is There An International System?" *International Studies Quarterly* (March 1978), pp. 143-166.

Lindberg, Leon, and Stuart Scheingold. *Europe's Would-Be Polity.* Englewood Cliffs, N.J.: Prentice-Hall, 1970.

McGowan, Patrick, and Michael K. O'Leary. "Methods and Data for the Comparative Analysis of Foreign Policy." In *International Events and Comparative Analysis of Foreign Policy,* edited by Charles W. Kegley Jr. et al. Columbia, S.C.: University of South Carolina Press, 1975.

Meadows, Donella, Dennis L. Meadows, Jorgen Renders, and William W. Behrens. *The Limits of Growth.* New York: Universe Books, 1972.
Miller, T. B. "On Writing About Foreign Policy." In *International Politics and Foreign Policy*, edited by James Rosenau, pp. 57-64. New York: Free Press, 1969.
Morgan, Patrick. *Deterrence: A Conceptual Analysis.* Beverly Hills, Calif.: Sage, 1977.
O'Leary, Michael, and William Coplin. *Quantitative Techniques in Foreign Policy Analysis and Forecasting.* New York: Praeger, 1975.
Nixon, Richard. *U.S. Foreign Policy for the 1970's: The Emerging Structure of Peace.* A Report to the Congress. Washington, D.C.: U.S. Government Printing Office, 1972.
———. *U.S. Foreign Policy for the 1970's: Building for Peace.* A Report to the Congress. Washington, D.C.: U.S. Government Printing Office, 1971.
Paige, Glenn. *The Korean Decision.* New York: Free Press, 1968.
Pirages, Dennis, ed. "International Politics of Scarcity." *International Studies Quarterly* (December 1977), Special Issue.
Rosecrance, Richard. *Action and Reaction in World Politics.* Boston: Little, Brown, 1963.
Rosenau, James. "The Study of Foreign Policy." In *World Politics*, edited by James Rosenau, Kenneth Thompson, and Gavin Boyd, pp. 15-35. New York: Free Press, 1976.
———. "Foreign Policy As Adaptive Behavior." *Comparative Politics* (April 1970), pp. 365-387.
———. ed. *Linkage Politics.* New York: Free Press, 1969.
Sarbin, Theodore, and Vernon Allen. "Role Theory." In *The Handbook of Social Psychology*, 2nd ed. vol. 1, edited by Gardner Lindzey and Eliot Aronson, pp. 488-567. Reading, Mass.: Addison-Wesley, 1968.
Smoke, Richard. "Theory for and about Policy." In *In Search of Global Patterns*, edited by James Rosenau, pp. 185-191. New York: Free Press, 1976.
Snyder, Richard C., Charles F. Hermann, and Harold K. Lasswell. "A Global Monitoring System: Appraising the Effects of Government on Human Dignity." *International Studies Quarterly* (June 1976), pp. 221-260.
Snyder, R., and Glenn Paige. "The United States Decision to Resist Aggression in Korea." *Administrate Science Quarterly* 3 (1958).
Steinbrunner, John. *The Cybernetic Theory of Decision.* Princeton University Press, 1976.
Sullivan, Michael. *International Relations: Theories and Evidence.* Englewood Cliffs, N.J.: Prentice-Hall, 1976.
Wilkinson, David. *Comparative Foreign Relations.* Belmont, Calif.: Dickenson Publishing Company, 1969.
Wish, Naomi. "Relationships between National Role Conceptions and Foreign Policy Behavior." Prepared for delivery at the annual meeting of the International Studies Association, St. Louis, March 16-20, 1977.

Young, Robert, ed. "International Crisis: Progress and Prospects for Applied Forecasting and Management." *International Studies Quarterly* (March 1979), Special Issue.

Zajonc, Robert. "Cognitive Theories in Social Psychology." In *The Handbook of Social Psychology*, 2nd ed., vol. 1, edited by Gardner Lindzey and Eliot Aronson, pp. 320-411. Reading, Mass.: Addison-Wesley, 1968.

Zinnes, Dina, and John Gillespie, eds. *Mathematical Models in International Relations.* New York: Praeger, 1976.

8
Elite Values and Foreign Policy Analysis: Preliminary Findings

Gerald W. Hopple

Overview

At least implicitly, the classical political philosophers Plato, Aristotle, Machiavelli, Locke, Hobbes, Rousseau, and Marx were all "psychopoliticists." Theories from political philosophy incorporate a number of assumptions about human nature, national character, the impact of personality characteristics, and other phenomena that can be housed within the domain of political psychology. In contrast, Thucydides, one of the earliest students of foreign policy strategy, can be viewed as an embryonic rational choice theorist (Hernes 1977).

This tension between psychologistic interpretations of statecraft and rationalistic postulates has recurred in discourse about international relations and foreign policy. Rational actor presuppositions have coexisted with Freudian and other depth-psychological models of world politics. In modern political science, Lasswell's (1930, 1948) seminal work has provided the foundation for a series of explorations of the nexus between psychology and politics.

Early critics of the "war begins in the minds of men" conflict-resolution school questioned the relevance of psychology to the study of international relations. The most common criticism invoked the criteria of "theoretical parsimony and research economy" (Holsti 1976:125; see also Bonham 1975): variance in international behavior can allegedly be accounted for by employing other clusters of determinants; psychological factors are thus superfluous.

A more reasonable question is not are psychological variables relevant, but how successfully do such factors explain behavior compared to other clusters? Advocates of relative potency testing (e.g., Hopple et al. 1977; Rosenau 1966; Wilkenfeld et al. 1978a) attempt to ascertain the explanatory contributions of sets of determinants. An early example of this genre of research juxtaposed role against individual-level or belief-set variables (Rosenau 1968; Stassen 1972).

The other dominant theme in empirical research involves efforts to specify the interaction patterns of clusters of factors (East et al. 1978; Powell et al. 1974). The ultimate application of this strategy entails the construction and testing of causal models of foreign policy behavior. Psychological variables would be among the inputs to a causal model, although the paucity of cross-national, individual-level data has precluded this approach.

Across-the-board relevance is a sterile question when one recalls that the psychological domain features sets of phenomena. Hermann (1977, 1978) groups the phenomena into four basic clusters. The types include: beliefs, motives, decision style, and interpersonal style.

Beliefs constitute the decision-maker's basic assumptions about the world and various aspects of it. Motives refer to basic needs and the reasons for action (see Winter and Stewart 1977). Decision style features preferred methods of making decisions. Confidence, preference for certain levels of risk, and preference for compromise exemplify the decision style realm. Interpersonal style refers to characteristic modes of dealing with others. Paranoia and Machiavellianism are two personality constructs that represent ways of interacting with others.

The Hermann scheme neglects certain types of variables and provides no criteria for distinguishing unambiguously among some of the categories. A more inclusive scheme posits three distinct types of factors: (1) psychodynamic analysis; (2) the personality trait approach; and (3) belief systems.

1. Psychodynamic reconstructions of personality and behavioral patterns refer to determinants that operate at a deep level within the policy maker's personality system. Psychodynamic or psychobiographical analyses are generally elaborate, in-depth psychological case studies, which explain the genesis and describe the dynamics of operative patterns in the individual's personality. The classic example of this genre of inquiry is the monumental George and George (1964) study of Woodrow Wilson.

2. Considerable empirical research has accrued on the personality traits of decision-makers. Here the concern is not with the genesis of personality processes and dispositions; the analyst

simply attempts to identify and measure key personality traits or characteristics. The latter are then employed as predictors of policy preferences or behavioral choices. The research of Hermann (1974, 1978) and Etheredge (1978) exemplifies this perspective.

3. What is a belief system? Consensus on the definition of this multifunctional, elastic term is far from unanimous. A panoply of competing concepts has also been employed: Brecher (1968) refers to the decision-maker's world view; George (1969) and McLellan (1969) discuss operational codes; Burgess (1968) examines elite images and strategic images; Winham (1970) focuses on the decision-maker's image of the situation; Axelrod (1972) simply discusses beliefs.

In general terms, a belief system consists of affective, cognitive, and conative concepts (Bonham and Shapiro 1977:57). Affective concepts are propositions with valences; Bonham and Shapiro classify policy objectives here. Cognitive concepts consist of beliefs about reality. Conative or "behavioral" concepts refer to the alternatives from which a decision-maker selects a policy recommendation.

Any belief system consists of a potentially infinite number of discrete elements. By definition, a *belief* system contains a set of propositions (statements about reality, predictions about the future, preferred events and outcomes, basic goals); the set ranges from specific beliefs ("The United States is allied with Britain") to higher-order end-states ("National security is essential").

A belief *system* is also an organized entity. An ideological belief system is tightly and coherently organized or constrained; the structuring is deductive in the sense that knowledge of higher-level elements (such as a preference for liberalism or conservatism) permits the observer to infer lower-level phenomena (such as specific policy preferences) with a degree of accuracy that departs very significantly from chance expectations.

Measurement of "mapping" of belief systems generally occurs via some form of content analysis. Alternatives include: computer simulation (Abelson and Carroll 1965; Bonham and Nozica 1976); in-depth interviews (Lane 1962); direct interviews and questionnaires (Semmel 1975, 1976).

Value Analysis

The Belief Systems Approach

Obstacles to data access invariably impose serious restrictions on the use of content analysis as a technique for the comparative study of decision-maker belief systems. Aside from the plethora of problems that plague any content analytic effort, there is the obvious limitation that only official, public documents can be employed. Private statements would undoubtedly be preferable, but such sources are unavailable to cross-national researchers.

The major issue that must be resolved is the choice of specific phenomena to measure in the cross-national content analytic research context. Attempts to map out the belief systems of dozens of foreign policy decision-makers would be excessively expensive and time-consuming. A belief system consists of at least several distinct subsystems and a potentially staggering number of discrete elements or propositions (such as statements about reality and other beliefs).

In order to avert the danger of a costly and ultimately unproductive "fishing expedition," it is necessary to adopt a framework for analyzing belief systems. Such a framework is provided by the belief system and value system research of Rokeach (1973).[1]

Rokeach's (1960) initial emphasis on the structural properties of belief systems was an outgrowth of his interest in ideological dogmatism and authoritarianism. In *Beliefs, Attitudes, and Values* (1968a), he extended his analysis of belief systems in an effort to incorporate other components. A belief system "represents the total universe of a person's beliefs about the physical world, the social world, and the self" (Rokeach 1968a:123). An attitude is one type of subsystem of beliefs; ideology is an organization of beliefs and attitudes shared with others and derived from external authority (Rokeach 1968a:123-24). The concept of organization or structuring is central to Rokeach's approach. Beliefs are organized within an attitude, attitudes within an attitude system, and all beliefs, attitudes, and values within a cognitive system (Rokeach 1968a:117, 162-63).

The value concept receives primary attention in Rokeach's *The Nature of Human Values*. The author asserts that each individual has a fairly small number of values (1973:3). Values can be subdivided into instrumental and terminal categories; terminal values are personal or social in nature; the instrumental category subsumes moral and competence values (Rokeach 1973:6-8). Values and value systems function as standards for action and general plans for conflict-resolution and decision-making (Rokeach 1973: 13-14).

A value is an enduring belief that a specific mode of conduct or end-state of existence is personally or socially preferable to an opposite or converse mode of conduct or end-state of existence. A value system is an enduring organization of beliefs concerning preferable modes of conduct or end-states of existence along a continuum of relative importance (Rokeach 1973:5).

Values, then, are basic orientations that structure perceptions and reactions. As Rokeach (1973:23-24) notes, culture, institutional socialization, and personal experience shape values, and values determine social attitudes, ideology, and behavior. Value differences that relate to attitude responses in diverse content domains provide impressive support for this proposition (see Rokeach 1973, Chapter 4). In an ingenious experiment on long-term attitude and value change, Rokeach (1973:263-71) offers more direct evidence that value change precedes attitude change.

Research on mass or elite belief systems will yield incomplete and distorted maps if the topography is not adequately described. The following guiding generalizations can be offered at this point: all individuals have belief systems; all belief systems include belief, attitude, and value subsystems; these subsystems are interrelated.

The value subsystem of a belief system emerges as a logical focus for cross-national content analysis. Values can be measured fairly easily; Rokeach's list of terminal values can be applied in diverse contexts. The value profiles of major institutions can be measured, as Rokeach (1975) demonstrated in his research on the institution of science. Values and value rankings can thus be obtained from individuals (through questionnaires and surveys) and from institutions (through content analyses of pertinent documents and sources).

Research Design

Figure 1 locates the value analysis technique in the context of an inclusive map for research on elite and social psychological phenomena (see Hopple 1978). The focus is on the psychological subdomain. Within that cluster, the specific emphasis is the belief system. In terms of the trilogy of attitudes, beliefs and values, the research here measures the latter.

For measuring the value subsystems of foreign policy elites, the *Daily Report* of the U.S. Foreign Broadcast Information Service (FBIS) is the only readily available source with appropriate data

FIGURE 1
Value Data Analysis: Research Design

Independent Variables	Intervening Variables	Dependent Variables
Psychological Component (18 variables)	1. Western Group	1. Constructive Diplomatic Behavior Sent
Societal Component (4 variables)	2. Closed Group	2. Non-Military Conflict Sent
Interstate Component (10 variables)	3. Unstable Group	3. Force Sent

for a significant number of states.[2] The *Daily Report* consists of material obtained through U.S. monitoring of foreign broadcasts. As would be expected, the source does not report on all states in a systematic and comprehensive, or even random, manner. Certain states—such as the Soviet Union, China, and most Middle Eastern and Eastern European states—receive an unusual amount of coverage, and other states are virtually ignored.

The initial task was to determine which states appeared with sufficient frequency to be included. The Interstate Behavior Analysis (IBA) Project, the initial basis for this work, had previously selected a sample of fifty-six states for the period from 1966 to 1970. The sample included all states that had initiated forty or more foreign policy events during the time-span between 1966 and 1969, according to the World Event Interaction Survey (WEIS) data set. The states comprising the IBA sample are listed in Table 1.[3]

Lists of heads of state (president, prime minister, etc.) and foreign ministers for all fifty-six states were then compiled.[4] Coders recorded every instance of a *Daily Report* speech (interview, broadcast, etc.) by members of the foreign policy elites (i.e., head of state and foreign minister) of all fifty-six states in the IBA sample.[5]

For the annual samples, all states for which there were three or more "cases" or speeches were included. The thirty-nine states that satisfied this criterion one or more times during the 1966 to 1970 time-span are listed in Table 2.[6]

The annual state samples vary from thirty-one (in 1966 and 1967) to twenty (1969). Certain states appear with regularity, whereas others are included rarely or not at all. States in the latter category include Canada, Brazil, some European states, Ghana, Ethiopia, the Union of South Africa, Turkey, Lebanon, and

TABLE 1

List of States

State	Code	State	Code
Western Hemisphere:		**Middle East:**	
1. United States	USA	33. Algeria	ALG
2. Canada	CAN	34. Iran	IRN
3. Cuba	CUB	35. Turkey	TUR
4. Brazil	BRA	36. Iraq	IRQ
5. Chile	CHL	37. United Arab Republic	UAR
		38. Syria	SYR
Europe:		39. Lebanon	LEB
		40. Jordan	JOR
6. United Kingdom	UNK	41. Israel	ISR
7. Netherlands	NTH	42. Saudi Arabia	SAU
8. Belgium	BEL	43. Yemen	YEM
9. France	FRN		
10. Spain	SPN	**Asia:**	
11. Portugal	POR		
12. West Germany	GMW	44. China	CHN
13. East Germany	GME	45. South Korea	KOS
14. Poland	POL	46. Japan	JAP
15. Hungary	HUN	47. India	IND
16. Czechoslovakia	CAE	48. Pakistan	PAK
17. Italy	ITA	49. Thailand	TAI
18. Albania	ALB	50. Cambodia	CAM
19. Yugoslavia	YUG	51. Laos	LAO
20. Greece	GRC	52. South Vietnam	VTS
21. Cyprus	CYP	53. Malaysia	MAL
22. Bulgaria	BUL	54. Philippines	PHI
23. Rumania	RUM	55. Indonesia	INS
24. U.S.S.R.	USR		
25. Sweden	SWD	**Oceania:**	
26. Denmark	DEN		
		56. Australia	AUL
Africa:			
27. Ghana	GHA		
28. Nigeria	NIG		
29. Zaire	COP		
30. Kenya	KEN		
31. Ethiopia	ETH		
32. South Africa	SAF		

Yemen, and such Asian countries as South Korea, Japan, Malaysia, the Philippines, and Australia.

Table 3 highlights the states that appear with the greatest frequency. Fourteen states are in all five samples; this core group will obviously yield the most useful data for such research questions as value subsystem stability across time. The fourteen states include many of direct interest to U.S. policy makers during the 1966 to 1970 period (e.g., Cuba, Czechoslovakia, the United Arab Republic, Jordan, Israel, China, and South Vietnam).

Generally, the states that comprise the yearly samples overrepresent the Middle East and the Communist states. However, there is at least some variety. Third World states such as Indonesia and India are included in four of the five samples; France and West Germany also appear on four of the five lists; such diverse states as Algeria, Indonesia, Poland, and Syria are listed three or

TABLE 2

State Samples (1966 to 1970)[a]

STATE	1966[b]	1967[c]	1968[d]	1968[e]	1970[f]	TOTAL
1. United States[g]	171	62	69	92	87	481
2. Cuba	20	10	6	10	11	57
3. Chile	4	9				13
4. France	13	7		8	7	35
5. West Germany	5	11	3		27	46
6. East Germany	20	15	11	22	26	94
7. Poland	4	9	11	12	14	50
8. Hungary	4	10		5	10	29
9. Czechoslovakia	7	11	41	52	19	130
10. Yugoslavia	15	19	30	20	41	125
11. Greece	12	8				20
12. Cyprus		4			4	8
13. Bulgaria					9	9
14. Rumania	9	7	16	17	26	75
15. U.S.S.R.	38	49	32	36	62	217
16. Ghana	12					12
17. Nigeria	7	21		6		34
18. Kenya	9					9
19. Algeria	8	8			6	22
20. Iran		4	3			7
21. Turkey	3	4				7
22. Iraq	21	16	11			48
23. United Arab Republic	18	16	20	14	37	105
24. Syria	10	14	5		5	34
25. Lebanon					6	6
26. Jordan	18	28	8	11	30	95
27. Israel	5	33	21	9	60	128
28. Saudi Arabia	7	3				10
29. Yemen		5				5
30. China	30	26	20	9	27	112
31. South Korea		7				7
32. Japan	4		9			13
33. India	24	4		7	4	39
34. Pakistan	27	6				33
35. Thailand			4	4		8
36. Cambodia	42	19	16	5	10	92
37. Laos					7	7
38. South Vietnam	46	4	13	10	3	76
39. Indonesia	42	3		6	4	55

[a]The figure is the number of speeches.
[b]$N = 31$.
[c]$N = 31$.
[d]$N = 21$.
[e]$N = 20$.
[f]$N = 25$.
[g]The source for the United States is the Department of State Bulletin.

TABLE 3

Most Frequently Included States

State	All Years (1966 - 1970)	Four Years	Three Years
United States	X		
Cuba	X		
France		X	
West Germany		X	
East Germany	X		
Poland	X		
Hungary		X	
Czechoslovakia	X		
Yugoslavia	X		
Rumania	X		
U.S.S.R.	X		
Nigeria			X
Algeria			X
Iraq			X
United Arab Republic	X		
Syria		X	
Jordan	X		
Israel	X		
China	X		
India		X	
Thailand			X
Cambodia	X		
South Vietnam	X		
Indonesia		X	

more times. Although the lists obviously reflect FBIS data collection biases and U.S. focus-of-attention idiosyncracies (such as the relative neglect of Western Europe and Africa in the 1966 to 1970 period), the sample does contain some heterogeneity.

For the value content analysis of the FBIS material, the list of thirteen terminal values from Rokeach et al. (1970) was employed. Exploratory content analyses suggested the addition of five foreign policy–specific values: progress, unity, ideology, cooperation, and support of government. The nineteen terminal values (and their respective definitions) are listed in Table 4.

Descriptive Data

For the purpose of providing some illustrative descriptive data, the results for 1970 will be presented. The descriptive data in Table 5 have been aggregated across all FBIS *Daily Report* states

TABLE 4

Values For Content Analysis[a]

1. A comfortable life (a prosperous life; economic stability; economic security; raising living standards).

2. A world of peace (free of war and conflict).

3. Equality (brotherhood; equal opportunity for all; impartiality; free from extremes).

4. Freedom (democracy; independence; free choice; liberty; absence of coercion).

5. Happiness (felicity; contentedness).

6. Governmental security (stability of government; sufficient governmental control).

7. Honor (feeling honorable; having self-esteem).

8. Justice (state of just dealing or right action; people receiving their due).

9. National security (protection from attack; sovereignty; serving national interests; integrity of borders).

10. Public security (protection of the rights of the people; law and order).

11. Respect (worthy of high regard).

12. Social recognition (admiration as a result of social status).

13. Wisdom (mature understanding of life).

14. Progress (goal achievement; economic/social/cultural development).

15. Unity (absence of opposition).

16. Ideology (balance; struggle; reference to Marx or Mao).

17. Cooperation (friendship; coexistence).

18. Support of government (sacrifice for government; patriotism; loyalty).

[a]The first 13 values are adopted from Rokeach et al. (1970)

TABLE 5

1970: Value Frequencies[a]

Value[b]	AF^{C^0}	RF^C	AF^{C^1}	RF^C	AF^{C^2}	RF^C	$AF^{C^{3+}}$	RF^C
A comfortable life	377	82.9	46	10.1	12	2.6	20	4.4
A world of peace	170	37.4	89	19.6	55	12.1	141	40.9
Equality	364	80.0	49	10.8	15	3.3	27	5.9
Freedom	232	51.0	93	20.4	47	10.3	83	18.3
Happiness	396	87.0	40	8.8	12	2.6	7	1.6
Governmental Security	385	84.6	34	7.5	15	3.3	21	4.6
Honor	365	80.2	52	11.4	14	3.1	24	5.3
Justice	336	73.8	75	16.5	18	4.0	26	5.7
National Security	162	35.6	92	20.2	60	13.2	141	31.0
Public Security	286	62.9	71	15.6	29	6.4	69	15.1
Respect	348	76.5	70	15.4	23	5.1	14	3.0
Social recognition	421	92.5	17	3.7	7	1.5	10	2.3
Wisdom	417	91.6	27	5.9	8	1.8	3	0.7
Progress	132	29.0	74	16.3	55	12.1	194	42.6
Unity	265	58.2	72	15.8	37	8.1	81	17.9
Ideology	256	56.3	51	11.2	41	9.0	107	23.5
Cooperation	147	32.3	56	12.3	39	8.6	213	46.8
Support of government	371	81.5	40	8.8	23	5.1	21	4.6

[a] Total N = 457 speeches for 24 states; excludes United States

[b] Results have been aggregated into the categories of 0 (no references to the value), 1, 2, and 3 or more.

[c] AF = Absolute Frequency; RF = Relative Frequency

with at least three speeches for 1970; frequencies are given for all eighteen values.

It should be emphasized that this particular aggregation strategy is unusually crude since it simply sums the value totals across all states. Actual analyses of the data set will entail the aggregation of value totals by individual states. In other words, value profiles will consist of state A's totals for each of the eighteen values, state B's totals for each of the eighteen values, and so on.

Table 5 provides absolute and relative frequencies for four categories: 0 references to the value, 1 reference, 2 references, 3 or more references. The fourth category simply combines all totals greater than 2 into one aggregate total.

The relative frequencies in the 0 column isolate the values appearing rarely; the least frequently appearing values include happiness, social recognition, and wisdom. The values "a world of peace," freedom, national security, progress, and cooperation appear most often in the 1970 data set. As would be expected, different institutions (religion, science, etc.) display strikingly different value patterns (see Rokeach 1975). The fourth column in Table 5 explicitly highlights the values that were most prominent in the FBIS-monitored speeches in 1970.

A summary descriptive profile of the value data set is presented in Table 6, where overall means for the eighteen values for all of the states and years in the data set are presented. Eight values have means above 1: a world of peace, freedom, national security, public security, progress, unity, ideology, and cooperation. Especially noteworthy is the mean of 4.54 for the value progress. The values with the lowest means are wisdom, social recognition, equality, and respect.

Validity

In order to determine the validity of the value scheme as applied to the comparative study of foreign policy, we could perform validity tests of one or more of the following types: content validity, criterion-related validity, and construct validity (Bohrnstedt 1970). Two criterion-related validation strategies have been pursued in prior value research. One entails the assessment of whether or not value rankings discriminate among subgroups; the other evaluates the relationship between values and behaviors.

The first approach is exemplified in a recent study of value rankings in the British House of Commons. Searing (1978:75) focuses on the capacity of the technique to differentiate among

TABLE 6

Value Means and Standard Deviations (1966-1970)

Value	Mean	Standard Deviation
A comfortable life	.66	1.01
A world of peace	1.74	1.80
Equality	.34	.53
Freedom	1.60	1.36
Happiness	.47	.65
Governmental security	.65	.61
Honor	.47	.53
Justice	.63	.69
National security	2.32	1.64
Public security	1.19	1.01
Respect	.38	.36
Social recognition	.29	.43
Wisdom	.22	.51
Progress	4.54	4.16
Unity	1.52	1.30
Ideology	3.10	3.60
Cooperation	3.65	2.88
Support of Government	.77	.85

politicians from different political camps. He compares a party's candidate with its parliamentary members and also compares Conservative and Labour members. The results offer striking support for the validity of the technique:

> Candidates are a faithful image of MPs from their own political camp. By contrast, Conservative and Labour members of Parliament are poles apart. They refer to one another as "the other side," and so they are: Unlike the family resemblance between candidates and MPs, every value comparison save one produces differences which are statistically significant, usually at the .001 level (Searing 1978:76).

Relative ranks for the core political values of freedom and social equality show the expected differences; 85 percent of the Conservative MPs rank freedom over social equality, and 79 percent of the Labour members rank the latter value higher than freedom (Searing 1978:77).

The value-behavior relationship is considered in detail in Rokeach (1973). Three general conclusions emerged:

- The behavior-value nexus is robust in magnitude. Of 360 correlations, 134 are statistically significant.
- The expected specific values exhibit strong relationships with given behaviors. Equality, for example, is the value which predicts various forms of behavior in the arenas of civil rights and discrimination.
- Certain values show an especially large number of significant relationships to the behavioral items. Among these are a comfortable life, equality, family security, national security, and salvation. The socioeconomic, political, and religious values of a comfortable life, equality, and salvation may be the most powerful overall determinants of both attitudes and behaviors, as Rokeach (1973:159) concludes. In contrast, the values freedom, inner harmony, self-respect, social recognition, true friendship, and wisdom exhibit no (in the case of the latter) or few potent correlations with behaviors.

Findings

Initial Relationships: Discrete Indicators and Variable Clusters as Determinants of Foreign Behavior

In order to gauge the impact of articulated values on foreign behavior, we initially determined the discrete relationships between the dependent variable of foreign behavior and four predictor domains (i.e., the psychological, societal, interstate, and global components). Then, the predicted values that were generated by these four regression analyses were entered into a regression equation which predicted foreign behavior; this provided a direct estimate of relative potency. We conducted tests both for the entire sample (i.e., the thirty-nine states that appear in the value state sample one or more times between 1966 and 1970) and for the clusters of states which had been identified in a Q-factor analysis of a state attribute data set (see Wilkenfeld et al. 1978b).

The state attribute data set consists of various static characteristics of states, grouped into three distinct areas: economic structure; capability (size, military power, resource base); and governmental structure (political development, structure, stability). There are twenty-three discrete variables in the data set. Examples include gross national product (economic structure), total area (size), defense expenditures (military power), percent of energy consumed that was domestically produced (resource base), number of political parties (political development), legislative selection (political structure), and average number of coups per year, 1946-1965 (political stability).

There is one important modification in the research design. Whereas five distinct groupings were isolated in the original Q-factor analysis (i.e., Western, closed, large developing, unstable, and poor), here we report results for only four groupings. Since the totals for the large developing and poor states were so low, it was impossible to perform separate analyses of these clusters; as a result, the two were collapsed into an "others" category.[7] Thus, we present results for the Western, closed, unstable, and (primarily) Third World categories.

The value data set has already been described. The other variables include societal, interstate, and global factors (independent variables) and dimensions of foreign behavior (dependent variables). The latter are derived from the World Event Interaction Survey or WEIS events data set.[8] Instead of employing the twenty-two discrete WEIS categories as dependent variables, the analyses will focus on three general dimensions that emerged in a factor analysis of the WEIS behavior set data (see Hopple et al. 1978).[9]

The first factor—"constructive diplomatic behavior"—explained 49 percent of the total variance. Fourteen of the WEIS events loaded on this dimension: yield, comment, consult, approve, promise, grant, reward, agree, request, propose, reject, deny, warn, and impose negative sanctions. The second dimension, which was designated "non-military conflict," accounted for 23 percent of the total variance. Clustered here were the action categories: accuse, protest, demand, threaten, demonstrate, expel, and seize. The third factor, labelled "force," explained only 9 percent of the total variance and consisted exclusively of the force category. Conflict thus bifurcated into "moderate" and "extreme" dimensions. There are three distinct dependent variables: constructive diplomatic behavior; nonmilitary conflict; and force.

The societal indicator realm consists of two indices of internal unrest and instability, a measure of economic performance, and a demographic variable. The domestic conflict indicators were selected from the time-series data set collected by Banks (1971). Cross-tabulations between all possible pairs of variables identified two distinct clusters: societal unrest (riots, antigovernment demonstrations, and general strikes) and governmental instability coups; changes in the executive, the cabinet, or the constitution; revolutions; and purges). General annual economic performance was assessed indirectly by the merchandise balance-of-payments situation within each state. Rate of population growth has also been included to represent the demographic aspect of the societal domain.

Data have been collected on a variety of measures of interstate economic involvement (see Rossa and Fountain 1977). Each variable in the interstate realm is briefly described below.

1. International economic involvement (total value of merchandise trade):

    total exports + total imports.

2. Food dependency index:

$$\frac{\text{food imports} - \text{food exports}}{\text{food imports} + \text{food exports}}$$

3. Export concentration index:

$$\frac{(Si)^2 - 1/10}{1 - 1/10},$$

    where Si is the percentage share of export income percentages in commodity class i, where ten categories exist.

4. Import concentration index:

$$\frac{(Si)^2 - 1/10}{1 - 1/10},$$

    where Si is the percentage share of import expenditures in commodity class i, where ten categories exist.

5. Energy dependence index (energy consumption dependence index:

$$\frac{\text{energy imports}}{\text{energy consumption} + \frac{\text{energy exports}}{\text{energy production}}}$$

6. Energy interdependence index:

$$\frac{\text{energy imports} + \text{energy exports}}{\text{energy consumption}}$$

7. Energy seller index (energy market strength or energy market supplier ability index):

$$\frac{\text{energy exports}}{\text{energy production} + \text{imports}}$$

8. Neo-colonial dependency index:

$$\frac{(\text{industrial imports} + \text{unrefined exports}) - (\text{unrefined exports} + \text{industrial imports})}{\text{total imports} + \text{total exports}}$$

The eight indices specified above for the purpose of empirically measuring sources of foreign behavior in the sphere of interstate economic relations incorporate the following types of information: (1) export and import flow data; (2) production and consumption within states; and (3) commodity-specific and overall relationships. Four of the indices focus on one specific commodity (energy or food); one concerns the overall relations of a state; and three attempt to combine commodity-specific information into single scales of overall relationships. The indicators describe state interdependency, dependency, and economic domination or advantage within the interstate system as reflected in dyadic or interstate relationships.

Massive conceptual and data collection problems confront researchers who attempt to analyze the impact of global determinants of foreign behavior (see East 1978). Cross-national data have been amassed for this study in two disparate global realms: borders and intergovernmental organization (IGO) memberships.

The research of Starr and Most (1976) on the subject of borders and the occurrence of war suggests that simple contiguity may be a source of interstate conflict and violence. In order to generate data on borders, we dichotomized the WEIS conflictual events into the categories of force and other conflict (the latter includes the event types: reject, accuse, protest, deny, demand, warn, threaten, demonstrate, give negative sanctions, and seize). The total number of events sent and received by all of a state's neighbors was recorded for each border category and for the force and conflict categories. This yielded eight discrete variables for a given state: (1) total number of conflictual events sent and received by states with direct land borders with the state; (2) total number of force events sent and received by states with direct land borders with the state; (3) total number of conflictual events sent and received by states with colonies land-bordering the state; (4) total number of force events sent and received by states with colonies land-bordering the state; (5) total number of conflictual events sent and received by states with direct sea borders with the state; (6) total number of force events sent and received by states with direct sea borders with the state; (7) total number of conflictual events sent and received by states with colonies sea-bordering the state; and (8) total number of force events sent and received by states with colonies sea-bordering the state.

IGO membership data are of two forms: the total number of intergovernmental organizations to which a state belongs and the number of new memberships for a state during a given year. The two variables tap a state's static and varying commitments to global mechanisms and provide an indirect measure of willingness to work within a global framework.

Figure 2 summarizes the overall research design. Regression results for each of the four variable realms are presented in Tables 7, 8, and 9 (psychological), 11 (societal), 12 (interstate), and 13 (global). In each table, the numbers in the columns are beta weights; each table also presents the proportion of variance explained (R^2) for that particular component. Beta weights and R^2's statistically significant at the .05 level are identified by asterisks.

Perhaps the most striking finding for the prediction of constructive diplomatic behavior by the eighteen values (Table 7) is that the overall R^2 of .24 conceals significant variations by group. The values explain 93 percent of the variance in diplomatic behavior for the Western group, 73 percent for the closed group, 80 percent for the unstable group, and only 39 percent for the fourth Third World cluster.

For the total group, eight of the eighteen values are significant; these include "a world of peace," equality, honor, justice, national security, progress, ideology, and cooperation. Three of the betas are negative in direction; expressions about the values of justice,

FIGURE 2

Value Analysis in the Context of the Command Psychophysiology Terrain

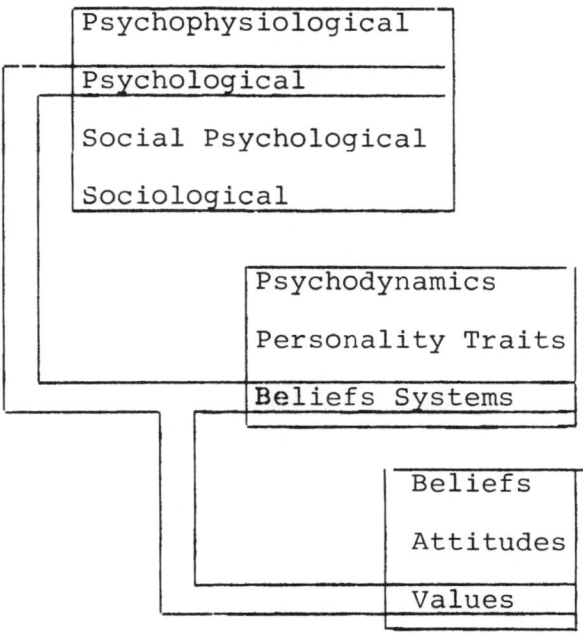

progress, and cooperation all tend to diminish acts of constructive diplomacy.

These overall results mask the kaleidoscopic patterns for the state clusters. Half of the values are significant for the Western group; especially noteworthy are the beta weights for wisdom (-2.64) and, to a lesser extent, a comfortable life (1.89).[10] In the case of the closed states, national security is the dominant value in relation to events of a constructive diplomatic nature. Interestingly, a concern with two internal values—public security and progress—depresses foreign behavior sent. Unity, however, correlates positively with external behavior. The most noteworthy finding for the unstable states is the negative relationship between articulations about progress and diplomatic behaviors. Few of the relationships for the fourth category are substantively meaningful or statistically significant.

For nonmilitary conflict as predicted by the psychological

TABLE 7

Constructive Diplomatic Behavior As Predicted By
The Psychological Component
(Nation-Years Aggregated, 1966-1970)[a]

	Total Group	Western Group	Closed Group	Unstable	Others[b]
Comfortable life	.15	1.89*	.58	.87*	-.35
Peace	.20*	.52*	.18	-.25	-.18
Equality	.37*	-.31	-.16	-.39	.02
Freedom	-.15	1.20*	.01	.39	.37*
Government Security	-.09	.41*	-.36	.05	-.22
Happiness	-.09	-.35	-.59*	-.50*	-.38*
Honor	.27*	1.26	.24	-.23	.17
Justice	-.22*	--	.05	-.44	-.18
National security	.19*	-.32	1.15*	.45	-.06
Public security	.07	-.19	-.86*	.40	-.21
Respect	.02	1.06*	-.01	.10	-.01
Social recognition	-.09	.62	-.37*	1.05*	.10
Wisdom	-.03	-2.64*	-.55*	-.52	.02
Progress	-.20*	.12	-.67*	-1.32*	.53*
Unity	-.15	.11	1.01*	-.21	.47*
Ideology	.32*	-.75	-.15	1.20*	-.44*
Cooperation	-.26*	-1.24*	-.36	.48	-.26
Support of Government	-.01	-1.23*	.20	-.84	-.20
R^2	.24*	.93*	.73*	.80	.39
N =	131	24	35	27	45

[a] Numbers in the first eighteen columns are beta weights.

[b] This group consists of all large developing, poor, and unclassifiable states

*Beta of R^2 significant at the .05 level.

TABLE 8

Non-Military Conflict as Predicted by The Psychological Component
(Nation-Years Aggregated, 1966-1970)[a]

	Total Group	Western Group	Closed Group	Unstable	Others[b]
Comfortable life	.09	3.18*	.74*	.43	.08
Peace	.23*	1.01*	.18	.60	-.52
Equality	.09	-.51*	-.13	-.28	-.11
Freedom	.11	-.18*	-.06	.49	.17
Government security	-.04	.56*	-.36*	.04	-.18
Happiness	-.14	-.46	-.58*	-.11	-.41
Honor	.17*	.54	.18	-.21	.10
Justice	-.18*	-.23	.02	-.47	-.06
National security	.13	.80*	1.04*	.15	---
Public security	-.09	-.37	-.99*	.08	-.19
Respect	-.02	.04	.03	-.05	.02
Social recognition	.02	.17	-.29	1.19	.27
Wisdom	-.09	-3.76*	-.57*	-.01	.18
Progress	-.13	1.18*	-.74*	-.74	.46*
Unity	-.07	.12	1.18*	-.13	.41*
Ideology	-.01	-2.11*	-.14	.53	-.58*
Cooperation	-.20*	-.15	-.30	.29	-.01
Support of government	.19*	.75*	.19	-.70	-.43
R^2	.17*	.94*	.78*	.53	.39
N =	131	24	35	27	45

[a]Numbers in the first eighteen columns are beta weights.
[b]This group consists of all large developing, poor, and unclassifiable states.
*Beta or R^2 significant at the .05 level.

component (Table 8), the same general finding emerges. The aggregate R^2 of .17 contrasts sharply with the fluctuating R^2's of .94 (Western group), .78 (closed group), .53 (unstable group), and .39 (others). For both the Western and the closed states, the values are significant determinants of this particular form of foreign behavior.

Again, half of the eighteen values are significant for the Western states. As in Table 7, the largest single beta weight is wisdom (-3.76). Other large betas include a comfortable life (3.18) and ideology (-2.11). Within the closed group, national security (1.04) and unity (1.18) are the primary determinants of nonmilitary conflict. None of the results is significant for the unstable states, although social recognition exerts some impact (a beta of 1.19).

TABLE 9

Force as Predicted by the Psychological Component
(Nation-Years Aggregated, 1966-1970)[a]

	Total Group	Western Group	Closed Group	Unstable	Other[b]
Comfortable life	.06	.90	.16	.11	.25
Peace	-.04	.15	.59*	-.44	-.30
Equality	.17*	-.29	.65*	-.03	-.23
Freedom	.02	.21	-.61*	.35	-.03
Government security	-.10	.02	-.10	.21	-.08
Happiness	-.09	-.14	-.28	-.26	-.20
Honor	.01	.97	-.07	-.91	-.30
Justice	-.05	-.95	.33	.71	.03
National security	.35*	.16	.60	1.13*	-.05
Public security	-.14	.95	.10	-.31	-.23
Respect	-.02	-.18	-.46	.35	.08
Social recognition	.12	-.73	-.14	.65	-.09
Wisdom	-.03	.27	-.24	-.98	.39
Progress	.04	-.01	-.16	-.78	-.18
Unity	-.08	-.48	-.23	-.50	.23
Ideology	-.04	.08	.30	.86	-.31
Cooperation	-.14	-.26	-.35	-.23	.28
Support of government	-.09	-.46	.40*	-.92	-.22
R^2	.19	.72	.76*	.50	.30
N =	131	24	35	27	45

[a]Numbers in first eighteen columns are beta weights.

[b]This group consists of all large developing, poor, and unclassifiable states.

*Beta or R^2 significant at the .05 level.

TABLE 10

Internal Values and Foreign Behavior[a]

	Constructive Diplomatic					Non-Military Conflict				
	Total	West.	Closed	Unstb.	Oth.	Total	West.	Closed	Unstb.	Oth.
Comfortable life		P	P	P		P	P			
Happiness		N	N	N			N			N
Public security		N					N			
Progress	N		N	N	P	P	N			P

[a]P denotes a significant positive beta weight; N denotes a significant negative beta weight; a blank denotes a nonsignificant beta weight.

TABLE 11

Foreign Behavior as Predicted by The Societal Component
(Nation-Years Aggregated, 1966-1970)[a]

	Societal Unrest	Governmental Instability	Population Growth Rate	Economic Performance	R^2
Total Group N=131					
Constructive Diplomatic	.55*	-.13*	---	.03	.31*
Non-Military Conflict	.17*	-.09	.09	.03	.03
Force	.14*	.10	.16*	---	.06
Western Group, N=24					
Constructive Diplomatic	.22*	.12	.13	.80*	.87*
Non-Military Conflict	-.22	.21	.32	.27	.11
Force	.40*	.65*	.14	-.29	.63*
Closed Group, N=35					
Constructive Diplomatic	.80*	-.10	.03	-.01	.61*
Non-Military Conflict	.76*	-.07	-.03	-.04	.55*
Force	.46*	-.23	.07	.01	.22*
Unstable Group, N=27					
Constructive Diplomatic	.14	-.15	-.14	.63*	.62*
Non-Military Conflict	-.41*	-.04	-.26	.44*	.21
Force	.16	-.10	-.17	.17	.05
Others, N=45[b]					
Constructive Diplomatic	.04	-.19	---	.19	.08
Non-Military Conflict	.10	-.19	.07	.11	.05
Force	-.18	-.04	-.25*	.28	.16

[a] Numbers in the first four columns are beta weights
[b] This group consists of all large developing, poor, and unclassifiable states.
*Beta or R^2 significant at the .05 level.

TABLE 12

Foreign Behavior as Predicted by The Interstate Component (Nation-Years Aggregated, 1966-1970)[a]

	INTER-NATIONAL INVOLVEMENT	ENERGY DEPEN-DENCY	ENERGY MARKET STRENGTH	ENERGY INTER-DEPENDENCY	FOOD DEPENDENCY	EXPORT CONCEN-TRATION	IMPORT CONCEN-TRATION	NEO-COLONIAL DEPEN-DENCY	R^2
Total Group, N = 131									
Constructive Diplomatic	.44*	−.13	−.22*	.14	−.07	−.01	.12	—	.26
Non-Military Conflict	.17*	−.19*	−.31*	.23*	−.09	−.08	−.10	.13	.13
Force	−.08	−.03	−.09	.10	−.08	−.01	.29*	−.03	.08
Western Group, N = 24									
Constructive Diplomatic	.54*	.03	.03	−.08	−.09	−.06	−.01	−.32	.39
Non-Military Conflict	−.09	−.40	−.20	−.37	−.33*	−.40*	−.31	−.14	.45
Force	−.19	.58*	.55	−.39	.03	.02	−.33	−.18	.31
Closed Group, N = 25									
Constructive Diplomatic	.36*	−31.70*	−7.31*	29.10*	−.06	.30	.02	.08	.66*
Non-Military Conflict	.35*	−33.96*	−7.86*	31.12*	.01	.19	−.03	.06	.66*
Force	.21	−18.67*	−4.25*	17.02*	−.16	−.05	.35	−.09	.37*
Unstable Group, N = 27									
Constructive Diplomatic	.65*	−.01	−.16	.03	.12	−.03	.19	.06	.49
Non-Military Conflict	.51*	−.12	−.33	.30	.08	−.31	−.40	.39	.45
Force	−.11	−.24	−.03	−.04	.10	−.01	.37	−.14	.09
Others, N = 45[b]									
Constructive Diplomatic	.57*	.16	−.40	.41	−.17	−.12	−.19	.32	.24
Non-Military Conflict	.42*	−.10	−.53*	.47*	−.25*	−.02	−.34	.43	.23
Force	−.14	−.13	−.27	.39	−.12	.02	.53*	.04	.31

[a] Numbers in first eight columns are beta weights.
[b] This group consists of all large developing, poor, and unclassifiable states.
*Beta or R^2 significant at the .05 level.

TABLE 13

Foreign Behavior as Predicted by The Global Component
(Nation-Years Aggregated, 1966-1970)[a]

	TOTAL IGO	NEW IGO	DLBC[b]	DLBF[b]	CLBC[b]	CLBF[b]	DSBC[b]	DSBF[b]	CSBC[b]	CSBF[b]	R^2
Total Group, N = 131											
Constructive Diplomatic	.32*	.04	.03	.09	.70*	-.29*	.44*	-.15*	-.29*	.08	.44*
Non-Military Conflict	-.05	-.01	.25*	.01	.75*	.46	.44	.11	-.12	.07	.40
Force	.15*	-.08	-.15*	.41*	.11	-.09	-.07	.24*	-.05	-.17	.22
Western Group, N = 24											
Constructive Diplomatic	-.22*	-.18	.07	-.01	.06	1.32*	.09	.21*	-.41*	-.14	.93*
Non-Military Conflict	-.41*	-.09	.26	-.23	1.45*	-.62*	.19	.26*	-.42*	.25	.83*
Force	-.14	-.04	-.42	.74*	.55	-.32	-.06	-.05	-.39	.15	.38
Closed Group, N = 35											
Constructive Diplomatic	.20	-.04	.08	-.03	2.97*	-1.55*	.51*	-.29*	-1.54*	.40*	.77*
Non-Military Conflict	-.06	-.05	.15	-.03	3.25*	-1.62*	.54*	-.33*	-1.59*	.46*	.78*
Force	.27	-.29	-.01	-.04	1.20	-.79	.29	-.25	-.46	-.03	.28
Unstable Group, N = 27[c]											
Constructive Diplomatic	.13	.06	.10*	.20*	-.18	.97*	.47*	-.25*	-.33*	.07	.96*
Non-Military Conflict	.25*	.29*	.11	.54*	1.71*	-1.39*	.65*	-.29*	-.34	-.47	.88*
Force	.08	-.05	-.13	1.18*	-1.27*	-1.02	-.21*	-.19*	.27	.17	.91
Others, N = 45											
Constructive Diplomatic	-.25*	-.17	.29	-.19	-.36	-.06	.73	.26	-.03	.07	.77*
Non-Military Conflict	-.30	-.17*	.28*	-.24	-.42	.19*	.43	.52*	.09	-.02	.67*
Force	-.03	-.04	-.10	.29	-.12	.05	-.33*	.80*	.12	-.61*	.43*

[a] Numbers in first ten columns are beta weights.
[b] Direct Land Borders Conflict (DLBC); Direct Land Borders Force (DLBF); Colonial Land Borders Conflict (CLBC); Colonial Land Borders Force (CLBF); Direct Sea Borders Conflict (DSBC); Direct Sea Borders Force (DSBF); Colonial Sea Borders Conflict (CSBC); Colonial Sea Borders Force (CSBF).
[c] This group consists of all large developing, poor, and unclassifiable states.
* Beta or R^2 significant at the .05 level.

Five of the betas are significant within the others category, although the R^2 is insignificant.

Finally, we can consider the findings for force behavior (Table 9). Generally, the elite values are not significant predictors of this extreme form of foreign conflict. This finding conforms to the pattern unearthed in prior work (Wilkenfeld et al. 1978a; Hopple et al. 1978), where it was discovered that force received accounts for force sent, whereas the other variable realms exert almost no impact.

The one exception to this generalization is the closed group; the values account for a significant 76 percent of the variance in force behavior sent by the members of this cluster. The main contributors to this are: a world of peace (.59); equality (.65); freedom (-.61); and support of government (.40). The positive relationship between the first two values and acts of force suggests that closed states may emphasize these values rhetorically as justifications for and rationalizations of force behaviors.[11]

The relationship between values referring to internal states of affairs and foreign behavior is of interest because of its potential relevance to the internal-external nexus question. Extensive research has accrued on the subject of linkages between external and interal conflict. In a more general sense, scholars, journalists, and other students of public policy have frequently alluded to the putative nexus between internal politics and foreign policy. The alleged propensity for diverting attention from domestic fiascoes and crises by becoming embroiled in foreign adventures and imbroglios is a popular illustration of this general hypothesis. In a more academic context, the research on linkage politics is based on a recognition of the interplay (and even fusion) between domestic and foreign affairs (see Rosenau 1969).

At least four of the eighteen values presumably concern the internal dimension of politics: a comfortable life, happiness, public security, and progress. The relationships between these endstates and foreign behavior are depicted in Table 10; a P denotes a significant positive relationship and an N a significant negative relationship.

Much of the traditional conjectural speculation on the subject suggests that the relationships would be almost uniformly negative in direction, with emphasis on an internal value reflecting a diminution in foreign behavior. Alternatively, the linkage politics perspective simply predicts that there will be robust interrelationships; the advocates of a "subsystem autonomy" interpretation would expect the absence of any relationships.

With respect to the latter controversy, the results offer support for neither position; nineteen of the relationships are statistically significant and the other twenty-one fail to attain significance. Of the nineteen significant beta weights, eleven are negative in direction and eight are positive.

The patterns in Table 10 can be summarized in a series of propositions. First of all, there is a clear tendency for the value of a comfortable life to covary with increases in both constructive and nonmilitary conflict behaviors. Secondly, the other relationships are predominantly negative; this generalization is especially applicable to the closed states, where rhetorical emphases on happiness, public security, and progress all presage a decrease in external behavior and a turning inward process. Thus, articulations about prosperity and economic stability (the value of a comfortable life) predict increases in general, primarily constructive and mildly conflictual foreign acts together, undoubtedly reflecting the reality of economic interdependence in a world of sovereign states. This phenomenon, however, has not spilled over into domestic politics generally, at least for closed and, to a lesser extent, unstable states.

A final observation about the results for the value data is warranted. Debates about the explanatory potency of psychological factors become sterile exercises when one recognizes that the key questions concern *when* psychological forces exert an impact and *which* particular variables are relevant. Regarding the former issue, it is obvious that certain situations and variable configurations maximize the impact of psychological factors. Among these are the organizational context, level in the hierarchy, decisional and situational attributes, and the type of state. The available evidence suggests that psychological source factors would exert maximal impact in closed states (because of concentration of power) and developing systems (because roles are less clearly institutionalized).

The prediction for closed systems is clearly supported in Tables 7, 8, and 9. However, the beta weights and R^2 values for the two "developing polity" categories are rarely large in size or significance. The two North clusters in terms of the North-South dimension—the Western and closed states—feature the majority of the noteworthy findings. This issue will be confronted again in the relative potency section.

The results for the other three components can be dealt with in a more cursory fashion, since the focus here is on value data. The impact of the societal component is assessed in Table 11. As is the case with other results for the entire state sample of fifty-six (see Hopple et al. 1977; Wilkenfeld et al. 1978a), many of the relationships are anemic in magnitude. The principal exceptions involve societal unrest for the total group of thirty-nine (all three forms of behavior), the Western cluster (constructive and force acts), the closed category (all three dimensions), and the unstable group (nonmilitary conflict). Governmental instability shows a clear relationship to force for the Western states; population growth rate correlates negatively with force behaviors within the others cluster; economic performances predict constructive diplomacy within the Western Q-group and both constructive and nonmilitary conflict behaviors with the unstable subset.

Results for the eight variables comprising the interstate component are presented in Table 12. As a general indicator, international involvement performs well, predicting both constructive and nonmilitary conflict behaviors for three clusters (closed, unstable, and others) and constructive diplomacy for the Western group. Especially significant is the unusual sensitivity of the closed states to the three energy measures.[12]

Table 13 zeroes in on the variables employed to operationalize the global component. A number of significant beta weights can be gleaned from the table. Among the more influential factors are total IGO memberships, colonial land-borders conflict, colonial land-borders force, direct sea-borders conflict, direct sea-borders force, and colonial sea-borders conflict. The percentage of total variance explained ranges from 22 to 96. Ten of the fifteen R^2's are significant, including constructive diplomatic behavior for the total group and all four of the state clusters, nonmilitary conflict for all of the subgroups, and force behavior for the others category.

Relative Potency

The assessment of relative potency here involves four distinct components. A single indicator is developed for each of the variable clusters; the latter is based on the combined effects of all of the variables within the cluster on the dependent variables. Whereas the test in Hopple et al. (1977) yielded a single dominant conclusion—that the interstate factors (with the action-reaction or foreign behavior received variables) account for an overwhelming portion of the variance in a direct "contest" with the societal realm—the results in Table 14 are much more complex. This test,

TABLE 14

Relative Potency of Predictors of Foreign Policy Behavior
(Nation-Years Aggregated, 1966-1970)[a]

	P[b]	S[b]	I[b]	G[b]	R^2
Total Group					
Constructive Diplomatic	.18	.28	.15	.42	.56
Non-Military Conflict	.21	.04	.15	.49	.46
Force	.29	.15	.14	.29	.34
Western Group					
Constructive Diplomatic	-.03	.58	.01	.30	.61
Non-Military Conflict	.07	-.05	.10	.72	.61
Force	.24	.29	.09	.31	.43
Closed Group					
Constructive Diplomatic	.28	.48	.13	.20	.74
Non-Military Conflict	.25	.47	.29	.15	.68
Force	.55	.16	.17	.07	.45
Unstable Group					
Constructive Diplomatic	-.05	.09	-.01	.90	.86
Non-Military Conflict	.09	-.10	.30	.50	.56
Force	.41	.29	.04	.18	.26
Others[c]					
Constructive Diplomatic	.28	.48	.13	.20	.74
Non-Military Conflict	.25	.47	.29	.15	.68
Force	.55	.16	.17	.07	.45

[a] Numbers in the first four columns are beta weights.
[b] Psychological (P); societal (S); interstate (I); global (G).
[c] This group consists of all large developing, poor, and unclassifiable states.
*Beta or R^2 significant at the .05 level.

of course, involves a different sample of states (a subset of the sample in Hopple et al. 1977), a drastically modified interstate cluster, and two additional indicator domains.

The lowest percentage of variance-explained figure is 26 (the force dimension for the unstable cluster); the highest is 86 (constructive diplomatic behavior for the same cluster). All of the R^2's, however, are significant.

What emerges from an examination of Table 14 is the relative priority of the two internal clusters. Psychological variables are significant in ten of the fifteen cases (with the exceptions of the Western group and two dimensions for the unstable states) and societal in seven of the fifteen instances. The two internal predictor realms are especially potent within the closed and others categories.

The stronger external variable domain is the global, with six significant betas. Aside from the significant, but far from impressive betas for the total group, the interstate forces exert a significant impact only on nonmilitary conflict behavior in the unstable and others clusters.

In contrast to the results reported in the preceding section, the psychological domain is important for the Third World (i.e. others) group, rather than for the Western states. The value data remain potent for determining the external behavior of the closed actors. These findings conform to the expected pattern for the relative influence of leadership beliefs by type of state.

Perhaps the most striking single finding in the entire table is the relationship between force acts and the psychological or value data. The beta weight is statistically significant for the closed polities as well as for both of the developing groups. In each instance, in fact, the psychological forces are the sole determinants of the overall significance of the force equations. Given our previous inability to account for the domain of force behavior (aside from the pervasiveness of the action-reaction syndrome), this finding is both nontrivial and unexpected.

Conclusion

In a fundamental sense, this chapter has been designed to go beyond the prior examples of relative potency testing on psychological and other variable areas. Aside from the research of Rosenau (1968) and Stassen (1972) on the individual vis-à-vis role variables, few comparative empirical analyses have dealt with this question.

Equally central to this analysis has been the explicit goal of providing a preliminary assessment of the validity of the value data set. The validation strategy pursued here emphasizes the behavioral relevance of the values of foreign policy making elites. Table 15 summarizes the relevant findings. For the three forms of foreign behavior and the eighteen values, there are 69 significant relationships out of 270 possible entries in Table 15. If we disregard the force results—for which we discovered only seven significant betas—then there are 62 entries out of a possible total of 180. The first proportion is about 25 percent; the second is over one-third. It is unlikely that these results are attributable exclusively to chance.

The results are somewhat encouraging, yet we must recognize

TABLE 15

Significant Value-Behavior Relationships: Foreign Behavior

	Constructive Diplomatic					Non-Military Conflict					Force				
	Tot	West	Clsd	Unstb	Oth	Tot	West	Clsd	Unstb	Oth	Tot	West	Clsd	Unstb	Oth
Comfortable life								*							
Peace	*	*		*			*	*				*			
Equality	*							*					*	*	
Freedom		*			*		*							*	
Gov't security		*						*	*						
Happiness			*	*	*				*	*					
Honor	*	*				*				*					
Justice	*					*									
Nat'l security	*		*				*		*					*	
Public security			*					*	*						
Respect		*													
Social Recognition			*	*			*								
Wisdom		*	*				*		*						
Progress	*		*	*	*		*	*		*					
Unity			*	*	*			*	*	*					
Ideology	*			*	*		*								
Cooperation	*	*				*									
Support of gov't		*				*									*

Tot = Total; West = Western; Clsd = Closed; Unstb = unstable; Oth = Others.

the potential problems with the data set. Aside from the obvious caveat that the direction of influence may be from behavior to value rather than the reverse, perhaps the most troublesome issue concerns the question of inferring from the source (FBIS *Daily Reports* based on monitoring foreign broadcasts and speeches) to the realm of behavior.

The entire issue revolves around the contrasting representational and instrumental models of communication (see Pool 1959). As Holsti describes the dilemma:

> analysts will be forced to rely on documents that are in the first instance intended to convey information to the public, to legislatures, or to foreign governments. As likely as not, they are also intended to persuade, justify, threaten, cajole, manipulate, evoke sympathy, or otherwise influence the intended audience. Words may convey explicit or implicit clues about the author's "real" beliefs, attitudes, and opinions; they may also be intended to serve his practical goals of the moment (Holsti 1976:133).

These words concisely describe the instrumental model, which involves "reading between the lines" in an attempt to determine what the message conveys, given its context and circumstances (Pool 1959:3). The representational model accepts articulations "at face value." As Pool (1959:209) concludes, every act of communication has representational and instrumental aspects.

Articulated values may be no more than rhetorical devices or meaningless shibboleths. In some instances, values may be used to deceive or obfuscate, as the relationship between force behavior and the value of peace for the closed group illustrates. To the extent that values are meaningless aphorisms, the utility of cross-national content analyses of public elite articulations is reduced to zero. Also, to the extent that elite value references are employed to confuse or mislead target(s), analysts can search for deception strategies. Even a pattern of lies can be of some importance in monitoring and attempting to predict elite behavior.

A factor that complicates this problem is the finding that the nature of the audience influences both the decision-maker's style of presentation and the substance of what is presented. Generally, statements for public consumption are less "truthful" than private statements (Bonham 1975:8). Empirical support is provided by Gilbert's (1975:15) research on Secretary of State John Foster Dulles's perceptions of the People's Republic of China. In his statements to the general public, Dulles gave high assessments of

Chinese hostility and strength; statements to the press ranked between those to the public and to Congress.

This implies that there is a validity-related hierarchy ranging from elite articulations directed at the mass public to: an attentive or elite subgroup in the public (e.g., the press); other actors within the political system (e.g., the legislature); and perhaps personal aides and confidants within the executive branch. Since the FBIS data consist of statements directed to the public and/or press, inescapable problems of image projection, manipulation, and distortion intrude.

Public statements can impose constraints on a state's future freedom of action. Officially enunciated foreign policy doctrines exert this impact in at least two distinct ways: by contributing to expectations within the state and by influencing the basis upon which the other actors make their decisions (Brodin 1972:105).

In addition, critics of content analyses of public documents may exaggerate the amount of distortion that occurs. We should recognize that manipulative (and distorting) communications, subtle cues, and direct messages are all lockstitched into the fabric of interstate diplomatic interaction; instrumental and representational elements coexist. We should also distinguish between routine articulations and statements that occur during a crisis period. The value approach assumes that each individual has (at least implicitly) a ranked scale of preferred end-states. In a series of articulations over time, basic values will presumably be revealed. Values are not consciously manipulated by the speaker, who, of course, is unaware that someone is planning to construct a profile of his or her value system.

Other validity criteria should be applied, but for both validation and policy-relevant purposes, the critical litmus test is the value-behavior relationship. As Marvick asserts in his review of elite research:

> Those who attempt empirically grounded work have produced ingenious and thought-provoking findings about elite perspectives. At best, these specify the distinctive ways in which elite figures plausibly behave in real-life arenas—how they analyze problems, view strategies, treat rivals, use resources, and achieve results. Evidence of actual elite behavior is seldom keyed to evidence of elite beliefs (1977:124).

This chapter has presented a preliminary assessment of that relationship; future inquiry will attempt to pursue this issue in a more systematic fashion and further ascertain the reliability, validity, and explanatory-predictive utility of the foreign policy elite value data.

Notes

This is a revised version of a paper which was presented at the 1978 Annual Meeting of the International Studies Association. I am indebted to Paul J. Rossa for his helpful comments and research assistance. I would also like to thank Amy Favin for typing the chapter and Judith Paris for editorial assistance. The value data were collected by Dorette Feit, Stuart Perry, and Helene Rubinstein. This research was initially supported by the Defense Advanced Research Projects Agency/Cybernetics Technology Office (DARPA/CTO) and was monitored by ONR under Contract No. N00014-76-C-0153. More recently, support was provided by DARPA/CTO under Contract No. MDA 903-78-C-0341, monitored by DSSW. The views and conclusions in this work are those of the author and do not necessarily represent the official policies, either expressed or implied, of DARPA or the U.S. Government.

1. See also Rokeach (1968b, 1968-1969); Bishop et al. (1972); Rokeach et al. (1970); Searing (1978).
2. This poses a problem for the case of the United States, since the United States is obviously not included in FBIS *Daily Reports*. As a substitute source, we employed the *Department of State Bulletin* to generate U.S. value data. Each weekly issue of the *Bulletin* generally contains one or more speeches by the head of state and/or the foreign minister (i.e., secretary of state).
3. This sample has subsequently been expanded to a total of seventy-seven states. Updated value content analyses for the period since 1970 will employ this master list for generating annual state samples. See Hopple et al. (1978).
4. The sources for the lists were the *Political Handbook and Atlas of the World* and the *International Yearbook and Statesmen's Who's Who*. In some cases, there was ambiguity about the appropriate official to list as the *effective* head of state. In countries with both a president and a prime minister (such as France), the "real" head of state in an operational decision-making sense was selected. In most Communist states, the first secretary of the Communist party (or the functional equivalent) was listed (rather than the occupant of the formal head of state position). In several cases, more than one head of state was listed for a given country. The actual lists are provided in Hopple (1977).
5. A copy of the data-generating code sheets appears in Hopple (1977). Speeches of less than 100 words were automatically excluded, as were joint communiques and purely congratulatory or ceremonial telegrams or messages.

For each entry, coders recorded the date, decision-maker, state, and pages in the *Daily Report.*

6. The annual samples are discussed in detail in Hopple (1977).

7. This new group is essentially a merger of the large developing and poor groups; six states from the total group of fifty-six—Thailand, Ghana, Kenya, Saudi Arabia, Greece, and Nigeria—could not be classified by any of the factors extracted. Thailand appears in the value sample twice (1968, 1969), Ghana once (1966), Kenya once (1966), Greece twice (1966, 1967), and Nigeria three times (1966, 1967, 1969). With the exception of Greece, all of these states are clearly developing or Third World countries.

8. On WEIS, see Burgess and Lawton 1972, McClelland 1968, and McClelland and Young 1969.

9. The factor analysis involved the time-span from 1966 to 1970. Each country year constituted a separate case, yielding 56 (states) x 5 (years) or 280 cases. (The 56 states are listed above in Table 1.) A principal component solution was employed with communality estimates replacing the main diagonal elements of the correlation matrix, and a varimax rotation. See also Young (1975).

10. The result for wisdom is unusual, since that particular value appears rarely in the data set (see Table 6); what this finding means is that on the infrequent occasions when a reference is made to wisdom in the speeches of Western leaders, it reduces the amount of constructive diplomatic behavior sent.

11. This foreshadows a critical issue discussed in the conclusion of this section in the context of the instrumental versus representational debate: are articulated elite values nothing more than rhetorical devices employed to deceive other actors and generally obfuscate reality? If we conceive of the values as a monitoring or forecasting tool rather than a scientific data set (i.e., a set of variables for explaining foreign behavioral patterns), then it is important to recognize that states may say x and do y. That is, a positive relationship between the value of a world of peace and acts of force may be expected (from an instrumental frame of reference) rather than anomalous (given a representational perspective).

12. The unusually large beta weights for energy dependency and energy interdependence mean that even an occasional fluctuation in this area exerts a large effect on external behavior. Note that the direction of the effect for energy dependency is strongly negative (resulting in decreases in all forms of behavior), while the relationship in the case of energy interdependence is equally strong but in a positive direction.

References

Abelson, R., and J. D. Carroll. "Computer Simulation of Individual Belief Systems." *American Behavioral Scientist* 8 (1965):24-30.

Axelrod, R. "Psycho-Algebra: A Mathematical Theory of Cognition and

Choice with an Application to the British East India Committee in 1918." *Papers, Peace Research Society (International)* 18 (1972):113-131.

Banks, A. S. *Cross-Polity Time-Series Data.* Cambridge, Mass.: M.I.T. Press, 1971.

Bishop, G. F., A. M. Barclay, and M. Rokeach. "Presidential Preferences and Freedom-Equality Value Patterns in the 1968 American Campaign." *Journal of Social Psychology* 88 (December 1972):207-212.

Bohrnstedt, G. W. "Reliability and Validity Assessment in Attitude Measurement." In *Attitude Measurement,* edited by G. F. Summers, pp. 80-99. Chicago: Rand McNally, 1970.

Bonham, G. M. "Cognitive Process Models and the Study of Foreign Policy Decision-Making." Paper presented at the Annual Meeting of the International Studies Association, Washington, D.C., 1975.

Bonham, G. M., and M. J. Shapiro, eds. *Thought and Action in Foreign Policy.* Basel and Stuttgart: Birkhauser Verlag, 1977.

Bonham, G. M., and G. J. Nozica. "A Cognitive Process Model of Foreign Policy Decision-Making." *Simulation and Games* 7 (June 1976):123-152.

Brecher, M. *India and World Politics: Krishna Menon's View of the World.* New York: Praeger, 1968.

Brodin, K. "Belief Systems, Doctrines, and Foreign Policy." *Cooperation and Conflict* 7 (1972):97-112.

Burgess, P. M. *Elite Images and Foreign Policy Outcomes: A Study of Norway.* Columbus: Ohio State University Press, 1968.

Burgess, P. M., and R. W. Lawton. *Indicators of International Behavior: An Assessment of Events Data Research.* Beverly Hills, Calif.: Sage, 1972.

East, M. A. "The International System Perspective and Foreign Policy." *Why Nations Act: Theoretical Perspectives for Comparative Foreign Policy Studies,* edited by M. A. East, S. A. Salmore, and C. F. Hermann, pp. 143-160. Beverly Hills, Calif.: Sage, 1978.

East, M. A., S. A. Salmore, and C. F. Hermann. *Why Nations Act: Theoretical Perspectives for Comparative Foreign Policy Studies.* Beverly Hills, Calif.: Sage, 1978.

Etheredge, L. "Personality Effects on American Foreign Policy 1898-1968: A Test of Interpersonal Generalization Theory." *American Political Science Review* 72 (June 1978):434-451.

George, A. L. "The 'Operational Code': A Neglected Approach to the Study of Political Leaders and Decision-Making." *International Studies Quarterly* 13 (1969):190-222.

George, A. L., and J. L. George. *Woodrow Wilson and Colonel House: A Personality Study.* New York: Dover, 1964.

Gilbert, J. D. "John Foster Dulles's Perceptions of the People's Republic of China: An Assessment of Accuracy." Paper presented at the Annual Meeting of the Southwestern Political Science Association, San Antonio, Texas, 1975.

Hermann, M. G. "Effects of Personal Characteristics of Political Leaders on

Foreign Policy." In *Why Nations Act: Theoretical Perspectives for Comparative Foreign Policy Studies*, edited by M. A. East et al., pp. 49-68. Beverly Hills, Calif.: Sage, 1978.

——, ed. *A Psychological Examination of Political Leaders*. New York: Free Press, 1977.

——. "Leader Personality and Foreign Policy Behavior." In *Comparing Foreign Policies: Theories, Findings, Methods*, edited by J. N. Rosenau, pp. 201-234. New York: Halsted, 1974.

Hernes, H. "Classical Theories of Foreign Policy Making as Cognitive Archetypes." In *Thought and Action in Foreign Policy*, edited by G. M. Bonham and M. J. Shapiro, pp. 242-262. Basel and Stuttgart: Birkhauser Verlag, 1977.

Holsti, O. "Foreign Policy Decision Makers Viewed Psychologically: 'Cognitive Process' Approaches." In *In Search of Global Patterns*, edited by J. N. Rosenau, pp. 120-144. New York: Free Press, 1976.

Hopple, G. W. "Mapping the Terrain of Command Psychophysiology: A Preliminary Design for an Emerging Applied Science." McLean, Va.: International Public Policy Research Corporation Technical Assessment Report 78-2-1, August 1978.

——. "Psychological Determinants of Foreign Policy Behavior: A Cross-National Data Set." College Park, Md.: Interstate Behavior Analysis Project Data Package Number 5, University of Maryland, 1977.

Hopple, G. W., J. Wilkenfeld, and R. N. McCauley. "Societal and Interstate Determinants of Foreign Conflict." *Jerusalem Journal of International Relations* 2 (Summer 1977):30-66.

Hopple, G. W., P. J. Rossa, and J. Wilkenfeld. "Progress Report on the Cross-National Crisis Indicators Project." College Park, Md.: University of Maryland, 1978.

Lane, R. *Political Ideology*. New York: Free Press, 1962.

Lasswell, H. D. *Power and Personality*. New York: Viking, 1948.

——. *Psychopathy and Politics*. Chicago: University of Chicago Press, 1930.

Marvick, D. "Elite Politics: Values and Institutions." *American Behavioral Scientist* 21 (September/October 1977):111-134.

McClelland, C. A. "Access to Berlin: The Quantity and Variety of Events, 1948-1963." In *Quantitative International Politics*, edited by J. D. Singer, pp. 159-186. New York: Free Press, 1968.

McClelland, C. A., and R. A. Young. "World Event/Interaction Survey Handbook and Codebook." Los Angeles, Ca.: University of Southern California, WEIS Technical Report No. 1, January 1969.

McLellan, D. S. "Comparative 'Operational Codes' of Recent U.S. Secretaries of State: Dean Acheson." Paper presented at the Annual Meeting of the American Political Science Association, September 1969.

Pool, I. S. *Trends in Content Analysis*. Urbana, Ill.: University of Illinois Press, 1959.

Powell, C. A. et al. "Determinants of Foreign Policy Behavior: A Casual

Modeling Approach." In *Comparing Foreign Policies: Theories, Findings, Methods*, edited by J. N. Rosenau, pp. 151-170. New York: Halsted, 1974.

Rokeach, M. "Value Images of Science and the Values of *Science*," mimeographed. Pullman, Wash.: Washington State University, 1975.

———. *The Nature of Human Values*. New York: Free Press, 1973.

———. "The Role of Values in Public Opinion Research." *Public Opinion Quarterly* 32 (Winter 1968-69):547-559.

———. (1968a). *Beliefs, Attitudes, and Values: A Theory of Organization and Change*. San Francisco: Jossey-Bass, 1968.

——— (1968b). "A Theory of Organization and Change Within Value-Attitude Systems." *Journal of Social Issues* 24 (January 1968):13-33.

———. *The Open and Closed Mind: Investigations into the Nature of Belief Systems and Personality Systems*. New York: Basic Books, 1960.

Rokeach, M., R. Homant, and L. Penner. "A Value Analysis of the Disputed Federalist Papers." *Journal of Personality and Social Psychology* 16 (October, 1970):245-250.

Rosenau, J. N., ed. *Linkage Politics: Essays on the Convergence of National and International Systems*. New York: Free Press, 1969.

———. "Private Preferences and Political Responsibilities: The Relative Potency of Individual and Role Variables in the Behavior of United States Senators." In Quantitative International Politics, edited by J. D. Singer. New York: Free Press, 1968.

———. "Pre-Theories and Theories of Foreign Policy." In *Approaches to Comparative and International Politics*, edited by R. B. Farrell. Evanston, Ill.: Northwestern University Press, 1966.

Rossa, P. J., and L. Fountain. "The Interstate Component: Data and Indices." Interstate Behavior Analysis Project Research Report Number 30, University of Maryland, College Park, Md., 1977.

Searing, D. D. "Measuring Politicians' Values: Administration and Assessment of a Ranking Technique in the British House of Commons." *American Political Science Review* 72 (March 1978):65-79.

Semmel, A. K. "Some Correlates of Attitudes to Multilateral Diplomacy in the U.S. Department of State." *International Studies Quarterly* 20 (June 1976):301-324.

———. "Deriving Perceptual Data from Foreign Policy Elites: A Methodological Narrative." *Political Methodology* 2 (1975):29-49.

Starr, H., and B. A. Most. "The Substance and Study of Borders in International Relations Research." *Inernational Studies Quarterly* 20 (December 1976):581-620.

Stassen, G. H. "Individual Preference Versus Role-Constraint in Policy-Making." *World Politics* 24 (October 1972):96-119.

Wilkenfeld, J., G. W. Hopple, P. J. Rossa, and S. J. Andriole (1978a). Final Report of the Interstate Behavior Analysis Project, University of Maryland. College Park, Md, 1978.

Wilkenfeld, J., G. W. Hopple, S. J. Andriole, and R. N. McCauley (1978b).

"Profiling States for Foreign Policy Analysis." *Comparative Political Studies* 11 (April 1978):4-35.

Winham, G. R. "Developing Theories of Foreign Policy Making: A Case Study of Foreign Aid." *Journal of Politics* 32 (February 1970):41-70.

Winter, D. G., and A. J. Stewart. "Content Analysis as a Technique for Assessing Political Leaders." In *A Psychological Examination of Political Leaders*, edited by M. G. Hermann, pp. 28-61. New York: Free Press, 1977.

Young, R. A. "A Classification of Nations According to Foreign Policy Output." In *International Interactions: Theory and Practice of Events Analysis*, edited by E. Azar and J. Ben-Dak. London: Gordon and Breech, 1975.

9
Small-Group Dynamics and Foreign Policy Decision-Making: An Experimental Approach

Andrew K. Semmel
Dean Minix

Recent efforts to more fully understand the enormous complexities of foreign policy have motivated scholars to pay closer attention to the nature and dynamics of the decision processes preceding national actions. Accordingly, more systematic scrutiny is now given to the role and influence of cognitive processes, small group behavior, and organizational dynamics in the shaping of the content and quality of foreign policy decisions. This chapter follows in this research vein by focusing on the critical role that small groups play in the making of foreign policy decisions. Specifically, it highlights one of the potential pathologies that may be inherent in small group deliberations, the so-called "choice-shift" phenomenon.

Whatever its label—ad hoc committee, special action group, task force—the small decision unit is frequently the locus of important foreign policy activity. Small group deliberations are involved in virtually every phase of the decision process, ranging from information collection and assessment to option identification and recommendation to implementation and post-decision evaluation. In many cases, the small decision group is the principal and final decision body itself (see Janis 1972).

The major purposes of this chapter are to explore and explain substantive differences in decision outcomes arrived at by individual decision-makers and small groups and to illustrate, by

---

This chapter is a revised version of a paper originally presented at the "Workshop Conference on Military Policy Evaluation: Quantitative Applications" at the Strategic Studies Institute of the U.S. Army War College, June 2-4, 1977 and appears in Richard Farkas et al. *Military Decision-Making: Approaches and Evaluation* (Alphen a/d Rijn, The Netherlands: A. W. Sijthoff International Publishing Company, 1978).

example, the utility of experimental research in the study of foreign policy. Accordingly, we will present some experimentally derived decision data to buttress our contention that group-based decisions will differ significantly from individual decision outcomes. The issue is more than an academic one, for if the content of foreign policy decisions rendered by individual decision-makers systematically differs from the substance of small group choices, it is obviously important to find out which decision unit is responsible for foreign policy decisions. As we hope to show, our main objective is to measure choice shifts that occur between the two decision units and to analyze some of the possible sociopsychological effects of group interaction and discussion on individual behavior and collective choice-making.

The unique characteristic of small groups in decision-making studies is that they are likely to be populated with members with multiple policy preferences. Given this almost certain likelihood, how do the individual group members combine and sort out their conflicting preferences, to arrive at a final agreed-upon decision? How does this final decision reflect their initial or personal preferences? Is there a consistent pattern within the small group decision process whereby the multiplicity of options is somehow shifted from a more (or less) risky one to a less (or more) risky one? Or, to reiterate, how does the final group decision differ from the average or pooled preferences of the individuals comprising the group? Do foreign policy choices emanating from small decision units resemble the private preferences of the group's membership?

Choice Shifts

The most appropriate theoretical framework for addressing the individual-group dichotomy, the changes and shifts in final decisions, and the effects of idiosyncratic and group attributes on decision processes and outcomes can be found in the sociopsychological literature of "choice shift" (see Pruitt 1971a, 1971b). This literature (summarized below) treats as hypotheses, not as givens, the conventional wisdoms that groups lack boldness, that they tend to be conservative and cautious, and that they are motivated toward incrementalism in their actions. Considerable experimental evidence amassed from scores of studies suggest that groups have a propensity to opt for decisional alternatives that are both more risky and more cautious than the average preferences of their individual members. It is this bidirectional tendency of group decisions that has prompted us to systematically evaluate the choice-shift phenomenon in a foreign policy context.

Choice shifts have been measured among liberal arts students (Wallach, Kogan, and Bem 1962), graduate students in business administration (Stoner 1968), business executives (Marquis 1962), workers (Jamieson 1968), and experimental subjects in a dozen foreign countries: in Europe (Bateson 1966; Kogan and Doise 1969; Lamm and Kogan 1970), Canada (Ferguson and Vidmar 1971), Israel (Rim 1964), New Zealand (Jamieson 1968), and Uganda (Carlson and Davis 1971). Despite the intense interest of social psychologists in choice-shift research, there are infrequent references to it in the literature of political science and foreign policy (DeRivera 1968; Janis 1972; Hermann et al. 1974; George 1975; Kirkpatrick 1975a, 1975b; Kirkpatrick et al. 1976).

There are several excellent summaries and critiques of the literature on choice shifts the interested reader can consult: Kogan and Wallach 1967; Kelly and Thibault 1968; *Journal of Personality and Psychology* 20, no. 3 (1971); Vinokur 1971; or Kirkpatrick et al. 1976. The accumulated research over the past decade and a half has resulted in an impressive array of conflicting explanations and multiple findings—not unlike the findings derived from the more heterogeneous research seeking to identify the causes and correlates of foreign policy behavior (see, for example, McGowan and Shapiro 1973). Vinokur's (1971) survey of the field provides a useful review of the plural hypotheses and conflicting findings of this research. He identified four broad, overlapping types of hypotheses or models used to explain choice shifts in groups: the affective, the cognitive, the interactive, and the statistical (see also Cartwright 1971 and Kirkpatrick and Robertson 1976).

Affective models of choice-shift behavior include most research that interprets individual behavior change as a consequence of having to decide in the presence of others (i.e., in a group context). One explanation centers on the "sharing" or "diffusion of responsibility" thesis. Here, individuals are shielded from repercussions of their actions by their group anonymity.[1] The collective setting, in other words, distracts attention from individual responsibility and diverts it, instead, to the collectivity, thereby making it easier for the individual to endorse more risky (or more cautious) decisions. Should the outcome decision be regarded a success, the individual and the group could claim whatever credit is forthcoming (Wallach, Kogan, and Bem 1962; Melgram 1974; and Stoner 1968).

A second and very engaging affective explanation looks to the larger cultural attributes of society or subculture and relates risk-taking behavior to dominant values favorable or unfavorable to risky or cautious behavior. Thus, the rhetoric of risk and the centrality of risk-taking virtues (e.g., masculinity, youth, toughness) in a society or subsociety may render risky behavior a positive value.[2] In such a cultural setting, peer pressures can operate to allow a member of a group to behave in ways enabling him to regard himself at least as willing to take risks as any other group member (Brown 1965:698-706; Teger and Pruitt 1967; Pruitt 1971a).

Cognitive models judge choice shifts as a consequence of the situation at hand rather than of the conditions under which a decision is discussed and made. One variant of the model explains changes in individual judgment in rational or subjective utility terms: the individual alters his preference ordering and reassesses the value of success or the consequences of failure as a result of group discussion and then changes his behavior to accommodate these new values (Vinokur 1971). Another explanation falling under this set of cognitive models looks at the content of information exchanges and arguments raised in group discussions relating to the problem-task. When new information and persuasive arguments are introduced, they contribute to a different understanding of such things as the costs of negative consequences and the probability of success. These new elements tend to reduce uncertainty and increase familiarity with an issue and thereby encourage boldness and risk-taking or caution (Pruitt and Teger 1969; Vinokur 1971; Silverthorne 1971; Myers and Bishop 1971; see also Holsti 1976).

The third set of explanatory models, the *interactive*, focuses on the social or leader-follower processes in the group. High initial risk-takers tend to be highly committed to more risky alternatives and are more forceful, more confident in their views, and judged by others in the group as having more influence in the group discussion (Wallach, Kogan, and Bem 1962). The behavior of influential high-risk-takers (or influential low-risk-takers) within the group pulls along or releases others from the social constraints of the group and helps move them in the direction of the dominant members of the group (Pruitt 1971). This latter interpretation is slightly reminiscent of Asch's (1952) well-known study of conformity, where deviation from the norm by a determined individual made it easier and more probable that others in the group would follow the "leader."

The final hypothesis is a *statistical* one. Rather than affect, interaction, or informational influence within the group, this hypothesis accounts for choice shifts in terms of decision rules or the distribution of individual choice preferences at the outset. Choice shifts here are simply artifacts of the various experiments that are designed to explain them (Cartwright 1971; Zajonc, Wolosin, and Wolosin 1972).

More recently, choice-shift and related decision studies have been reinterpreted from the perspective of the *group* polarization hypothesis. This hypothesis holds that average group responses become extreme in the direction indicated by the average of the initial individual preferences (see Moscovici and Zavalloni 1969; and Myers and Lamm 1976). Decisional situations evoking initial risk-oriented responses generally elicit further shifts in the risky direction. Those items that produce shifts to caution are those that elicited initial cautious means. The group polarization hypothesis is regarded as a subset of the extremization phenomenon, which predicts movement away from some neutral point but does not predict the direction of the shift. A very recent review of attitude research, negotiations, juridical decisions, choice shifts, and related decision-making studies involving small group discussions lends strong support to the view that group polarization effects (e.g., choice shifts) are traceable to information exchange and influence and to interpersonal comparisons within the group (Myers and Lamm 1976). This conclusion, as we will see, is generally consistent with the findings we discovered in our own small-group experiments.

The current state of this research is marked by considerable dissension over which model or which explanatory variable best explains the phenomenon of choice shifts. The only major area of consensus is that such changes regularly do transpire. As one set of reviewers noted, choice shifts are "more easily replicated than explained" (Hinton and Reitz 1971:277).

In foreign policy literature, applications of choice shift are confined to the multiple "groupthink" case studies of Irving Janis (1972) and to de Rivera's discussions of U.S. risk-taking during the Korean intervention decision (1968). In addition, Crow and Noel (1965) and Hermann et al. (1974) found that subjects participating in simulation experiments tend to opt for risky alternatives when aggressive acts are initiated by others; in the Hermann et al. exercise, it was discovered that increased group interactions were likely to lead to the choice of more risk alternatives under conditions of a contrived nuclear strike.

Most of the evidence of choice shifts, however, comes from anecdotal accounts, case studies, memoirs, and case studies of actual foreign policy decisions. Arthur Schlesinger, for example, recalled a conversation with President Kennedy over events leading up to the U.S. decision in the Cuban missile crisis that illustrates the risk-taking potential of group interactions: "The trouble is that, when you get a group of senators together, they are always dominated by the man who takes the boldest and strongest line. That is what happened the other day. After Russell spoke, no one wanted to take issue with him. When you can talk to them individually, they are reasonable" (Schlesinger 1965:812).

Other accounts of the decision dynamics during the missile crisis suggest that several participants in EXCOM altered their views in the days preceding the final decision to implement the naval quarantine (Sorenson 1965; Abel 1966). For example, Secretary McNamara's commitment to the side of caution may have influenced others to follow a less risky course of action. It should be noted that McNamara initially had proposed a do-nothing response but shifted his advice to a sea blockade; others in EXCOM retreated from their original riskier proposals, such as invasions or selective air strikes, to endorse the final compromise decision (Allison 1971).

Sorenson (1965) has also recorded the changing effects of the group advice coming from the advisors surrounding President Kennedy. During the Bay of Pigs decision, they argued very little restraint and showed little caution concerning the dangers of an invasion of Cuba. Two years later, however, Kennedy's advisors apparently convinced the president to pursue a more moderate, though still risky, course of action. During the planning of the Bay of Pigs invasion, Chester Bowles, Arthur Schlesinger, and Senator Fulbright each expressed reservations over the CIA-sponsored invasion plan, but for a variety of reasons (many group-induced) they failed to articulate them before the group meetings. Bowles's memorandum to Secretary Rusk that "the chances of success are not greater than one out of three" (Halberstam 1972:85), and Schlesinger's own account of his reluctance to speak out against the invasion plan (1965:252-256), indicate that private criticism seldom found its way into active consideration during group discussions.

These examples serve to complicate the issue, since it is very difficult to sort out the positive or negative effects of group-induced shifts on foreign policy decisions solely from case studies or from anecdotal accounts, as valuable as both are.[3] Generalizations are hard to come by.[4] However, the methodology of controlled experimentation is well-suited to analysis of small-group decision processes and to making generalizations about group-induced outcomes.

Experimental Research

Alternative research strategies abound in the comparative study of foreign policy and foreign policy processes. Each strategy contains unique advantages and disadvantages likely to vary depending on the design and objectives of the research. First, a researcher can consult experts familiar with a given subject matter by carefully culling the existing literature for insights, data, and generalizations. This research mode may involve post facto library research or other forms of secondary analysis similar to the comparative case studies researched by Irving Janis (1972). As a research strategy, resort to experts is limited by the available resources at hand and may be subject to or influenced by prevailing orthodoxies.

A second strategy involves field research, which embraces a variety of empirically based methodologies. Surveys of elites (e.g., Deutsch, et al. 1967) or specialized interviews (Dexter 1970; Lane 1964) with active or former participants can lead to valuable data-based findings. These in turn can build to generalizations across cases or across individuals or can be utilized for the reconstruction of a given policy decision or decision process. Scholars especially concerned with the external validity of their findings have found field studies a preferred research methodology. Some fundamental difficulties exist, though. Researchers familiar with field studies involving attitudinal data, for example, are painfully aware of the problems of access, sampling, and secrecy, to say nothing of the financial and time costs of such research (Dexter 1970; Semmel 1975). Frequently, these obstacles translate into frustration and limited scholarly payoffs. Numerous exceptions exist, but the entrenched problems of reliability and validity cannot be easily dismissed and have deterred many analysts from adopting this particular research mode.

A third research strategy relies largely on unobtrusive measures devised to analyze foreign policy outcomes and/or processes from a distance. Typically, this strategy can involve a content analysis of documents, official records, or varying kinds of interpersonal, intergroup, or internation communication (see Holsti 1969, 1972; North et al. 1963). Events surveys, which focus on the kinds, the frequency, and the direction of nation actions and interactions illustrate a second type of unobtrusive research method (see Azar 1970; Rosenau 1974). Various national attributes have been used to measure internation distances or national capabilities or to construct other theoretically relevant nation typologies (see Rummel 1969; Rosenau 1969; Moore 1974). Although scores of studies have utilized content analysis, events surveys, or national attribute theory, they tend to focus on outcomes to the exclusion, or at least, minimization, of the process leading up to decision outcomes.

A final research strategy—the one employed in our study—is experimental research. Experimentation involves the more or less artificial recreation or reconstruction, through analogy or modelling, of the foreign policy phenomenon under investigation. The advantages of laboratory research have long been recognized by scholars outside political science—who have benefited enormously in their research on decision-making at both the micro and macro levels. Indeed, much of the data-base for individual and sociopsychologically oriented study of foreign policy and international relations has its intellectual genesis in experimental research (see Kelman 1965; Singer 1965; de Rivera 1968; Jervis 1968). Regrettably, experimental research "remains in relative infancy in political science, including the decision-making field" (Kirkpatrick et al. 1976:56). Nonetheless, its advantages are unique and make it a valuable instrument for conducting foreign policy research.

Laboratory research allows for close inspection, observation, and measurement of decisional behavior generally not available to researchers in their natural settings. Experimental research enables one to design controls and impose management over the interaction of the variables and the effects they are thought to produce—e.g., choice shifts. By structuring the experiment so extraneous factors can be accounted for and independent variables manipulated, hypotheses can be tested and rival explanations of decision processes and outcomes subjected to more precise analysis and evaluation.

When controls are carefully built into the experiment, they tend to increase internal validity and allow for the testing of causal relationships between the treatment variables and the effects they are intended to produce. Finally, replication permits an analyst to observe and assess similar processes more than once, a luxury rarely enjoyed in other research modes. Repeated observation can assist in establishing greater reliability and confidence in one's findings and in establishing criteria for evaluating external validity (see Campbell and Stanley 1963).

The drawbacks of experimentation are well-known. Controlled experiments generally have low external validity, making it hazardous to generalize findings to a population beyond the subjects in the experiment. The credibility of the pretense and the goodness of the fit between the laboratory and the natural setting as well as the differences in the "stakes" involved for real and temporary role players are only some of the critical problems relating to external validity.

Admittedly, these are serious questions that raise doubts about the validity and utility of experimental studies designed to investigate foreign policy outputs and processes. These problems, however, need not be a deterrent to imaginative research and creative testing of hypotheses. Weighting the liabilities heavier than the advantages of experimentation ignores the disadvantages of alternative research strategies. As two analysts of collective behavior have noted, "Short of this (experimentation), hypothesis testing must wait upon when, and what, the natural world chooses to yield" (Marx and Wood 1975) and/or what we choose to or are able to observe. We think a compelling argument can be made for preempting the natural world rather than permitting it to direct and dictate scholarly interest and activity.

Experimental studies are no substitute for direct observation if direct observation is possible. Important determinants of foreign policy outcomes, such as small-group processes, however, are almost always immunized from direct observation and measurement. Indeed, access to small groups involved in foreign policy making is ordinarily more difficult to achieve than access to individual-level or organizational-level data. Transcripts of small-group meetings—if kept at all—are rarely made available for public consumption; outside consumers are only occasionally invited to participate in or to witness the decisional activity of small groups. Experimentation is clearly the "least worst" research strategy available to our needs. These comments are not intended to detract from the genuine problems of substituting surrogates—our students, ROTC cadets, and junior military officers—for real-life decision-makers; rather, they are intended to highlight the obstacles to systematic research inherent in foreign policy analyses.

Methodology

The design for this study departed from the conventional choice-shift design in a number of ways.[5] First, the subjects who participated in the exercise were drawn from three contrasting populations: (1) U.S. army officers (N = 28) enrolled in the Fall 1976 Armor Officers Advanced Course at the U.S. Armor School at Fort Knox, Kentucky[6]; (2) student ROTC cadets (N = 39) enrolled in the army and air force reserve officers training programs at the University of Cincinnati[7]; and (3) a larger sample of students (N = 56) at the University of Cincinnati. Each experiment was conducted in the "natural" or "quasi-natural" environments of the three groups. In all, 123 individuals participated in the experiment. When combined into small groups, this resulted in twenty-six decision groups.

Several officers had combat experience and/or served one or more tours of duty overseas prior to their participation in the advanced course at Fort Knox. The advanced course is a regular career component for army Armor officers and includes in its core curriculum instruction in principles of decision-making, leadership, motivation, and related subjects. The cadets similarly received instruction in decision-making and training in leadership assertion. The student sample too was heavily exposed to instruction in decision processes. Although we anticipated different levels of initial risk-taking across the three samples, the differences in the direction (risky or cautious) and the magnitude (size) of their choice shifts were open to speculation.

As we noted earlier, there have been only a few direct applications of choice-shift research to foreign policy research (see Semmel 1976; Minix 1976). A novel feature of the experimental design, therefore, includes the use of six foreign policy scenarios designed to pose varying degrees of threat to the United States—threats which could conceivably occur in the contemporary international system. Although each scenario was contrived explicitly for the exercise, we were reassured of its utility by the fact that the various participants overwhelmingly endorsed it as credible (see Appendix A). Summarized, the six scenarios are:

1. A Soviet naval blockage of the strategic Strait of Hormuz (Persian Gulf).
2. The downing and capture of a U.S. reconnaissance plane and its crewmen in Cambodia (Cambodia).

3. An overt military threat to South Korea and U.S. personnel and dependents from North Korea (South Korea).
4. The collapse of SALT negotiations and the discovery of major Soviet breaches of SALT I agreements (SALT).
5. The boarding of a U.S. navy cruiser at the entrance to the Panama Canal by the Panamanian navy (Panama).
6. The occupation of a European embassy by Arab guerrillas resulting in several casualties (Hague).

Each scenario was followed by an identical set of ten possible responses. These options ranged from those judged to be least risky (e.g., engage in bilateral talks) to those which were clearly more extreme (e.g., the threatened or actual use of nuclear weapons). The ten-point options scale was determined by means of the paired-comparisons technique (Torgerson 1958; North et al. 1963; Smith et al. 1976).[8] This scale was developed because we were interested in the level of risk each participant was willing to recommend in order to accomplish a common desired outcome—the protection of U.S. interests. After selecting a course of action, each participant was also asked to estimate the choice his peers (officers, students, cadets) would make for each scenario.

In addition to the responses generated by the foreign policy scenarios, we collected a variety of demographic, personality, and experience data from each of the participants. These measures included a flexibility or rigidity scale (the California Psychological Inventory, or CPI) a political belief index (PBS), and a political involvement abroad scale (PIN).[9] Each decision group was profiled according to the unique combination of attributes among its membership.

Findings

The experiment was designed to test a number of hypotheses comparing individual and group choice-making behavior. Specifically, we wanted to identify and explain differences in the direction (to risk or to caution) and in the magnitude of decision shifts for persons deciding alone and then deliberating in a small group. The main treatment variable is the group membership (GROUP)—that is, the three subsamples studied in this research. Analysis of variance and arithmetic mean and shift scores are presented below. They show that differences between the two types of decision units are significant across the three experimental groups. The differences are statistically significant for each of the "pre-test," "post-test," and "shift" scores observed in the experiment. In addition, we calculated a set of regression coefficients to measure the relative effects of several independent variables on the three decision responses. Together these statistics can provide a useful description and a possible explanation of the pattern of decision responses observed in the experiment.

Analysis of Variance

Presented here are findings that enable us to state whether or not the respective decision responses were derived from the same population; that is, whether or not the dependent variables are statistically significantly across the three subsamples. Our main hypothesis, therefore, is:

H1. The decision responses will each be statistically significant across the three experimental groups.

To test intersample differences, we utilized an analysis of variance program with a 3 x 5 (6) x 1^{10} factorial design, with repeated measures on the first two factors.[11] Thus, the five (or six) crisis scenarios and the three experimental groups were treated as repeated measures. Tables 1a, 1b, and 1c on the following page present F-statistics and probability levels showing that intersample differences for each of the three decision scores are all statistically significant ("pre-test": $F = 5.88$; $df = 2$; $p < .01$; "post-test": $F = 17.01$; $df = 2$; $p < .01$; "shift": $F = 11.44$; $df = 2$; $p < .01$). The practical meaning of these statistics is that the response scores for each decision variable are significantly different across the three sets of subjects involved in the experiment.

We do not want to make more out of these tables than is due. F-statistics do not and can not directly tell us the magnitude of differences across the treatment variable, nor can they tell us the direction of the differences (Iverson and Norpoth 1976). They can suggest that there are important differences between and among the sample subjects. These tables permit us to conclude that the first hypothesis (H1) is supported.

Direction and Size: Mean and Shift Scores

In two earlier papers (Semmel 1976; Minix 1976), we reported briefly on both the direction and the magnitude of the choice shifts within and among the three experimental groups. Looking at

TABLE 1

A. ANOVA for "Pre-Test" Responses for Three Experimental Groups

	Sum of Squares	Degrees of Freedom	Mean Square	F Ratio	Significance
Groups	23.79	2	11.89	5.88	0.009
Residual	46.49	23	2.03		

B. ANOVA for "Post-Test" Responses for Three Experimental Groups

Groups	182.27	2	91.14	17.01	0.000
Residual	123.25	23	5.36		

C. ANOVA for "Shift" Scores for Three Experimental Groups

Groups	74.49	2	37.24	11.44	0.000
Residual	74.86	23	3.25		

the differences between the "pre-test" and the "post-test" decision responses for *all* scenarios (N = 148), we reported that the twenty-six groups shifted to a more risky option 54 percent (N = 80) of the time, moved to caution 44 percent (N = 65) of the time, and failed to register any shift in only 2 percent (N = 3) of the cases.

When we computed the average shift responses per group across the set of six crisis scenarios, the results were far more suggestive and revealing. All the military groups shifted to risk when they deliberated as a small decision unit and all but one of the ROTC cadet groups recorded riskier preferences than they expressed in private. The college students, however, behaved in a mixed and ambivalent manner: five of the twelve groups endorsed more risky choices, while seven moved in a more cautious direction. In terms of direction of choice shift, the students represent the deviant cases.

The principal directional hypotheses we tested include the following:

H2. The military officer group will shift to risk more often than the ROTC cadet groups and more often than the college student groups.

H3. The ROTC cadet groups will shift to risk less often than the military officer groups and more often than the college student groups.

In a sense, hypotheses H2 and H3 assert that the direction of the choice shifts will vary with the personnel composition of the small group. Here, we expected the military units to express the highest levels of risk-taking and the college students to endorse the lowest levels of riskiness. Accordingly, we posed two closely related hypotheses:

H4. The military officer groups will elicit choice preferences on both the "pre-test" and the "post-test" decision responses that are higher than the ROTC cadet groups and the college student groups.

H5. The ROTC cadet groups will elicit choice preferences in both the "pre-test" and the "post-test" decision responses that are lower than the military officer groups and higher than the college student groups.

Table 2 presents a comprehensive overview and summary of the response patterns for each crisis scenario by each experimental group. Included are the "pre-test" scores, the "post-test" responses, and the "shift" scores for each subsample across the six crisis situations. On the whole, the officer groups not only supported greater levels of risk-taking in both the individual and group decision settings but also shifted greater distances and more often to risk than did both the ROTC cadets and the student groups. In almost every scenario, the officers recommended options which required the actual or threatened use of force to protect U.S. national security. By contrast, the twelve student groups preferred to negotiate with the adversary and to recommend the use of diplomatic moves on all but the South Korean crisis (see Appendix A). The ROTC cadets recorded preferences which were, as hypothesized, somewhat more cautious than the officer groups, but more risky than the student decision units.

Figure 1 graphs the mean shift scores on each scenario for each experimental group. The pattern of movement is a clear one. In all but three instances, the differences in decision shifts are as hypothesized. The officer groups failed to register a shift response greater than the ROTC groups on only one scenario (Item 4: SALT). The ROTC groups recorded smaller shifts to risk than the students on two scenarios (Item 1: Persian Gulf; and Item 3: South Korea). These three results were unexpected and deviant cases, but it should be borne in mind that shift scores only represent the size of the difference between the individual and group-based decision units. They do not represent the riskiness of the option actually selected. A closer look at Table 2, for example, would show that a shift of +1.55 from a "pre-test" of 6.79 (Military

TABLE 2

"Pre-Test," Post-Test," and Shift" Decision Responses for Each Experimental Sample

Scenario	Officers (N=28)			ROTC-Cadets (N=39)			Students (N=56)		
	Pre	Post	Shift*	Pre	Post	Shift*	Pre	Post	Shift*
Persian Gulf	4.28	7.17	+2.89	3.11	2.13	-0.99	3.74	3.75	+0.01
Cambodia	3.66	5.00	+1.35	4.60	5.88	+1.28	3.75	1.92	-1.84
South Korea	6.79	8.33	+1.55	5.39	5.98	+0.59	4.37	5.17	+0.80
SALT	3.28	3.83	+0.55	2.89	3.63	+0.74	2.68	2.08	-0.60
Panama	6.89	7.85	+0.95	5.60	6.00	+0.40	4.91	4.25	-0.66
Hague	5.27	5.83	+0.56	----	----	-----	3.96	3.67	-0.29
$\bar{X}$	5.03	6.33	+1.31	4.32	4.72	+0.40	3.90	3.47	-0.43

* A positive shift value indicates a shift-to-risk and a negative shift value a shift to caution.

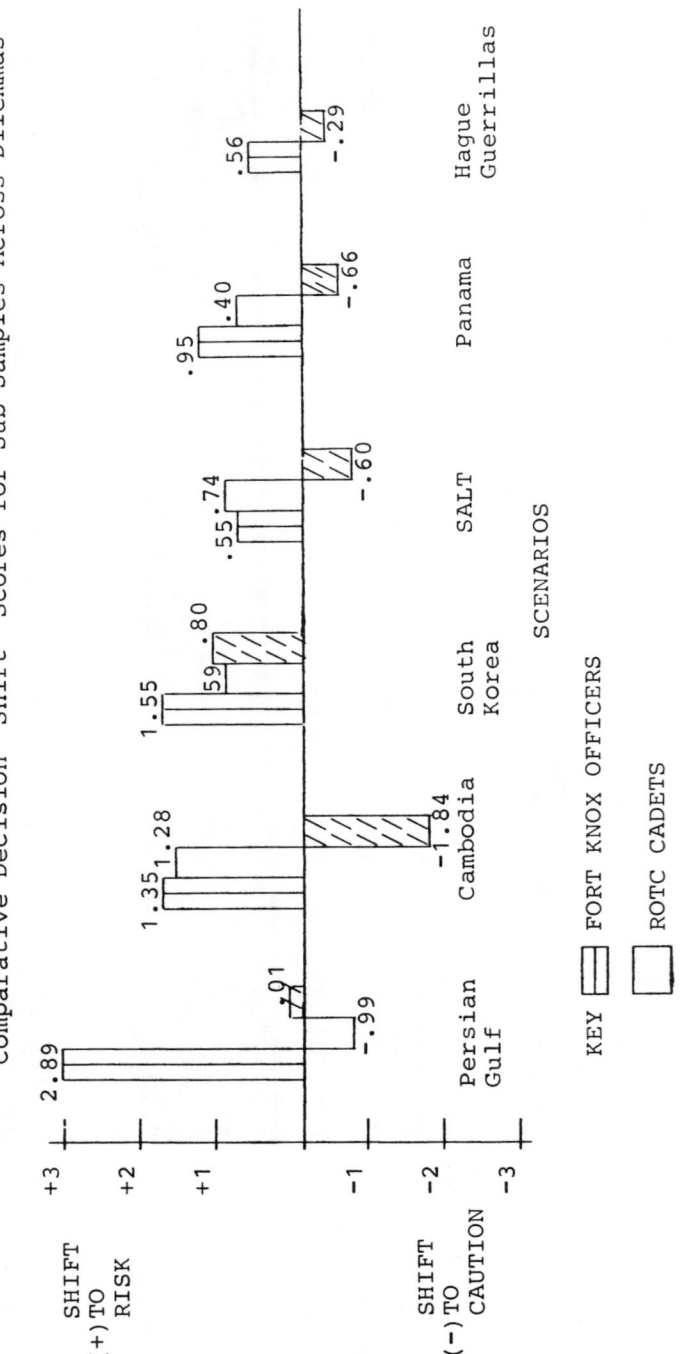

Blockade) is substantially different from a hypothetical but identical shift of +1.55 from a "pre-test" base of, say, 2.00 (Call a meeting of the UN Security Council). The former shift score clearly involves a greater commitment of resources, planning, and risk than the latter, even though the two shift scores are identical.

In sum, we can conclude that hypotheses H2 through H5 are supported by the evidence presented. Some exceptions exist, but the comparative levels of risk-taking in the "pre-test," the "post-test," and the direction and size of the decision shifts do conform to what we hypothesized.

It must be strongly emphasized that we do not and cannot claim to know which level of risk or caution is appropriate or inappropriate for any given scenario. We cannot say, for example, that the army officers were unnecessarily supporting levels of risk in excess of that required for a resolution of a given crisis or that student groups were endorsing undue caution when less restraint was called for. A recommendation of a more extreme option in one situation may reflect proper judgement, while an identical recommendation in another situation may indicate poor judgment. These findings only indicate the pattern of choice-making across individual and small-group decision settings within and across the subsamples included in the study. Nevertheless, the results do indicate that efforts to reconcile differences among group members eventuate in contrasting decisions for the military and ROTC groups on the one hand and the students on the other.

Measures of Strength

One question remains: Which explanatory variable or variables best account for the pattern of decision responses found in Table 2 and pictured in Figure 1? Put differently, what best explains the variance in each of the three dependent decision variables? To derive a measure of strength, we computed separate regression coefficients for each decision response variable. In addition to our core explanatory variable, group membership (GROUP), we analyzed the separate and combined effects on the decision scores of the following independent variables: (1) psychological rigidity (CPI); (2) political beliefs (PBS); (3) support for U.S. political involvement abroad (PIN); (4) group size (GRSIZE); and (5) type of decision rule used (DECRULE).

Here we had no specific hypothesis or set of hypotheses in mind. Frankly, the analysis in this section involved a fishing excursion into the data. However, we would be surprised if the

GROUP factor failed to correlate highly with the decision variables or failed to explain a considerable proportion of the variance in each of the decision responses. As for the remaining explanatory variables, we had no ironclad expectations. These variables were included in the analysis because they represent possible rival explanations of the decision responses. We anticipated that the index of rigidity (CPI) would correlate highly with the frequency and magnitude of shifts, regardless of direction. More flexible subjects and groups composed of flexible members are likely to be more susceptible to interpersonal influence and more likely to agree to group decisions different from their own preferences. Similarly, we reasoned that subjects and groups expressing stronger support for U.S. involvement abroad would endorse higher levels of risk-taking on both the "pre" and the "post" test responses.

The political belief, group size, and decision rule variables were analyzed because we wanted to ascertain their independent and relative effects as well. Considerable evidence exists that conservatism correlates positively with activism abroad or with the use of more coercive instruments of foreign policy (see McClosky 1967). There is also evidence that the size of the group will affect the decision process and the quality and content of outcomes (Bales 1950; Collins and Guetzkow 1964; Hare 1962:224-25). Finally, several studies have shown that the type of decision rule (unanimous versus majority vote) employed elicits different response patterns (Kirkpatrick and Robinson 1976; Semmel 1976; Scheff 1963). Some studies have explicitly pointed out that majority-vote decision rules are more conducive to risky decisions or, at least, to larger choice shifts. To repeat, we anticipate that the GROUP variable will be the most potent of these explanatory factors.

The three multiple regression tests in Table 3 show the relative and cumulative effects of the explanatory variables on the three decision variables. The explanatory variables are arranged in hierarchical order according to their relative contribution to the cumulative percentage of variance explained (R^2 change). Pearson product-moment correlation coefficients (r) are also presented to show the simple bivariate association between each variable and each decision score—without considering the additional effects of the remaining variables. The beta coefficients are standardized beta statistics and indicate the amount of change in each dependent variable for every unit change in the independent variable

TABLE 3

Multiple Regression

"Shift"

	Multiple R	R^2	R^2 Change	r	Beta
GROUP	0.705	0.497	0.497	0.705	0.744
DECRULE	0.719	0.518	0.021	-0.152	-0.167
PIN	0.731	0.535	0.017	-0.077	0.201
PBS	0.747	0.558	0.023	0.066	0.152

"Post-Test"

	Multiple R	R^2	R^2 Change	r	Beta
GROUP	0.769	0.593	0.593	0.769	0.593
CPI	0.791	0.626	0.034	-0.643	-0.301
GRSIZE	0.806	0.649	0.023	-0.024	-0.135
PBS	0.813	0.661	0.011	0.103	0.124

"Pre-Test"

	Multiple R	R^2	R^2 Change	r	Beta
CPI	0.611	0.373	0.373	-0.611	-0.490
PIN	0.662	0.438	0.065	-0.185	-0.133
GROUP	0.675	0.455	0.018	0.577	0.221
PBS	0.681	0.464	0.008	0.117	0.103

with all other independent variables held constant. Each table, finally, lists only those explanatory variables that account for at least 1 percent of the variance in the decision responses.

The tables reinforce the conclusions discussed earlier. Group membership, and presumably group dynamics, account for most of the variance in both the "post-test" scores ($R^2 = .59$) and the choice-shift differences ($R^2 = .49$). In each case, the multiple R^2 is almost solely determined by the robust size of the R^2 for group membership. The one exception is found in Table 3 where the GROUP variable explains only 2 percent of the total variance. The negligible effect of GROUP membership on the "pre-test" decision scores is traceable to the fact that, in this experimental phase, the GROUP variable only refers to the mean of the individual "pre-tests." Although the strength of the GROUP variable on the "post-test" may be traceable to actual group processes, its impotence in explaining "pre-test" results can be traced to the absence of any possible group-induced effects.

The GROUP and CPI variables have the strongest and most consistent bivariate relationship with the three decision responses. Table 4 reproduces the Pearson product-moment correlations for these two variables; the entries in the table show that the correlation between GROUP membership and each decision response is strong and positive while the r's for the CPI index are strong, but

TABLE 4

Pearson r Coefficients for GROUP and CPI-Index

	Pre-Test	Post-Test	Shift
GROUP	+.58	+.77	+.71
CPI	−.61	−.64	−.50

negatively related. These latter correlations would suggest that more flexible subjects or experimental groups are less likely to register risk-oriented preference than rigid subjects. The remaining variables—PBS, PIN, DECRULE, GRSIZE—all have weak bivariate relationships and contribute little to the overall variance in the three decision scores.

Discussion

The three sets of statistical findings presented above all point to group membership as the critical explanatory variable. The analysis of variance showed that statistically significant differences exist in the decision responses across the three experimental samples. The mean and shift scores displayed in Table 2 portrayed the overall pattern in the direction and magnitude of the three decision responses within and across the sampled groups. Finally, the bivariate and multivariate analyses helped sort out the relative strengths of several independent variables and to identify which variable(s) accounted for the explained variance in the decisions scores. In all cases, the GROUP setting proved to be the most potent variable on which to anchor an explanation of our findings.

The statistical findings are impressive in their consistency, yet they do not, by themselves, account for the process or dynamic that shaped the actual decision results. It should be clear by now that factors must have been operating in the student groups that were different from those in the officer and ROTC cadet decision units. The question we must now pose is: How can we further explain the effects of decision dynamics on the pattern of choice shifts among the three experimental groups?

Earlier, we summarized a number of models or explanatory modes extant in the choice-shift literature. Here, we propose to link our findings to decision processes by combining elements of the "cultural value" thesis (Brown 1965; Carleson and Davis 1971) and the "group polarization" thesis (Myers and Lamm 1976; Moscovici and Zavalloni 1969). Briefly, the former looks at the peculiar cultural or value milieu of a decision unit and predicts that the direction and content of its decision will reflect relevant group values. The group polarization thesis simply explains choice shift as an enhancement of the dominant value already expressed by group members in the initial, or "pre-test," phase of the experiment. When combined, these two theses explain choice shifts in terms of the reinforcement of dominant values within the group and among group members. Through the media of group discussion, information exchange, and exposure to relevant arguments about the desirability of certain outcomes, cognitive learning takes place among group participants. The new information is processed by individuals to reinforce and enhance pre-existing dispositions. Recalcitrants are pulled along by the strength of persuasive arguments. Options may be revised, but, depending on the value milieu of the small group, revisions tend to move in the direction of the already preferred pole—i.e., to more risk or to more caution. Such a hybrid explanation has the theoretical advantage of being able to embrace both shifts to risk and shifts to caution in experimental studies and in actual foreign policy processes.

This explanation would seem superficial if it were not for the fact that the decision responses of the officer and the ROTC groups were so different from those of the students. When this reasoning is reformulated into hypotheses, we have the following:

H6. Decision groups that shift to risk will have higher "pre-test" scores on average than those groups that shift to caution;

H7. Decision groups that shift to caution will have lower "pre-test" scores on average than those groups that shift to risk;

and,

H8. The direction and size of choice shifts can be explained by the content of the information exchanged during group discussions.

Hypotheses H6 and H7 compare the average individual "pre-test" scores with the mean "post-test" responses and assess directional changes between them. In conformity with the group polarization thesis, those groups recording high (low) on the initial decision runs would score higher (lower) on the group-based decision choices.

Figure 2 visualizes the "pre-test" and the "post-test" marginals (from Table 2) of each experimental sample and vividly illustrates the direction of the changes between the two decision results. The officer groups shift sharply upwards (to risk), as do the ROTC cadets, although the incline of the latter is less pronounced. On the whole, the student groups show a reduction in risk-taking when they deliberate as small groups—hence, the downward or negative directional slope. Unlike the military and quasi-military groups, the effect of deciding in small groups for the students was to lessen the level of risk they expressed in private settings.

The officer groups shifted to more risky alternatives as anticipated by hypothesis H6; the ROTC groups did the same, although they registered a less dramatic movement to more extreme options. The student groups, on the other hand, changed to less extreme preferences, as hypothesis H7 suggests. Generally, those decision units which recommended diplomatic options at the outset did not shift to military options and those which preferred force-related alternatives in private were inclined to the increased use of military solutions in their small group discussions.

Unfortunately, we did not collect the kind of systematic evidence from the group discussions that is required to support or refute hypothesis H8. We did tape-record all the discussions of the military groups. What follows is by no means systematic or definitive. Yet a qualitative content analysis of the recorded discussions yields some valuable clues—which tend to confirm our last hypothesis.

The discussions within the officer groups were generally marked by considerable rhetoric of risk.[12] Typically, a discussion began with an individual describing the scenario and expressing his personal preference: "I think 8 is the bare minimum (Korea)," or "I can go with 10 based on this information. Do you want to go with 10 (Korea)?" The thematic content of the interchange within the officer groups pertained mostly to: (1) the strategic importance and the security threats of each situation to the United States; (2) recent and historic analogies and previous action taken or not taken (e.g., Munich 1972; *Mayaguez*; *Pueblo*; Entebbe); (3) the needs to establish or reestablish U.S. credibility through action; and (4) intense discussion of the potential gains and likely costs of selecting a given option in a given crisis. The following

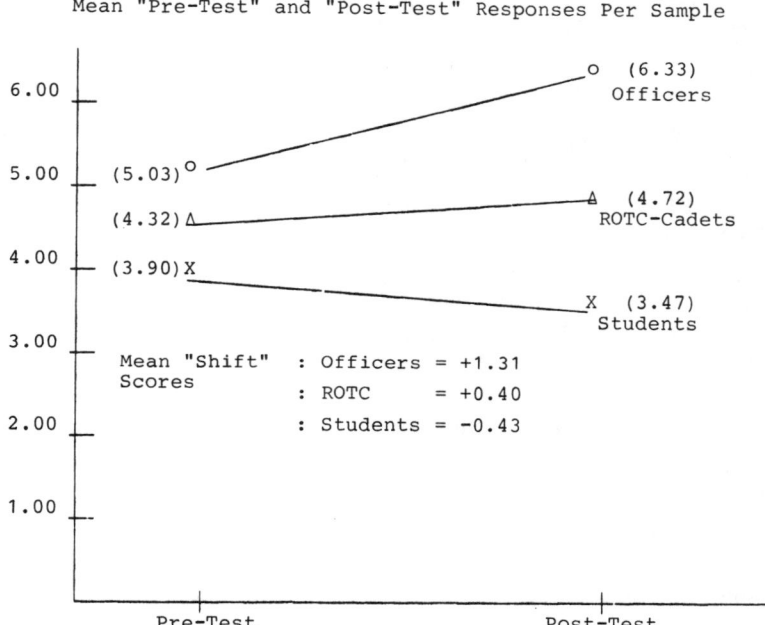

FIGURE 2

Mean "Pre-Test" and "Post-Test" Responses Per Sample

excerpt illustrates one exchange within one officer group deciding how to respond to a terrorist occupation of the U.S. embassy in the Hague:

> Subject 1: I'd use whatever force is necessary on them. I want them out.
> Subject 2: Well, I wouldn't play games with them.
> Subject 1: If we lose a few, we lose a few ... we want immediate action.
> Subject 3: There will be a lot of repercussions. I would accede to their demands.
> Subject 4: Eight months ago, we had some terrorists lock themselves in the Hague. You really have to admire the Israelis ... I'd say, another raiding party.
> Subject 3: We're becoming more militant as we go along.

Although the specifics of this exchange are unique, the direction and the content were not atypical.

Additional illustrations of the prevailing value of the officer groups could be cited, but they would closely resemble this example. "Wait and see" suggestions were rarely raised in the officer groups; instead, the discussions nearly always centered on the imperatives of committing the United States to some course of action. As one officer concluded, "You either throw in the towel or come out fighting." Many of the student groups, by contrast, discussed the utility of "riding out" the crises and/or resolving them through negotiation and diplomatic intercourse. We have no detailed record of these discussions, but some post-experiment debriefings do indicate that information introduced into discussions was persuasive in altering downwards the initially risky private preferences of some student subjects.

Information exchange in the form of persuasive arguments about the desirability of a given option or a given outcome appears to have been the most influential factor shaping group decisions. From the fragmentary evidence we gathered, the content of the information exchanged in the student and officer groups disposed the latter to move to riskier and the former to shift to more cautious decisions. Group polarization apparently did take place in the direction of the dominant values of each experimental sample, since the initial individual values or preferences were apparently strengthened and enhanced by the small group deliberation.

Conclusion

What, finally, are the policy inferences or lessons to be drawn from this research? We believe that the quality and content of foreign policy decisions can be judged most feasibly by an analysis of the quality of the processes which precede them (see Janis and Mann 1977). Only after the impediments to optimal information processing or rational choice-making are identified can one hope to devise means for rendering higher quality foreign policy decisions.

Several researchers have identified a potential "group-pathic" tendency in small-group decision-making. Irving Janis, for one, noted that the advantages of making decisions in small groups are often lost because interpersonal pressures among closely knit, like-minded individuals may lead to premature closure and defective decision-making. Based on his analyses, Janis (1972, Chapter 9) recommends the institutionalization of a devil's advocate, the introduction of outside participants, the use of second-chance reconsiderations, and other devices to spur more discussion and greater independent thinking. Other scholars, noting similar defects in small deliberative groups, recommend a restructuring of the decision process so the acknowledged advantages of diversity, information recall and exchange, and option identification are not lost. Several innovative techniques such as Delphi (Brown et al. 1974; Schweitzer 1977), the Nominal Group Technique (Delbecq et al. 1975), and Multiple Attribute Utility Theory (see Edwards 1976; Laurence 1977) are decision strategies intended to enhance the positive advantages of small-group exchange of ideas without having to contend with the corrosive pressures of interpersonal dynamics.

The most general recommendation for avoiding or moderating excessive choice shifts is to alter the decision culture of the groups themselves. One suggestion is for acknowledged leaders to refrain from overly directive behavior and to promote decision recommendations that truly reflect the calculations of the group, rather than deference to its leader(s). Short of changing the group norms and ambiance—largely a function of leadership style, tolerance, and personality—our findings suggest that higher quality decisions are more likely when they are made by groups composed of a heterogeneous mix of individuals recruited from different organizational subunits or backgrounds. Although we did not integrate our three samples, it is likely that the magnitude and the direction of the choice shifts would have been less extreme had we done so. Greater diversity would increase the probability that the quality and quantity of information exchange, considered as a variable, would rival or surpass the "group" variable as the best predictor of the "post-test" group response and the size and direction of choice shifts.

Outsiders who are not wedded to specialized interests and who do not stand to gain by promoting one view over another would contribute further to group diversity. Ideally, the group members would have reasonably comparable resources and prestige to lend weight to their inputs, but this can rarely be approached (see George 1972). Nonetheless, greater diversity is likely to introduce a broader range of perspectives in group discussions so no one perspective can easily dominate. The advantages of an intragroup adversary process, with structured conflicts over multiple biases, may not always minimize faulty decision-making or avoid excessive shifts to risk or caution. Indeed, it may compound them by creating endless debates, by consuming valuable time, or by permitting the chief executive the latitude to choose his own preferences over those of his hopelessly deadlocked advisors. Despite these real problems, the small cosmopolitan group carries with it the potential for expanding search and appraisal, for increasing the range of choice, for introducing competing interpretations of events, and for teasing out the underlying assumptions the members hold about foreign policy and/or the case at hand. Should any of these changes develop because of conscious efforts to broaden the composition of the decision units—mixing military with diplomatic decision-makers, specialists with generalists, and/or insiders with outsiders—the prospects for improved quality of decision should be enhanced (though by no means guaranteed). Each of these suggestions is, of course, likely to introduce costs or problems of its own. Regrettably, there are no panaceas in foreign policy or no certain ways to avoid decision error or miscalculation.

We can conclude that the findings generated by this project may provide useful insights into foreign policy behavior at the individual and small-group levels of analysis. Linking the two levels of analysis with an emphasis on decision processes should be a research priority among those analysts who believe, as we do, that much of the variance in foreign policy behavior can be explained by sociopsychological-type variables and theories.

Appendix A

The following is the scenario format used in the test and retest packets. The question at the bottom of each scenario was deleted in the group or retest packet. Note, also, that the directions and options are not included for scenarios 2-6 in the Appendix, but are included in the test and retest packets.

Situation 1

The Persian Gulf, the heartline of the Western world's oil supply, is connected to the Indian Ocean by the tiny stretch of water known as the Strait of Hormuz. The Soviet Union, which is the most prominent naval power in the area, has decided to block the strait and deprive the Western world of its vital energy source. As a member of the National Security Council, your recommendation to the president would be to:

A number of alternatives for action have been made. Some are more decisive and involve more risk to the United States, but are also more likely to bring about the desired outcome. If necessary, how far down the list of options below would you be willing to go in order to protect the interests of the United States?

Note that the alternatives are listed in the order of the extremity of the action involved. The first item is the least extreme and the last the most extreme. CHECK ONLY ONE ITEM!

_____ 1. Engage in bilateral negotiations or talks with the adversary to settle the crisis.
_____ 2. Call a meeting or special session of the United Nations Security Council.
_____ 3. Support (nonmilitarily) opposition elements in the area or nation in which the national interests and security of the United States is threatened.
_____ 4. Discontinue diplomatic relations with the adversary and attempt to sway world public opinion to the side of the United States.
_____ 5. Create economic turmoil in the adversary's country to substantially weaken his war effort.
_____ 6. Send military *advisors* to the area that is threatening to U.S. interests and security. These are noncombatant personnel only.
_____ 7. Establish a military or naval blockade of the adversary's country.
_____ 8. Use conventional ground forces to repel the adversary's threat.
_____ 9. Engage in limited *strategic* bombing of noncivilian, military sites only.
_____ 10. Use the nuclear capability of the United States to eliminate the possibility of many American deaths and to bring the adversary to the point of negotiation.

What option do you think most officers at or above your rank would be likely to recommend? (No. ___).

Situation 2

A U.S. reconnaissance aircraft recently strayed over the sovereign airspace of Cambodia. The plane was shot down with a Soviet-made surface-to-air missile and its highly secret, sophisticated technology and its two-man crew captured. Now, the government of Cambodia has secretly demanded that the United States commit itself to a $10 billion economic aid program over the next five years or risk the execution of the U.S. airmen as spies and the transfer of the secret aerial technology to the Soviet Union or China. As a member of the National Security Council, what is your recommendation to the President?

Situation 3

Three days ago, an ally of the United States—South Korea—thrust across the fortified border separating itself from North Korea. At the time, South Korea said that its military action was begun to prevent an attack from the North Koreans. This morning, it was learned that nearly 90,000 South Korean regulars have been encircled just north of the border. Included among the South Korean army are 200 U.S. military observers who followed the northward incursion. If the South Korean army is wiped out or forced to surrender, it would leave open a gap through which the North Koreans could push southward and threaten the safety of some 50,000 U.S. nationals in South Korea. As a member of the National Security Council, what is your recommendation to the President?

Situation 4

The Strategic Arms Limitation Talks (SALT) between the Soviet Union and the United States have attempted to produce an acceptable balance in the number, size, and capacity of missiles and bombers of the two countries. Such an agreement is based on the belief that both sides will abide by its provisions. Upon learning of drastic violations by the Soviets of this agreement, what would your National Security Council recommendation to the President be?

Situation 5

The Panamanian navy has detained and forcibly boarded a U.S. cruiser at the entrance to the Panama Canal. Its action has stalled all commercial and military traffic through the canal. Moreover, the Panamanian Government is holding the cruiser as "hostage" in order to compel the United States to yield to its demands for immediate nationalization of the

Canal Zone. As a member of the National Security Council, your recommendation to the President would be:

Situation 6

The U.S. Embassy in the Hague, Netherlands has been seized since early this morning by a militant faction of Arab nationalists who are a splinter group of a Chinese communist-supported organization that is headquartered in Damascus, Syria. Since the occupation, the guerillas have killed four and wounded two in a violent attempt to establish their credibility. The U.S. ambassador to the Netherlands is also a captive, but before his release, the guerrillas are demanding $10 million in cash, $3 million in medical supplies, and a safe exit out of the country via a Swiss airliner. As a member of the National Security Council, what is your recommendation to the President?

Notes

1. Similar explanations have been raised in trying to explain the collective behavior of crowds (e.g., Johnson 1974).

2. For a discussion of contrasting subcultures as they relate to decision style and risk-taking, see Henry T. Nash's (1973:96-99) comparison of military and nonmilitary approaches to conflict resolution.

3. Part of the problem, no doubt, stems from the difficulty in identifying what is meant by risk in concrete decision situations. In related research such as Asch's study (1952) or the so-called "Lost on the Moon Test" (see Hall 1971), which compares the correctness of individual and group decisions under survival circumstances, an objective or correct response is knowable. In actual foreign policy decision situations, the appropriate or correct level of risk is not always knowable, either before or after a decision response is made. Most analysts, moreover, agree that the quality of group-made decisions is higher than that of individuals acting alone. The intriguing problem, then, is to identify those group-based factors which lessen the advantages groups have in decision situations.

4. Risk-taking behavior may be associated with a host of other conditions: crisis situations, stress, uncertainty, a feeling of a loss of control, poor negative feedback (see Reedy 1970; Weisband and Frank 1975), groupthink (Janis 1972), the strategic decisional location of authoritarian or aggressive personalities (George 1969; Leites 1953), and cognitive rigidity (Garnham 1974), to mention a few possible sources.

5. The conventional design in choice-shift research typically utilizes (up to) twelve life dilemma decision situations incorporated in some version of a choice-dilemma questionnaire (CDQ). Subjects are asked to select a course of action that represents the lowest "probability of success' (e.g., 2 out of 10) they consider acceptable for a person to follow. They do so in private and again in small groups. The test-retest difference indicates the choice shift, with lower success probabilities (e.g., 1 out of 10) representing higher risk-taking and higher success probabilities indicating caution.

6. We would like to express our appreciation to the assistant commandant at Fort Knox, Brigadier General Paul S. Williams, and to Captain Keith Titus of the Leadership Department of the Advanced Course at Fort Knox for their cooperation and assistance in this exercise. The experiment was not conducted for or on behalf of the U.S. Army; the above graciously consented to our experiment uses only.

7. We want to express our appreciation also to Captain James Connell and Captain Paul Sefrin of the Military Science Department of the University of Cincinnati for their cooperation and assistance.

8. Paired-comparison scaling requires that all scale items (in this case, ten) be dyadically paired with every other item; using judges to select the more extreme item in that dyad; and calculating a frequency score for each option. In our research, this produced a relative scale of risk among all items ranging from low risk (bilateral talks) to high risk (threat or use of nuclear weapons) (see Smith et al. 1976).

9. The Political Belief Scale (PBS) profiles each subject's political ideology along the standard, seven-item, forced-choice scale that the Center for Political Studies (CPS) traditionally uses. The twenty-two item, true-false questionnaire from the California Psychological Inventory (CPI) measures a respondent's psychological rigidity or flexibility in accepting change. For an application to the study of foreign policy, see the studies by David Garnhan (1974). The Political Involvement Scale (PIN) was first used by Campbell et al. *The American Voter* (1960). This scale was obtained in Robinson, Rusk, and Head (1968:296-97).

10. The 5(6) entry in the factorial design indicates that the ROTC cadets were not asked to respond to scenario six (Hague Embassy). The officer and student samples were tested on all six scenarios.

11. The analysis of variance program that was used is part of the Biomedical Program Package (BMD) developed at the University of California at Los Angeles.

12. In writing about the Bay of Pigs decision, Schlesinger (1965:256) noted the importance of risk rhetoric among the supporters and opponents of the invasion plan: "[they] had a rhetorical advantage. They could strike virile poses and talk of tangible things. . . . To oppose the plan, one had to invoke intangibles."

References

Abel, Elie. *The Missile Crisis*. New York: Bantam, 1966.

Allison, Graham T. *Essence of Decision: Explaining the Cuban Missile Crisis.* Boston: Little, Brown, 1971.

Allison, Graham T., and Morton H. Halperin. "Bureaucratic Politics: A Paradigm and Some Policy Implications." *World Politics* (Spring 1972), pp. 40-79.

Asch, Solomon. "Affects of Group Pressure upon the Modification and Distortion of Judgment." In *Readings in Social Psychology*, edited by G. Swanson et al., pp. 2-11. New York: Henry Holt, 1952.

Azar, E. "Analysis of International Events." *Peace Research Reviews* 4 (November 1970).

Bales, Robert F. *Interaction Process Analysis*. Cambridge, Mass.: Harvard University Press, 1950.

Bateson, N. "Familiarization, Group Discussion, and Risk-Taking." *Journal of Personality and Social Psychology* (hereafter *JPSP*) 2 (1966):111-129.

Bem, Daryl, M. A. Wallach, and N. Kogan. "Group Decision-Making under Risk of Aversive Consequences." *JPSP* 1 (1965):453-460.

Brehm, D., and S. Cohen. "Re-evaluation of Choice Alternatives as a Function of Their Number and Qualitative Similarity." In *Dimensions in Social Psychology*, edited by W. E. Vinacke. Chicago: Scott-Foresman, 1964.

Brown, Rex et al. *Decision Analysis for the Manager*. New York: Holt, Rinehart, and Winston, 1974.

Brown, Roger. *Social Psychology*. New York: Free Press, 1965.

Campbell, D., and J. Stanley. *Experimental and Quasi-Experimental Designs for Research*. Chicago: Rand McNally, 1963.

Campbell, D. et al. *The American Voter*. New York: John Wiley, 1960.

Carleson, J., and C. Davis. "Cultural Values and the Risky Shift: A Cross-Cultural Test in Uganda and the United States." *JPSP* 20 (1971):392-399.

Cartwright, D. "Risk Taking by Individuals and Groups: An Assessment of Research Implying Choice Dilemmas." *JPSP* 20 (1971):361-378.

Collins, Barry, and H. Guetzkow. *Social Psychology of Group Processes for Decision-Making*. New York: John Wiley, 1964.

Crow, W., and J. Noel. "The Value Use of Simulation Results." Western Behavioral Science Institute Reprint, Contract No. DA-49-1460X2-110, June, 1965.

Delbecq, Andre et al. *Group Techniques for Program Planning: A Guide to Nominal Group and Delphi Processes*. Glencoe, Illinois: Scott Foresman, 1975.

De Rivera, Joseph H. *The Psychological Dimension of Foreign Policy*. Columbus: Charles Merrill, 1968.

Deutsch, K. et al. *France, Germany, and the Western Alliance*. New York: Scribner, 1967.

Dexter, L. *Elite and Specialized Interviewing.* Evanston, Ill.: Northwestern Press, 1970.

Dion, K. L., and N. Miller. "An Analysis of the Familiarization Explanation of the Risky Shift." *Journal of Experimental Social Psychology* (hereafter *JESP*) (1971):524-533.

Dion, K. L. et al. "Cohesiveness and Social Responsibility as Determinants of Group Risk Taking." *JPSP* 20 (1971):400-406.

Dion, K. L. et al. "Why Do Groups Make Riskier Decisions than Individuals?" *Advances in Experimental Social Psychology* 5 (1970):305-377.

Edwards, Ward. *How to Use Multi-Attribute Utility Measurement for Social Decision-Making.* Los Angeles: Social Science Research Institute, University of Southern California, 1976.

Eulau, H. "Problematics of Decisional Models in Political Contexts." *American Behavioral Scientist* 20, no. 1 (1976):127-143.

Ferguson, D., and N. Vidmar. "Effects of Group Discussion on Estimates of Culturally Appropriate Risk Levels." *JPSP* 20 (1971):436-445.

Festinger, Leon. *Theory of Cognitive Dissonance.* Stanford University Press, 1967.

Festinger, Leon et al. *Conflict, Decision, and Dissonance.* Stanford University Press, 1964.

Fisher, B. A. *Small-Group Decision-Making.* New York: McGraw-Hill, 1974.

Flanders, J. P., and D. L. Thistelwaite. "Effects of Familiarization and Group Discussion upon Risk Taking." *JPSP* 5 (1967):91-97.

Galtung, J. "Small Group Theory and the Theory of International Relations." In *New Approaches to International Relations*, edited by M. Kaplan. New York: St. Martin's, 1968.

Garnham, David. "State Department Rigidity: Testing a Psychological Hypothesis." *International Studies Quarterly* 18, no. 1 (1974):31-40.

George, A. "The Operational Code: A Neglected Approach to the Study of Political Leaders and Decision-Making." *International Studies Quarterly* 13, no. 2 (1969).

———. "The Case for Multiple Advocacy in Making Foreign Policy." *American Political Science Review* (hereafter *APSR*) 66 (Sept. 1972):751-785.

George, A. et al. Appendix D: The Use of Information. In *Appendices: Commission on the Organization of the Government*, vol. 2. Washington, D.C.: Government Printing Office, 1975.

Graham, W. K. and S. G. Harris. "Effects of Group Discussion on Accepting Risk and on Advising Others to be Risky." *Psychological Record* 20 (1970):219-224.

Halberstam, D. *The Best and the Brightest.* Greenwich, Conn.: Fawcett, 1972.

Hall, Jay. "Decisions, Decisions, Decisions." *Psychology Today* (Nov. 1971).

Hare, P. *Small Group Research.* New York: Glencoe, 1962.

Hermann, Charles F. "Some Consequences of Crisis Which Limit the Viability of Organization." *Administrative Science Quarterly* 8 (1963):61-82.

———. *Crisis in Foreign Policy Decision-Making: A Simulation of International Politics.* China Lake, Calif.: Project Michelson, Contract N123 (60530) 32779A (1965).
———. *Research Tasks for International Crisis Avoidance and Management.* Washington, D.C.: Office of Naval Research, 1975.
Hermann, Charles F., and Margaret G. "An Attempt to Simulate the Outbreak of World War I." *APSR* 61 (1967):400-416.
Hermann, Charles F., Margaret G., and Robert A. Cantor. "Counterattack or Delay: Characteristics Influencing Decision-Makers' Responses to the Simulation of an Unidentified Attack." *Journal of Conflict Resolution* 18, no. 1 (1974):75-106.
Hinton, B., and H. Reitz. *Groups and Organizations.* Belmont, Calif.: Wadsworth, 1971.
Holsti, Ole R. "The 1914 Case." *APSR* 59 (1965):365-378.
———. "The Belief System and National Images. . . ." In Rosenau, James. *International Politics and Foreign Policy.* New York: Free Press, 1969.
———. *Crisis, Escalation, War.* Montreal: McGill-Queens, 1972.
———. "Cognitive Process Approaches to Decision-Making: Foreign Policy Actors Viewed Psychologically." *American Behavioral Scientist* 20, no. 1 (1976):11-32.
Homans, George. *The Human Group.* New York: Harcourt Brace, 1950.
Hoyt, G. C., and J. Stoner. "Leadership and Group Decisions Involving Risk." *JESP* 4 (1968):275-284.
Iverson, G., and H. Norpoth. *Analysis of Variance.* Beverly Hills: Sage, 1976.
Jamieson, B. D. "The Risky-Shift Phenomena with a Heterogeneous Sample." *Psychological Reports* 23 (1968):203-206.
Janis, Irving L. *Victims of Groupthink.* New York: Houghton-Mifflin, 1972.
Janis, Irving, and Leon Mann. *Decisionmaking Psychological Analyses of Conflict, Choice, and Commitment.* New York: Free Press, 1977.
Jellison, J. M., and J. Riskind. "Social Comparison of Abilities Interpretation of Risk-Taking Behavior." *JPSP* 25 (1973):375-390.
Jervis, R. "Hypotheses on Misperception." *World Politics* 20 (1968):454-480.
Johnson, Norris. "Collective Behavior as Group-Induced Shift." *Sociological Inquiry* 44, no. 2 (1974):105-110.
Johnson, N., and James Stemler. "Collective Behavior as Risky Shift: A Laboratory Experiment," mimeographed. University of Cincinnati, 1974.
Johnson, N., and M. Glover. "Individual and Group Shifts to Risk: Two Laboratory Experiments on Crowd Polarization." Paper presented to the North Central Sociological Association, 1976.
JPSP 20, no. 3 (1971) (Special Risky-Shift Issues).
Kelly, H., and J. Thibault. "Group Problem-Solving." In *Handbook of Social Psychology*, vol. 4, edited by G. Lindzey and E. Aronson, pp. 1-202. Reading, Mass.: Addison-Wesley, 1968.
Kelman, H. *International Behavior.* New York: Holt, Rinehart and Winston, 1965.

Kirkpatrick, Samuel A. (1975a). "Risks in Political Decision-Making: An Experimental Analysis of Choice Shifts." *Experimental Study of Politics* 4 (January 1975):55-92.

———. (1975b). "Problems of Risk-Taking in Bureaucracies." Paper presented at the Annual Meeting of the International Studies Association, Washington, D.C., February 1975.

——— (1975c). "Epistemological Perspectives on the Social-Psychological Study of Political Decision-Making." Paper presented at the Annual Meeting of the American Political Science Assoc., San Francisco, September 1975.

——— (1975d). "Psychological Views of Decision-Making." In *Political Science Annual*, vol. 6, edited by C. P. Cotter. Indianapolis: Bobbs-Merrill, 1975.

Kirkpatrick, Samuel A., and Roby D. Robertson. "Choice Shifts in Political Decision-Making: An Experimental Test of Value Theory." Paper presented at the Annual Meeting of the Midwest Political Science Association, Chicago, April 20-May 1, 1976.

Kirkpatrick, Samuel A., et al. "The Process of Political Decision-Making in Groups: Search Behavior and Choice Shifts." *American Behavioral Scientist* 20, no. 1 (1976):33-64.

Kogan, N., and W. Doise. "Effects of Anticipated Delegate Status on Level of Risk-Taking in Small Decision-Making Groups." *Acta Psychologica* 29 (1969):228-243.

Kogan, N., and M. A. Wallach. "The Risky Shift Phenomenon in Small Decision-Making Groups: A Test of the Information-Exchange Hypothesis." *JESP* 3 (1967):75-85.

Laurence, Edward. "The International Transfer of Arms: Problems of Measurement and Conceptualization." Paper presented at the Annual Meeting of the Midwest Political Science Association, Chicago, 1977.

Lamm, H., and N. Kogan. "Risk-Taking in the Context of Inter-Groups Negotiation." *JESP* 6 (1970):351-363.

Lane, R. *Political Ideology*. New York: Free Press, 1964.

Leites, N. *A Study of Bolshevism*. Glencoe, Ill.: Free Press, 1953.

McClosky, H. "Personality and Attitude Correlates of Foreign Policy Orientation." In *Domestic Sources of Foreign Policy*, edited by J. Rosenau, pp. 51-109. Free Press, 1967.

McGowan, P., and H. Shapiro. *The Comparative Study of Foreign Policy*. Beverly Hills: Sage, 1973.

Madaras, G., and D. Bem. "Risk and Conservatism in Group Decision-Making." *JESP* 4 (1968):350-365.

March, James B., and Herbert A. Simon. *Organizations*. New York: John Wiley, 1965.

Marquis, D. G. "Individual Responsibility and Group Decisions Involving Risk." *Industrial Management Review* 3 (1962):8-23.

Marx, S., and J. Wood. "Strands of Theory and Research in Collective Behavior." In *Annual Review of Sociology*, edited by A. Inkeles, pp. 363-

428. Palo Alto: Annual Reviews, 1975.

Milburn, T., and R. Billings. "Decision-Making Perspectives from Psychology: Dealing with Risk and Uncertainty." *American Behavioral Scientist* 20, no. 1 (1976):111-12.

Milgram, S. *Obedience to Authority.* New York: Harper and Row, 1974.

Miller, N., and K. Dion. "An Analysis of the Familiarization Explanation of the Risky Shift." In *Proceedings of the Annual Convention of the American Psychological Association* (1970), pp. 337-338.

Minix, Dean A. "The Role of the Small Group in Foreign Policy Decision-Making: A Potential Pathology in Crisis Decision-Making?" Paper presented to the Southern Political Science Association (1976).

Moore, D. "Governmental and Societal Influence on Foreign Policy in Open and Closed Nations." In Rosenau, James. *Comparing Foreign Policies.* Beverly Hills: Sage, 1974, pp. 171-200.

Moscovici, S., and M. Zavalloni. "The Group as a Polarizer of Attitudes." *JPSP* 12 (1969):125-135.

Myers, D. L., and G. D. Bishop. "Enhancement of Dominant Attitudes in Group Discussion." *JPSP* 20 (1971):386-391.

Myers, D. L., and H. Lamm. "The Group Polarization Phenomenon." *Psychological Bulletin* (1976).

Nash, H. *American Foreign Policy: Response to a Sense of Threat.* Homewood, Ill: Dorsey, 1973.

North, R. C., O. R. Holsti, M. C. Zaninovich, and D. Zinnes. *Content Analysis: A Handbook with Applications for the Study of International Crisis.* Evanston, Ill.: Northwestern University Press, 1963.

Pruitt, Dean G. "The 'Walter Mitty' Effect in Individual and Group Risk Taking." *Proceedings of 77th Annual Convention of the American Psychological Association* 4 (1969):425-426.

Pruitt, Dean G., and Allan Teger. "The Risky-Shift in Group Betting." *JESP* 5 (1969):115-126.

Pruitt, Dean G. (1971a). "Choice Shifts in Group Discussion: An Introductory Review." *JPSP* 20, no. 3 (December 1971):339-361.

—— (1971b). "Conclusions: Toward an Understanding of Choice Shifts in Group Discussions." *JPSP* 20 (1971):495-510.

Reedy, G. *The Twilight of the Presidency.* New York: World, 1973.

Rim, Y. "Social Attitudes and Risk-Taking." *Human Relations* 17 (1964): 259-265.

Robinson, John P., J. Rusk, and K. Head. *Measures of Political Attitudes.* Ann Arbor: Institute for Social Research, 1968.

Rosenau, James. "Pre-Theories and Theories of Foreign Policy." In *Approaches to Comparative and International Politics*, edited by R. B. Farrel. New York: Harcourt, Brace, Janovich, 1968.

——. *International Politics and Foreign Policy.* New York: Free Press, 1969.

——. *Comparing Foreign Policies.* Beverly Hills: Sage, 1974.

Rummel, R. "Some Dimensions in the Foreign Behavior of Nations." In

Rosenau, James. *International Politics and Foreign Policy.* New York: Free Press, 1969, pp. 600-621.

St. Jean, R. L. "Information and Interaction in Group Risk Taking." *Dissertation Abstracts International* 31, no. 7-A (1971):3641.

Scheff, T. "Decision Rules, Types of Error, and Their Consequences in Medical Diagnosis." *Behavioral Scientist* 8 (1963):97-107.

Schlesinger, Arthur. *A Thousand Days: John F. Kennedy in the White House.* Boston: Houghton-Mifflin, 1965.

Semmel, Andrew K. "Deriving Perceptual Data from Foreign Policy Elites: A Methodological Narrative." *Political Methodology* 2, no. 1 (1975):29-49.

———. "Group Dynamics and the Foreign Policy Process: The Choice-Shift Phenomenon." Paper presented to the Southern Political Science Association, Atlanta, November 1976.

Schweitzer, Nicholas. "Delphi as a Technique in Intelligence." Paper presented at the Annual Meeting of the International Studies Association, St. Louis (1977).

Sherif, M. *The Psychology of Social Norms.* New York: Harper, 1936.

Silverthorne, C. P. "Information Input and the Group Shift Phenomenon in Risk-Taking." *JPSP* 20 (1971):456-461.

Singer, J. D. *Quantitative International Politics.* New York: Free Press, 1965.

Singer, J. D., and P. Ray. "Decision-Making in Conflict: From Interpersonal to International Relations." *Bulletin of the Menninger Clinic* 30 (Jan. 1966):300-312.

Smith, Barbara L. et al. *Political Research Methods.* Boston: Houghton-Mifflin, 1976.

Snyder, R., H. Bruck, and B. Sapin. *Foreign Policy Decision-Making.* New York: Free Press, 1962.

Snyder, R. C. *Deterrence, Weapons Systems, and Decision-Making.* China Lake, California: Project Michelson, 1962.

Sorenson, Ted. *Kennedy.* New York: Bantam, 1965.

Steinbruner, John D. *The Cybernetic Theory of Decision.* Princeton University Press, 1974.

Stokes, J. R. "Effects of Familiarization and Knowledge of Others' Odds Choices on Shifts to Risk and Caution." *JPSP* 20 (1971):407-412.

Stoner, J. "Risky and Cautious Shifts and Group Decisions." *JESP* 4 (1968): 442-459.

Teger, A., and D. Pruitt. "Components of Group Risk-Taking." *JESP* 3 (1967):442-459.

Torgerson, Warren G. *Theory and Methods of Scaling.* New York: John Wiley, 1958.

Verba, Sidney. *Small Groups and Political Behavior.* Princeton University Press, 1968.

Vinokur, A. "Review and Theoretical Analysis of the Effects of Group Processes upon Individual and Group Decisions Involving Risk." *Psychological Bulletin* 58 (1971):231-250.

Wallach, M. A., and N. Kogan. "The Roles of Information, Discussion, and

Consensus in Group Risk Taking." *JASP* 1 (1965): 1-19.
Wallach, M. A., N. Kogan, and D. J. Bem. "Group Influence on Individual Risk-Taking." *JASP* 65 (1962):75-86.
———. "Diffusion of Responsibility and Level of Risk-Taking in Groups." *JASP* 68 (1964):263-274.
Weiner, Anthony J., and Herman Kahn. *Crisis and Arms Control.* New York: Hudson Institute, 1962.
Weisband, E., and T. Frank. *Resignation in Protest.* New York: Grossman, 1975.
Zajonc, R., R. Wolosin, and M. Wolosin. "Group Risk-Taking under Various Decision Schemes." *JASP* (1972):16-30.

10
Psychological Models and Systemic Outcomes

Lawrence S. Falkowski

In 1960 James Rosenau waxed eloquent about a lake in Maine and the ability, for once, to see both the forest and the trees (Rosenau 1971:3). It is somewhat presumptuous of me to engage in similar musings, but I thought that before summing up we might reflect for a moment on the nature of this intellectual endeavor.

It may be that we are all "naive scientists" trying to make sense of a world that is too complex, too rapid in its changes, and too ambiguous in its manifestations. This volume began with an examination of the relationship between psychological variables and the study of international politics; in this chapter I wish to discuss whether or not there is a relationship between those variables and observable internatioal and foreign policy behaviors. In effect, we are trying not only to see both the forest and the trees but also to decide which trees will combine to make the most beautiful or most useful forest. Given the complexity of the task, how can we really develop the intellectual hubris needed to confront the questions, let alone answer them?

It is necessary to face one's own psychological predispositions and assumptions before speaking on the mental forces that cause others to act. My own intellectual motives not only give me the energy to work in this area of research but also cause me to question my own findings. At the most abstract level, the goals that I sought to achieve in this volume are best described by Jacob Bronowski: "Science is a very human form of knowledge. We are always at the brink of the known, we always feel forward for what is to be hoped. Every judgment in science stands on the edge of error and is personal. Science is a tribute to what we can know, although we are fallible" (Bronowski 1973:374). This volume stands as a modest attempt to discover what is known and to feel forward for what we hope will be known.

The Systemic Impact of Psychological Models

Let us now look at the question of whether the use of psychological variables can be shown to have an impact on international systems. We must immediately decide what an international system is and how we can determine if a particular observable behavior has an impact on the relationships contained within an international system. Only after we address those knotty problems can we speak of the relationship between psychological models and international systems.

The conceptual confusion and proliferation of systems theory are well known to scholars of international politics. It is not my purpose to debate whether international politics contains one or many systems, whether these systems are subsystem-dominant, or even whether and on what basis systems can be defined. Those concerns are important, but they are not directly relevant to our discussion and they have been discussed elsewhere (see Lampert, Falkowski, and Mansbach 1978). What we must do is determine the extent to which insights gained from the use of psychological models can be translated into systemic behavioral predictions.

If we are unsure which particular behaviors have an impact on the international system or systems, we must be willing to make empirical assessments of degree of impact rather than make a priori judgments. If, in turn, every observable behavior has the potential for systemic impact, the locus of our investigation will be the nexus between an individual's policy preferences, the decision reached, and the implementation of that decision into a behavior or set of behaviors. The impact of psychological variables is, then, the degree to which these variables are related to behavior, and not the degree to which these characteristics are responsible for overall system change.

Another issue that must be dealt with is the nature of political phenomena. Can we legitimately conceive of international politics as a subject encompassing many levels of analysis and thus requiring research designs that deal with several levels of analysis simultaneously? If we can break out of the level-of-analysis problem, it becomes much easier to plan strategies for investigating the impact of psychology on international behaviors.

Consider for a moment the following melding of decision-making and systemic theory. Let us say that the world is composed of a series of international systems, somewhat like Morgan's gaming tables (Morgan 1972:227-28). Further, let us assume that each actor (player) at each table is interacting with other players. Part of the requirements for the response of each player is a series of judgments concerning the motives of opposing players. For each person around any particular table, his perception of the motives of others becomes one of several possible explanatory variables for their behavior. The player may also take into account the degree to which the situation might affect the way his opponent weights the various factors to be considered in the decision. Thus psychological factors can transcend level of analysis in two ways; first, by being a relational property of the system—the distribution of attitudes, beliefs, and possibly operational codes becomes a systemic parameter vis-à-vis behavior—and second, the responses of any one actor in the system may be conditioned by his own psychological needs and his expectations of the psychological needs of other actors in the system. In short, the system becomes a vast information and behavior-processing machine very similar to Rosenau's description of linkage theory:

> An integrated linkage theory posits a vast feedback system. Variations at each level are seen to be systemically linked to variations at the other levels in such a way as to feed back into and become part of the behavioral sequences at the original level. . . . [S]uch developments would be data that fit readily into rather than undermine the across-system theories toward which our emerging conceptual tools are inexorably leading us (Rosenau 1971:23).

If this proposition is accepted, the role of psychological variables becomes one of impact—the amount of variation explained by these variables. In evaluating psychological variables we must decide which behaviors can be explained by reference to these variables and which by reference to other variables.

A more radical explanation is also possible. In this approach, the international system becomes part of the decision-making context and is not important in and of itself. According to this view, the decision is the most crucial unit for investigation, and personal traits and the nature of the system become two of many independent variables. In that case, if personal characteristics are found to be most important in a particular decision setting, the further question of systemic relevance need not be asked.

It does not seem necessary to accept any particular approach to international politics or internatioal systems or levels of analysis in order to address the relevance of psychological variables. It is possible to create an "ideal" method of evaluation without having to opt for any particular point of view. Admittedly, this mode of investigating may not yet be completely operational, but it can serve as the basis for comparing and evaluating the research included in this volume.

The Nexus between Psychological Models and International Behavior

Research in this area deals with a number of difficult problems. One has to do with which psychological variables are likely to be important; another with how important psychological variables are relative to other variables; and a third with how well psychological variables actually predict the behavior of individuals or groups in international politics.

When constructing a method to evaluate these factors, it is necessary to keep the principle of parsimony in mind at all times. In our discussions, we must try to reduce the number of variables to the minimum that will give us a satisfactory explanation or prediction. At the same time, it is not to our advantage to eliminate an important variable just because we believe that some other variable might work as well. We must also be aware of any situational or issue-oriented variables that might affect the results we are trying to achieve.

I owe a great deal to the processes-tracing method outlined by Alexander George. I would go slightly further than he in terms of evaluating the impact of psychological variables, but the basic concepts I employ come from George's insights. At the first level—"receptivity to an assessment of incoming information about the situation"—we have to look for the models that posit the degree to which an actor's perception is related to his predispositions, attitudes, beliefs, memory, and so forth. In order to accept a proposed relationship as valid, a researcher should be able to demonstrate that the same set of perceptions are not related to another set of personal variables. This is quite similar to what George calls a "necessary condition." Once we have determined what psychological mechanisms cause or are related to differences in perceptions, we can turn to the next step in the process: the definition of the situation.

Situational definition must take into account the possible effects of governmental (or organizational) variables, societal variables, cultural differences, systemic constraints, and the nature of perceptual constraints within the individual. A number of possible relationships could exist at this level. We may indeed discover that, in terms of defining a situation, several of these variables may be more than additive. It is also possible that the mechanism by which an individual receives information about the situation is causal in terms of his definition of that situation. Again, the caveat of necessary condition applies. If we were to discover that the only necessary condition for defining the situation was the variables associated with the perception of the situation, we might be able to convincingly state that the two steps outlined are, for research purposes, one. In that case, both the perception of information about the situation and the definition of the situation would be related to the same cause by a certain set of personal characteristics, be they belief systems, attitudes, or predispositions.

The procedure would be repeated at the next step of process tracing, identification and evaluation of options. At this stage, the governmental cluster of variables is likely to include various aspects of group dynamics as well as the more typical governmental variables. Once the processes of investigation and conclusion have taken place, the same mode of analysis would be repeated for examining the choice of action by the decision-maker involved or the group responsible for the decision. Here George stops. I would suggest we go one step further and perform a similar analysis for the processes by which the particular choice is implemented. In that way we might be able to compare the decision reached with the behavior actually exhibited by some collectivity.

Although relatively simple to describe, this procedure may be impossible to implement in any rigorous fashion. Part of the problem stems not from the complexity of the design or from its sequential nature but from the fact that in order to make definite and generalizable statements, this type of analysis would have to be repeated for a series of societies over a range of situations dealing with a wide diversity of issues. Only then would we be on firm ground in evaluating the impact of psychological variables.

It is quite possible, however, that after doing all this research and applying such evaluation procedures we might discover that psychological variables have little or no impact on internatioal politics. Yet a finding of that nature would be an important contribution to the field. It is my belief that we are likely to discover that psychological factors do play a role in international politics, but that the extent of the role may be attributable to variations in types of societies, issues, and situations.

The State of Psychological Models:
What We Know and What We Suspect

It is difficult to claim that we have definitive information on any of the variables or linkages discussed in this volume. Most of the studies contain interesting findings and conclusions, but all of the chapters indicate places where more research is needed. While suggestive, the findings are not conclusive. In discussing the findings I will try to use the mode of evaluation outlined above.

The first group of studies that need to be examined is that relating most directly to the decision-makers' perceptions and their definition of a situation. In this area we need to compare and contrast my work with that of Margaret Hermann and Thomas Wiegele.

Hermann deals with a question that may even precede the examination of decision-maker perceptions. Her work centers around what kinds of individuals become heads-of-state and whether different types of societies tend to select individuals with different personal characteristics and orientations for such a post. Her analysis indicates that societies that vary in terms of size, modernization, and regime-type do tend to choose different types of leaders. In another work not reported in this volume (see Hermann 1976), she finds that the orientations of leaders are somewhat related to foreign policy behaviors.

A number of questions raised by the study need careful consideration. The first and most important concerns the relationship between the leaders themselves and the societies of which they are a part. If the relationship between type of society and leaders chosen is strong, could we not eliminate the personal characteristics of the leaders? In other words, if a small modernizing society whose regime has come to power illegally always has as its leader a person who is extremely nationalistic, high in need for power, distrustful of others, and expansionist, perhaps we might be able to ignore personal characteristics and deal only with information about the type of society involved. That would tell us rather directly what kind of individual would be chosen for the leadership position, and possibly, how that individual would behave.

The results of such research to date are not strong enough to allow us to make those kinds of conclusions, and even if the results were definitive, it is not at all certain that personal characteristics would not play a role. We are dealing with the problem of causation, and it is unclear at this point if the societal variables are causal in the selection of leaders or if the causal arrow runs in the opposite direction. Hermann's study does not really address that question, and in evaluating her work we can only speculate on the matter.

Another question that is raised in Hermann's research is: what do these findings tell us about how a decision-maker gains information about a situation and then defines that situation? Again, Hermann does not speak directly to the question, but the results of the study are so interesting in this regard that a little speculation is warranted. She establishes that certain personal orientations are highly related to the leaders of certain types of societies. Furthermore, these orientations are perhaps the basis upon which the individuals in question select and filter information. On the basis of that premise, we should be able to hypothesize how variously orientated leaders are likely to handle information and, thus, how they will perceive and define situations. If such hypotheses can be tested and supported, we may be able to find a rather predictive link between leadership type and consequent behavior.

For example, consider the personal characteristic, "distrust of others." Say we wish to examine how a person who distrusts others is likely to perceive the world around him and how he is likely to define that which he perceives. Although we do not have firm empirical evidence to support a proposition or confirm a hypothesis, a preliminary hypothesis might be: the more a leader distrusts others, the more he will perceive hostility in the environment. A second hypothesis related to this insight is: the more hostility perceived in the environment, the more an individual will define decision situations as zero sum. The implications of defining a situation as zero-sum-like are that the leader involved will probably be rigid and highly committed, since he perceives a great deal as being on the line and he cannot afford to show any weakness or all will be lost. Ole Holsti's study of John Foster Dulles can be viewed in this light (Holsti 1962). We are not sure whether Dulles was distrustful of everyone; we are reasonably sure that he was rather distrustful of the Soviet Union. This orientation heightened his perception of hostility coming from the Soviet Union, regardless of the actual stimuli, and we suspect that the behavior he exhibited was more hostile and more committed than would have been the case if he had not perceived the USSR in that fashion. When we add to this description the fact that Dulles seemed to be the major force in U.S. foreign policy at that time, we can see the possible effects of his "distrust of others."

This extended example points up how Hermann's findings might be linked to questions of perception. Another part of her work indicated not only that these orientations are linked but also that there may be ways in which the weight of these orientations can be associated with systemic outcomes—in the terms of the chapter, with "national foreign policy behaviors." Given differences in the types of societies, two relationships may exist rather than just one. The first is the way in which a society recruits its leaders. The second is the degree to which personal characteristics and orientations will be related to foreign policy behavior due to variations in society. Hermann's analysis is sensitive to these relationships—for example, "One consequence of a low level of modernization is a small bureaucracy and, in turn, a greater chance for the head of state to exercise control over policy"—but does not deal with them in a comprehensive fashion. This is not a criticism of the work, since its major emphasis was elsewhere; rather it serves as an indication of the richness of the research and its potential overall impact. To conclude, because of its descriptive nature this particular work of Hermann's does do an excellent job of identifying and characterizing the heads of state of various countries as well as indicating what types of societies are likely to produce what kinds of leaders. By implication the study raises questions about the ways in which different orientations could lead to differences in perception and definition of situations and how these differences might be related to different observable foreign policy behaviors. Also the author suggests ways that other variables like types of government, size, societal stress, and modernity may enhance or diminish the effect of a leader's personal characteristics on the foreign policy of a society.

At this early stage, none of these relationships can be considered causal, nor can they be raised to the level of law. However, the results are such that the insights gained beg for additional study, and I suspect that as more evidence is compiled, the relationships will be supported.

The next study dealing with these questions is my own, which deals directly with peceptions and, by logical extension, with the definition of the situation. The results reported by Hermann and myself are in no way contradictory. Rather, in terms of the degree to which perceptions are influenced by personal characteristics, they are quite complementary. Hermann deals with a world survey and discovers different leaders. I deal with the leaders in one country and find differences in perceptions.

My argument is that even in large, developed, open countries, situations arise in which personal involvement by the leaders is quite likely. The study investigates whether leaders in those situations have different perceptions and whether those different perceptions lead to different behaviors. The model used is based on memory. It suggests that since perception and definition of a situation are filtered through memory, knowing a given subject's memory profile will allow us to predict whether the subject will change his behavior, and if so, to what extent. The study looks at one crisis failure for each presidential administration since World War II and analyzes the memory profile of each president and secretary of state. A prediction is then made, and the subsequent behavior of each individual is compared to see if the predictions are accurate.

The variable that is being predicted is "flexibility," and it is defined in terms of the direction and intensity of behavior change from a base line of activity prior to a crisis. I find that referents and congruence are indeed strong predictors of subsequent behavior change. In short, memory profiles are predictive of the ways in which a decision-maker perceives events and, by extension, how that decision-maker defines a situation.

My study does tend to suffer from a lack of explanation of the mechanisms by which this occurs; I did not deal with competing explanations of the data in a rigorous fashion. Rather, I attempted to set up a quasi-experimental design in which I argue that I have controlled for differences in situation, role, governmental variables, and the like. If you accept this argument, you can assign great importance to the findings; if you do not accept it, the findings become merely suggestive. However, the Hermann results and mine stand together and support one another. The combination suggests a mechanism that might be useful in the evaluation of perception and definition.

Evidently, personal characteristics *can* play a role in perception, and the mechanism of that role seems to be related to the memory profile of the individual. If the memory profile and the orientations of the individual are congruent, they provide a link with degrees of flexibility and behavior. Built into both these systems in a variety of ways are the effects of various intervening factors, including type of situation.

What we know and what we suspect diverge. In another study (Falkowski 1978:107) I dealt with how flexibility could be viewed in a goal-oriented context, but left unstated whether other factors might not impinge on the very nature of the goal hierarchy. To use Hermann's words: "Are our findings merely the result of the heads of state assuming the rhetoric of their particular roles, or would we find similar characteristics prominent in their responses to the press prior to coming to office?" An interesting, if unanswerable, question. In fact, my work might imply an answer in support of Hermann's findings by saying that individual variables are important. I study individuals who occupy the same role (U.S. presidents for example) and find very dramatic differences in the value orientation, goals, preferences, and behavioral style of these individuals. This might suggest that though we do not know how much impact the role constraints have, it is clear that at least some individual variation is present.

The picture we are creating of how individuals perceive is still somewhat incomplete. Hermann and I control for some extraneous factors, but Thomas Wiegele suggests that still other factors must be taken into account. While I assume that a crisis is a situation of high stress, Wiegele looks to see when stress is physically present and suggests what effects stress might have on decision-makers in terms of their perception and their subsequent behavior.

It might seem odd to compare two content analytic works with one that deals with developing unobtrusive ways to measure changes in voice patterns associated with stress. But in terms of the personal characteristics of elites, we must consider whether stress as well as the other variables have an effect on perception. Wiegele suggests that knowing when and about what a decision-maker is stressed may tell us a great deal about the ultimate behavior that he will exhibit. Although he does not provide hypotheses as to the effects of stress on political elites, the mode of analysis may be used in conjunction with my research design and Hermann's categorizing to answer questions such as: Do leaders of small countries with limited resources exhibit higher or lower degrees of flexibility in the presence of stress during crisis?

Although Wiegele's data on political elites are only exploratory in nature at this stage, some of the findings are quite revealing. For example, he finds that in various crises, U.S. presidents have tended to exhibit low stress when describing the crisis itself and high stress when specific measures were discussed, in response to the behavior exhibited by the opponent or behaviors that the president was suggesting. Although there are minor exceptions to this finding, the general pattern is clear. He also discovered that all presidents except Johnson indicated high levels of stress when discussing the determination of the United States to see that the outcome of the crisis would be acceptable to this country.

One wonders whether the stress aspects of these various decisions could be related to personal characteristics Hermann studies. Suppose we discovered that all presidents save Johnson were high on the variables Hermann calls "complexity." We might then say that high conceptual complexity was related to viewing the crisis decision and a favorable outcome as stressed, and that this, in turn, might be related to an orientation toward "lack of resolve" or some other indicator. At that stage, we could link all three studies into a related mechanism of perception and reaction to a given situation.

An unscientific impressionistic example may serve to indicate how we might construct and test such a mechanism. I found that prior to the Tet offensive, Johnson's primary foreign policy goals were quite nationalistic in their orientation. The three most frequently mentioned were: supporting the troops in Vietnam, resisting communism, and increasing U.S. security (Falkowski 1978:107). Hermann associates a number of dimensions of leaders with an expansionist orientation. Doris Kearns describes Johnson in a way that seems consistent with Hermann's work. After each of Kearns's statements (given below) the appropriate Hermann variable appears in parentheses:

> Success or failure was determined entirely by the individual himself (high belief in own control over events) ... the desire to benefit others was ever the prime motive for his quest for power (high need for power) ... good works, he believed, brought love and gratitude (low conceptual complexity) ... yet as he looked around him in 1967 and 1968 he saw only paralyzing bitterness and hatred ... he would seek the cause of his decline in personal animosity and motives of individual enemies (high distrust of others) (Kearns 1976:x-xi).

Kearns might argue that many of the variables associated with an expansionist orientation—except for high nationalism and low need for affiliation—were present in Johnson's character. My results may indicate high nationalism, but impressionistic evidence seems to indicate that Johnson had a high need for affiliation. In any case, for our example we might contend that Johnson seems to be quite close to being an expansionist. Wiegele discovers that only during the Gulf of Tonkin and Pueblo incidents did words associated with the determination of the United States have low stress. It might be possible to say that expansionists do not see the high commitment strategies associated with crisis as stressful, since they believe they control events and are highly nationalistic. Of course, I am not suggesting that this explains Wiegele's findings; in order to do so you would have to examine all the other presidents whom he studies. I am merely trying to illustrate how possible connections can be made and how these connections might lead to behaviors with systemic importance.

Thus, we have discovered that three of the chapters contain findings suggesting a relationship between personal characteristics, orientations, memory profiles, and possibly stress. Furthermore, we uncovered some interesting hints on how these findings might be interconnected and how, as a group, they might be related to observable foreign policy behaviors. The next series of studies indicates ways in which we might be able to integrate these factors with the choice of options and policy preferences.

One could argue that all the remaining studies in the volume address questions related to the identification and weighting of options, followed by the choice of policy. However, we need to be slightly more specific in our discussion. Because it deals with some of the theoretical and methodological problems of operational code analysis and because of its importance for process tracing evaluation techniques, the chapter by Alexander George precedes the empirical work dealing with individual attitudes and personal attributes.

George illustrates how advances in psychology—and especially in cognitive psychology—can lead to a model of man as naive scientist, an active element in decision-making. Since the decision-maker is a probelm solver, the various steps outlined in terms of process tracing seem quite appropriate. He then proceeds to outline the various philosophical and instrumental beliefs associated with operational code analysis. Given the theoretical premises of operational codes, he addresses the congruence and process-tracing methodologies that could be used. The value of this study cannot be overemphasized. Not only does it set the stage for the works that follow, it also indicates how we can evaluate these studies. George is sensitive to other variables that modify the effects of operational codes.

Admittedly, even in his work, problems arise. For example,

although operational codes are clearly at the individual level, their application seems most appropriate to the decisional group, which leaves the reader with the problem of aggregation. The problem may be more apparent than real, however, since some of the other research deals directly with it. Hoagland and Walker hold the opinion that:

> There is also evidence to indicate that a government's decision-making process in a crisis situation is likely to become more centralized under the control of its principal leader. Under these circumstances the beliefs of Stalin and Khrushchev are more likely to influence the actions of the Soviet government in this type of situation, making it less important to decide whether to attribute such beliefs to an individual leader or to other actors in the government. Similarly, within the American government the centralization of the decision-making process probably increased the influence of Truman's and Kennedy's beliefs upon the crisis behavior of the U.S. government.

In addition, the entire thrust of the work of Semmel and Minix is to determine the impact of choice shift, which is important for establishing the degree to which an individual operational code would translate for a group and in determining a group operational code.

Operational code analysis is an attempt to determine what belief systems are and how they are related to behavior. Steven Hoagland and Stephen Walker use the congruence approach to operational codes for an analysis of the two Berlin crises. They obtain a number of interesting results. The authors find that there is a link between beliefs and crisis behavior, even though there is some deviation from a pure relationship. They also discover that an actor's image of the opponent may be a "master belief," and the advisability of generalizing from individuals to groups is questionable under certain conditions. Their research design is so innovative that even these mixed results should be looked upon as an important advance. When their work is viewed in the context of results reported elsewhere in the volume, the nature of the results is made more understandable.

The finding that the image of the opponent may be a master belief is reasonably consistent with my own notion of the operation of perceptual filters. The way in which different factors are combined to move from the individual to the systemic level may be gleaned from the experimental work of Semmel and Minix. Although it can be argued that, viewed from the level of the system, operational code analysis is not all that potent, it remains an empirical question. Hoagland and Walker have taken the first important steps in answering that question. To the degree that they have discovered that certain beliefs contained within the operational code are more important than others, they have advanced the study of operational codes. If further analysis and study indicated that there is a hierarchy in the operational code structure, we may be able to eliminate less important variables in operational codes and get closer to the basic mechanisms that govern the perception of information and may also be highly or even causally related to the choice of options.

In connection with the research of Hoagland and Walker we must look at the research of Gerald Hopple and the role-conception work of Walker. Both of these efforts take off from the Hoagland and Walker research. If the findings concerning the hierarchy of beliefs are accurate, we will want to find out which values and role conceptions are most important in determining foreign policy behavior.

Hopple's notions of values are reasonably similar, if less elaborate, than notions of operational codes. He may be dealing with the identification of options and policy choices by indirection. Basically, he suggests that a relationship may exist between the values of top decision-makers and observable foreign policy behaviors. If this relationship does exist and the relationship is fairly strong, we may be able to combine two steps in process tracing. The stage at which options are evaluated would become relatively less important if a direct link between values and behavior were known to exist.

Hopple does find that values are somewhat related to behaviors, especially in the case of force. He also finds that a number of non-value-oriented variables (including societal, interstate, and global variables) are related to behavior. At this point, then, we cannot eliminate a step in our process tracing; we have to consider the relative weight of other factors. Hopple's work does suggest that we are beginning to narrow our focus somewhat and to see more clearly certain relationships in this area. Hopple and Hermann seem to agree on the hypothesis that Third World states are more likely to exhibit behavior that is highly related to psychological or value factors than are other types of states. Also Hopple discovers that his value data are quite potent for determining the behavior of closed regimes, a finding that corresponds to Hermann's analysis by extrapolation.

Working in a similar fashion, Walker seeks to examine the systemic impact of national role conceptions. With some modification, his notion of role conception can be seen as an elaboration of value or attitude analysis. Walker argues that different psychological models may be most appropriate to different stages in the decision process and that perhaps national role conceptions are most highly related to international events. The findings are somewhat mixed; although it seems that some nations are more consistent in their foreign policy than others and that role conceptions may play a part in this relationship, the data simply do not allow the kind of in-depth analysis necessary to make firm judgments. In short, the research design and the model construction and its execution are clearly worthwhile contributions; we await more explicit data in order to confirm or reject a number of the hypotheses discussed. As Walker concludes:

> If these analyses were based upon data sets collected explicitly for these purposes, it probably would be possible to conduct the analysis with little or no information loss by retaining the capability to disaggregate and aggregate across levels of generalization. Consequently, the potential value of role theory as an analytical tool for linking individual and systemic generalizations appears to be rather high.

The work of Semmel and Minix has been discussed earlier, but one additional point needs to be made. Their work can serve as a basis for creating research designs for the operational environment as well as for additional experimental work. In one sense there is a common concern in Walker's research and that of Semmel and Minix: the need and sometimes the inability to obtain good data unless we create it ourselves.

Finally, I think we must acknowledge that what we suspect currently takes up a great deal more space in the literature than what we know. Yet, what we know has increased dramatically in the last several years. It is a curious and I believe important fact that all the chapters in this volume are empirically oriented, and most of them present findings of ongoing studies. Up to this point I have been quite optimistic and very ready to examine connections, seek common interests, and formulate conclusions. Before we end our discussion, however, I should discuss, at least briefly, the possibility that our attempts may be so flawed that further advances in this area will be long in coming.

Let the Buyer Beware:
Correlation, Causation, and Spurious Relations

As a devotee and supporter of research in this area, I am all too willing to think the best of my colleagues, give the researcher the benefit of the doubt, and put greater stock in findings than I would if I were not actively involved in the field myself. Being keenly aware of the difficulty of the task, it is tempting to applaud too loudly at even moderate successes. I have tried not to be overwhelming in my enthusiasm for the results reported in this volume, yet I have waited until the very end to raise a number of questions that are germane to almost all of the studies. I think the first and most important question concerns the direction of the causal arrows.

In preparing and organizing this volume, I have assumed that causation begins with the individual and, through various mechanisms and levels of abstraction, results in systemic behavior. It may be that causation runs in the other direction. In fact it may be that an individual's perceptions, beliefs, attitudes, choices, and roles are being caused by environmental conditions and not the other way around. So far, it has not been possible to answer this question, but it is crucial that we do. Are we all creatures of our environment to the point where no variance is explained by reference to our individual cognitive processes? Have we all been socialized in a manner that leaves us as interchangeable parts?

If we do not have specific answers to these questions, at least we can take some solace in the fact that we can empirically demonstrate that individuals subjected to similar socialization processes have different perceptions of similar situations. As these perceptions vary so—we think—the behavior will vary; thus the causal sequence starts with the individual and not the environment.

Recent trends in the political socialization literature point toward a greater role for the individual:

> We argue, then, for a greater recognition of the role played by the individual in political socialization. His needs and attitudes are an integral element of the interaction, and attention to them will assist us in developing a more dynamic conceptualization and a more precise explanation of the process of political socialization (Schwartz and Schwartz 1975).

It may be too early to assume that the causal chain begins with the individual, but the results compiled to date seem to indicate that there is merit to that argument.

Another serious potential problem is the discovery and analysis of intervening variables at all levels of generality. Most of the authors talk about the relative impact of psychological variables as opposed to role constraints, environmental factors, and so forth, but much more work is needed before we can really assess the exact relationships between these factors. Until this work is accomplished we run the risk of becoming either reductionist or irrelevant.

A serious difficulty scholars in this area face is the charge that they are reducing the study of foreign policy to the study of psychology. This is a problem only if we accept the notion that human behavior is so segmented that no spill-over occurs. If political decisions can be explained and predicted by models and theories originally formulated in other social sciences, does that mean that the decision is no longer political or that the specific series of situations we are investigating might not, in some meaningful way, be different? The reduction criticism has merit if we lose sight of the subject matter of our investigation. This is a serious problem, but it is one that all the contributors to this volume have avoided. Their studies are directed toward relevant subject matters and address the subject at hand within the limits of the research.

Finally, the studies contained in this volume are all based either directly or indirectly on an implicit notion of stimulus-organism-response. Even the Hermann research, which seems not to have this dimension, tries to determine different states of the organism. Her other research goes on to associate the differences in the organism with differences in response. It is still not clear to what extent the organism itself is responsible for response variations, but the findings reported have given preliminary indications of this relationship.

Having mentioned a number of possible problems, we still need to deal with the question of systemic relevance. It is possible to duck the issue quite nicely by suggesting that since a number of scholars in international politics and foreign policy are working in this area it must be relevant, but that is more of an evasion than an answer. Can we really deal with the nexus between the psychological models we have discussed and the outbreak of war or overall instability in various international systems?

The answer to this question must be qualified, but it does

appear to be affirmative. We do not yet know the exact impact of these variables, but the results all show that relationships seem to exist. The fact that the correlation figures are relatively low does not mean that the relationship is irrelevant; it may mean that we simply have not reached the level of sophistication necessary to chart the exact sequence of events. The next step for us is to push ahead and develop that sophistication through further research.

References

Bronowski, Jacob. *The Ascent of Man.* Boston: Little, Brown, 1973.
Falkowski, Lawrence. *Presidents, Secretaries of State, and Crises in U.S. Foreign Relations.* Boulder: Westview Press, 1978.
Hermann, Margaret. "The Effects of Political Leaders' Orientations to Foreign Affairs on Foreign Policy Behavior." Paper presented at Peace Science Society, meeting (1976).
Holsti, Ole. "The Belief System and National Images: A Case Study." In *International Politics and Foreign Policy*, edited by James Rosenau. New York: Free Press, 1969.
Kearns, Doris. *Lyndon Johnson and the American Dream.* New York: Harper and Row, 1976.
Lampert, Donald, Lawrence Falkowski, and Richard Mansbach. "Is There an International System?" *International Studies Quarterly* (March 1978).
Morgan, Patrick. *Theories and Approaches to International Politics.* San Ramon, Calif.: Consensus, 1972.
Rosenau, James. "Theorizing across Systems: Linkage Politics Revisited." Presented at American Political Science Association meeting (1971).
———. *The Scientific Study of Foreign Policy.* New York: Free Press, 1971.
Schwartz, David C., and Sandra Kenyon Schwartz, eds. *New Directions in Political Socialization.* New York: Free Press, 1975.

Index

Affective models
  of choice shift, 253-254
Ambiguity, 107
Avoidance, 65

Balance, 185-188, 190-191, 195, 199
Bay of Pigs, 256
Beliefs, 212
  hierarchy of, 302
Belief systems, 213, 215
  defined, 214
  of decision-makers, 212
  of elites, 215
  mapping of, 213
Berlin, 85, 145
Berlin crises, 132, 145, 161, 301
Berlin crisis
  of 1948, 126, 130-131, 138
  of 1961, 126, 131, 138
Bounded rationality, 125
Brandt, Willy
  operational code of, 115-116

California Psychological Inventory (CPI), 261, 267-269
Cambodia, 260, 277-278
Capability, 224
Carter, James E., 66
Causal models
  of foreign policy behavior, 212
Chicken
  game of, 133-134
Choice shift, 251-252, 255, 260
  direction of, 263
Chou En-Lai, 34

Closed states, 237
Cognitive balance, 106
Cognitive dynamics, 182
Cognitive maps, 170
Cognitive models, 125
  of choice shift, 254
Cognitive organization, 96
Cognitive processes, 96, 251
Cognitive psychology, 97, 300
Cognitive structures, 96
Cognitive theory, 96
Cognitive variables, 95
College student groups, 271, 274
College students, 264
Commitments
  set of, 170
Comparative Research on the Events of Nations (CREON), 23
Complexity, 34, 299
  conceptual, 34
Conflict
  concerning colonial land borders, 238
  concerning colonial sea borders, 238
  concerning direct sea borders, 238
Congruence, 105-107, 126, 147-148, 180-181, 186, 192
  defined, 69
  lack of, 153
Congruity, 185, 187-188, 190-191, 193, 195, 199. *See also* Congruence
Constructive diplomatic behavior, 225
Content analysis, 8, 22, 24, 213-214, 219-220, 257
  of values, 219
Cooperation, 222

Coups
  per year, 225
Credibility, 138
Crisis, 52-53, 58, 60, 62, 63, 125, 132
Crisis behavior
  of the Soviet government, 147
  of the United States government, 147
Crisis failure, 55
Crisis outcomes, 156
Cuba, 88
  missile crisis in, 256
Cues, 178, 185, 199, 204
Cultural values, 271
Cybernetics
  concepts of, 170

Data access
  problems of, 7
Decision-makers, 49-50, 53, 65-66, 252
  beliefs of, 8, 109
  perceptions of, 109
Decision-making, 51, 71, 74, 95, 97, 103, 127, 129, 291
  in crises, 125
  faulty, 275
  frameworks of, 172
  in small groups, 251, 252, 274
Decision-making analysis, 49
Decision-making approaches, 95
Decision-making group, 6, 251
Decision-making processes, 251-252
Decision-making style, 242
Decision-making theories, 170
Decision rules, 267, 270
Decision situations, 255, 295
Decision units, 270
De-escalation, 133, 137
De-escalatory behavior, 137
Defense expenditures, 225

Economic structure, 224
Eisenhower, Dwight D., 34
Elite images, 213
Elite recruitment, 16
Elites, 3-4, 78, 89
  behavior of, 71
  personal characteristics of, 298
  psychological states of, 72
  survey of, 257
Elite values, 236

Energy
  percent consumed, 225
Energy dependence index
  formula for, 226
Energy interdependence index
  formula for, 227
Energy seller index
  formula for, 227
Environment, 1
  psychological, 172
Escalation, 133, 137
Escalatory behavior, 148
Events surveys, 258
EXCOM, 256
Expansionism
  in Africa, 42
  in Eastern Europe, 42
  in Middle East, 42
Experimental research, 258
  in foreign policy, 252
Experimental studies, 259
  of foreign policy outputs, 259
Experimentation
  drawbacks of, 259
Export concentration index
  formula for, 226

Failure, 58, 60, 63
FBIS *Daily Reports. See* Foreign Broadcast Information Service *Daily Reports*
Feedback, 54-55,
  second order, 54
Flexibility, 49, 54, 58, 66, 297
  degree of, 52, 55
  framework for, 52
  prediction of, 49
Flexible behavior, 59
Foreign Broadcast Information Service *Daily Reports* (FBIS), 23-24, 219, 242
Foreign policy, 49, 170, 172, 204
  forecasting, 171
  as rhetoric, 182
  rhetoric of, 170
Foreign policy behavior, 71
Foreign policy crisis, 74
Foreign policy decisions, 175
  processes of, 274
  quality of, 274

Index

Foreign policy elites, 71, 76
  psychological states of, 76
Foreign policy monitoring, 170
Freedom, 222

Goal orientations, 298
Goal theme, 60
Government
  type of, 296
Governmental instability, 226
Governmental variables, 293
Government structure, 224
Gross national product, 225
Group membership, 261, 267-270
Group polarization, 255, 271-272
Group size, 267, 270
Group think, 255
Gulf of Tonkin, 300

Hague, 261, 280
Heads of state, 17, 216
  orientations of, 44
High threat, 53, 63
Hostility
  of the Soviet Union, 295
Human interactions, 5

Import concentration index formula for, 226
Individual beliefs, in operational codes, 100
Influences
  regimes, 37
  societal, 37
Information
  nature of, 50
Information processing, 98, 102-103
Information processing tasks, 101
Instrumental beliefs, 103
Interactive models
  of choice shift, 254
Inter-coder reliability, 27
International actors
  nontraditional, 254
International behavior, 290
  impact of psychology on, 290
International economic involvement
  formula for, 226
International systems, 172, 290-291
Interstate Behavior Project (IBA), 216

Issues
  instrumental, 96, 100
  philosophical, 96, 100

Johnson, Lyndon B., 299

Key Word in Context (KWIC) Concordance, 24
Khrushchev, Nikita, 144, 162
  Kennedy's image of, 145
Kissinger, Henry A., 65
  operational code of, 109
Korea, 53, 88, 261, 272, 278
  United States risk-taking in, 255
  See also South Korea

Laboratory research
  advantages of, 258-259
Leadership
  nature of, 53
Leakage, 72-73
  defined, 72
Legislative selection, 225
Level of modernization, 32
Levels of analysis, 290
Lin Piao, 34
Liu Shao-chi
  operational code of, 114-115

Man
  as problem solver, 98
Mao Tse-tung
  operational code of, 114
Master belief, 301
Measurement techniques, 9
Mediator/Integrator orientation
  in Asia, 42
  in Atlantic Community, 42
  in Latin America, 42
  in Middle East, 42
Memory, 6, 54-57, 60, 297
Memory profiles, 11, 297
Military groups, 263
Military officer groups, 264, 267, 271-272
Military officers
  junior, 259-260
Modernity, 296
Modernization, 40
  level of, 296

Motivation, 1-2

Naive scientist, 98, 99, 289
Nation
  size of, 36, 225
National attributes, 170
National foreign policy, 44
Nationalism, 34
  in Africa, 42
  in Atlantic Community, 42
  in Middle East, 42
National level hypotheses, 186
National security, 222
National traits, 170
Nations
  closed group, 241
  unstable group, 231, 239
  western group, 231, 239
Neo-colonial dependency index
  formula for, 227
Newspaper editorials
  as data source, 61-62, 63-64
New York Times, 23, 61, 64, 227
Nixon, Richard M., 66-67
Nixon doctrine, 174-176
Nonmilitary conflict behavior, 240

OPCODE, 129, 143, 153, 156, 158, 160. *See also* Operational code.
OPCODE beliefs, 160
Operational code, 95, 127-128, 170, 213
  of decision-makers, 127
  of Harry Truman, 144
  of John Kennedy, 130, 144, 157
  of Nikita Khrushchev, 130, 140, 157
  of Soviet decision-makers, 131, 135, 139
  of United States' decision-makers, 131, 135, 139, 143
  See also OPCODE
Operational code beliefs, 99, 101-102, 104, 106
  causal weight of, 109
  explanatory power of, 109-110
  as necessary condition, 107-108
Opportunism
  in Africa, 42
  in Asia, 42
  in Atlantic Community, 42
  in Latin America, 42
Option development, 101

Organizational dynamics, 251
Orientations, 17, 22, 34, 295-296
  active independent, 17, 19, 40, 181, 191
  behavioral, 182
  bridge, 181, 191
  cluster of, 170
  expansionist, 17, 19, 30, 294
  to foreign affairs, 30
  independent, 181, 191
  influential, 17, 19
  isolate, 181, 191
  of leaders, 294
  mediator/integrator, 17, 20, 34, 37, 39-40, 42, 181, 191
  nationalism, 37
  neutralist, 191, 195
  opportunist, 17, 20, 34, 37, 39-40
  participative, 17, 21, 34, 36, 39, 40
  psychological, 76

Panama, 261, 278-279
Participative orientations
  in Atlantic Community, 42
  in Middle East, 42
Perception, 5, 50, 55, 215, 297
  of decision-makers, 294
  differences in, 292
  effected by personal characteristics, 297
  pattern of, 5
Perceptual filters, 55, 67
Perceptual screens, 55
Persian Gulf, 260, 264, 276-277
Personal characteristics, 15-17, 22, 27, 34, 37, 39-40, 44, 295-297, 299
  belief in ability to control events, 18, 27
  of citizenry, 44
  conceptual complexity, 18, 28
  distrust of others, 19, 44, 294
  of heads of state, 44
  nationalism, 18, 27, 40, 44, 294
  need for affiliation, 18, 28, 299
  need for power, 18, 28, 40, 44, 294
  of political leaders, 44
  by regions, 42
  training in foreign affairs, 18, 30
Personality, 212
  trait approach to, 97
Personality factors, 10
Personality inventories, 170
Personality variables, 9
Policy analysis, 173

Index

Policy makers, 99, 170, 172
  as naive scientists, 99
Policy making
  in Berlin crisis of 1961, 116-117
Political analysis, 2
Political belief index (PBS), 261, 267, 270
Political competition, 33, 40
  degree of, 33
Political elites, 298
Political involvement abroad scale (PIN), 261, 267, 270
Political leaders, 15
  emotional aspects of, 86
  number of, 225
Political psychology, 211
Political socialization, 304
Political values, 223
Power
  need for, 34
Predictors
  global, 224
  interstate, 224
  psychological, 224
  social equality, 223
  societal, 224
Press interviews, 23
Prisoner's Dilemma
  game of, 133-134
Process tracing, 105, 113, 292-293
  by controlled comparison, 114
Progress, 222
Psychoanalytical assessments, 170
Psychological analysis, 3
Psychological factors, 237, 294
Psychological mechanisms, 2, 5, 10
Psychological models, 1, 305
Psychological predispositions, 305
Psychological stress, 78
Psychological Stress Evaluator (PSE), 78, 81-86, 89
Psychological variables, 2, 4, 239, 290, 292, 305
Psychology, 300
Public documents
  as data source, 61
  validity of, 61
Pueblo crisis, 88, 89, 300

Rationality
  in decision-making, 50

Referents, 56
  domestic, 56
  foreign, 56-57
  future, 56
  negative, 57
  past, 57
  positive, 57
  present, 56, 66
Regime
  genesis of, 33, 36, 40
Regime influences, 31
Regime type, 294
Regional differences
  distrust of others, 42
  expansionist orientations, 42
  mediator/integrator, 42
  nationalism, 42
  opportunist, 42
  participative, 42
Regions
  of world, 33
Research
  policy-relevant, 169
Role, 16, 44
Role conceptions, 181-182, 184
  associated with the cold war, 181
  of the cold war, 183
  symmetry of, 187
  of target, 193
  of the unaligned, 191
  of the United States, 195
  valences, 204
Role conflict, 188
Role cues, 177
Role demands, 177
Role enactment, 185, 193, 199, 205
  valences, 195
Role expectations, 177
Role strain, 188
Role theory, 173-175, 177-178, 188
ROTC cadet groups, 271-272
ROTC cadets, 259-260, 263-264, 267

SALT I, 261, 278
Schemata, 96, 97
  defined, 97
Schumaker, Kurt
  operational code of, 115
Selection
  of political leaders, 16

Signal leakage
  examples of, 73-78
Situation, 110
  definition of, 6, 101-102, 292-293
Size
  of nation, 31, 36, 294, 296
Social psychology, 173
Social stress, 39
Societal indicators, 225
Societal stress, 39, 296
Societal unrest, 296
South Korea, 261, 264
Soviet-American confrontation, 146
Soviet Union, 183
  in Eastern Europe, 184
Spontaneous material, 23
Students, 259-260
Superpowers, 193, 195, 199. *See also* Soviet Union; United States
Surprise
  as element of crises, 63
Systemic level hypotheses, 187
Systemic outcomes, 172
Systems theory, 291

Theme, 56-57
  defined, 57

goal, 58, 62
policy, 58, 62
Threat
  perception of, 117
Thucydides
  as a rational choice theorist, 211
Trait reliability, 27

United States, 183
  in Western Hemisphere, 184
USSR. *See* Soviet Union

Value data, 222
Values, 215, 302
  articulated, 224, 242
  profiles of, 215
  terminal, 215
  vocal change, 78-81
  voice stress analysis, 78, 81

Western states, 231, 238
World Events Interaction Survey (WEIS), 62, 181, 216, 225, 227